P9-CMF-587

THE
METHODS OF HISTORICAL STUDY

EIGHT LECTURES

READ IN THE UNIVERSITY OF OXFORD IN
MICHAELMAS TERM, 1884

WITH THE INAUGURAL LECTURE

ON

THE OFFICE OF THE HISTORICAL PROFESSOR

BY

EDWARD A. FREEMAN, M.A., Hon. D.C.L. & LL.D.

REGIUS PROFESSOR OF MODERN HISTORY
FELLOW OF ORIEL COLLEGE
HONORARY FELLOW OF TRINITY COLLEGE

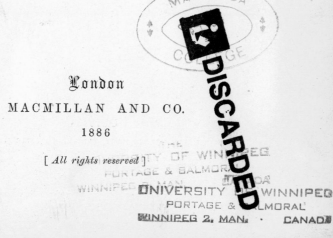

London
MACMILLAN AND CO.
1886

Oxford

PRINTED BY HORACE HART, PRINTER TO THE UNIVERSITY

PREFACE.

THE course of Lectures here printed, with the Inaugural Lecture prefixed, was meant as a call and an introduction to historical study in general. They were followed up in Easter Term 1885 by a course on the Chief Periods of European History. After these two general courses, I began in October 1885 the first of a series of more minute lectures, beginning at the point marked out in the present course as a provisional beginning for the special work of a Professor of so-called "Modern" History. That point is the great barbarian invasion of Gaul in 407, the beginning of Teutonic settlement, strictly so called, in the Western lands of the Empire. I had far rather have begun at 776 B.C. than at 407 A.D.; but I believe that I have chosen the best point that could be chosen, if an arbitrary division was to be made anywhere. But I feel more and more the utter worthlessness of the unnatural distinctions which are still drawn, in matters of history and language, between periods and subjects between which no natural distinction can be drawn. An advanced time of life has its drawbacks; but I daily feel, and I find that eminent contemporaries of mine feel with me, the great advantage of having spent our youth under the old Oxford system and not under the new. The changes of 1849-50 were premature. The old system needed expansion to bring it up to the actual level of knowledge; but its principle was good; it was sound within its own lines. Its examination in sixteen books at the end of four years was

a real test; it gave no such charming opportunities as are now provided for forgetting one subject before another is learned. It made no attempt to teach history or language beyond a certain point; but it gave a man habits of thought and study by which he might carry on his work further at pleasure. But, instead of enlarging that system so as to take in subjects later in date, the later subjects were set up as something distinct from the earlier, almost as antagonistic to them. It is against this state of things, to say nothing of other difficulties, that a historical Professor at Oxford has to fight. It is for others to judge whether I have won any ground in my early campaigns.

If really sound learning is to be our object, if the great discoveries of modern times are to be made available for the studies of the University, we must rise from the endless petty changes in which academic life seems to be frittered away, to a thorough recasting of our system. Learning must no longer be sacrificed to an unintelligible delight in an endless whirl of examinations. Instead of the diseased excitement of class-lists—a weak point of the old system which has been exaggerated under the new—we need such tests, in the form of examinations or otherwise, as shall make a bachelor's degree respectable, and a master's degree honourable. Instead of the present unnatural divisions, we need a School of History and a School of Language—better still a School of History and Language—in which both subjects may be studied without regard to artificial barriers which gender only to shallowness. This I hardly expect to see in my lifetime; but I do rejoice that, among many changes for the worse, there is hope of one change for the better, a change which may do something to bridge over the fatal gap, and which I trust may pave the way for a more thorough reform.

I speak of those subjects only of which I conceive myself to be able to judge. As to what may be best for studies other than those of history and language, I venture no opinion, because my opinion would be worthless. The University ought to welcome real knowledge of every kind, and to do for every branch of knowledge whatever is best for that branch. But that general cultivation and discipline of the mind which is the highest object of the University should surely not be sacrificed to mere specialism in any branch. And in every branch alike the aim should surely be knowledge for its own sake, knowledge as a discipline of the mind. It is surely not the business of the University to teach a man his calling in life, but to teach him something which may be good for him, whatever calling he may choose. In the most ancient system of all, the professional faculties, those of divinity, law, and medicine, could not be entered on till after long study in the more general faculty of arts. A degree in arts granted as the result of an examination in law or in divinity would have seemed a contradiction in terms. And however much the details of our studies may have changed from the studies of those days, the principle at least is a sound one.

On the relations of the professors to other teachers in the University I will not at present enlarge. In the more general lectures here printed, in the minute study of texts with a small class which I would gladly see larger, I have tried to show what I conceive the professor's duty to be. Teachers of other classes must do what they conceive to be their duty. But I am sure that college teaching—at least as college teaching was forty years back, when a college lecture was commonly a lecture on the text of a book carefully construed—might be brought into the closest harmony with professorial teaching. In my day there was very little professorial teaching; it was an evil that there was so little. The evil now is that there is so much of both kinds of teaching, but that the professor and the tutor seem to stand in no kind of relation to one another. In my small class with whom I have read Gregory and Paul, I have had graduates and undergraduates; I have had men but little younger than myself; I have had scholars of high renown, to whom on some points I am glad to look as my masters. Among these classes the professed teachers of history have supplied the smallest proportion. I merely state the fact; it is for them to explain it.

I trust that the present volume may be followed by my second course on the Chief Periods of European History. The lectures that have followed it, and others that may follow them, I do not propose to publish in the form of lectures; but I trust that their materials may be found useful in other shapes, as part of some of them has been already made use of in the first number of the English Historical Review.

St. Giles', Oxford,
    May 7, 1886.

CONTENTS.

INAUGURAL LECTURE.

THE OFFICE

OF THE

HISTORICAL PROFESSOR.

THE OFFICE OF
THE HISTORICAL PROFESSOR.

In coming forward for the first time, as I do
to-day, to fulfil the new duties which the highest
power in the land has laid upon me, I cannot forget
how soon my first words necessarily come after the
last words of the renowned scholar in whose place I
find myself. It is indeed matter of rejoicing for us
all that his last words were last words only in an
official sense. Our guide is taken from us, and yet
not wholly taken from us. Called to other and
higher duties, we feel sure that he will not forget
the studies of his earlier life; we feel sure that he
will still be ready, from time to time, to stretch out
a helping hand to those whose main work still lies
in the fields where his own once lay. And readiest of
all, I would fain hope, he will be to stretch forth a
hand to him who feels it his highest honour to stand
in his place, and to stand in it, I may make bold to
say, with his good will and something more. And
yet the fact in which we all rejoice that he in whose
place I stand still lives and flourishes does but in
some sort heighten the natural difficulties of my first
appearance before you. I am thereby driven into
more direct comparison than I otherwise might have

been with one with whom comparison is indeed dangerous. You have to hear my inaugural professions, while what I may call the exaugural confessions of the Bishop of Chester have as yet hardly passed from your ears. Let me only hope that, if I ever have the same privilege as he had, of parting from you, hardly, like him, to new duties, but when the time may come for me to lay all official duties aside, I may be able to make as good a confession as he made. I would fain hope that, when the time comes, I may part from you with as cheerful a confidence as his, that I may, like him, feel that I have at least done my best, and that you—or those who may then represent you here—have at least accepted the will, perhaps even, as in his case, the deed also.

There is one point of difference, whether I am to count it as a difference for gain or loss, between him who now speaks and him who spoke last in the same character, which comes strongly home to me when I am tempted to glance, as he did, at the history of the post in which I am called to succeed him. As a rule, the younger succeeds the elder. It is by a rather singular lot that I am called on to take the place which has been held in succession by two living men, by two personal friends, by two of the men of whom among all living men I think most highly, but to neither of whom can I look up with that particular form of reverence which we feel towards our elders and official teachers. Of the last two holders of this chair, the latter is certainly younger than I am by a few years, as even the former is by a few days. And this fact, a disadvantage truly in many ways, is no small advantage when I come to look back at times before either of them was called to it. My academic memory goes back further than that of the Bishop of Chester, and I cannot mourn that it does so. There can be but few here who can remember, as I can, listening to lectures from a Regius Professor of Modern History more than two-and-forty years ago. But those whose memory carries them so far back will assuredly not have forgotten the time when they listened to the voice of Arnold. Of that great teacher of historic truth, that greater teacher of moral right, I can speak as one wholly free from local, traditional, or personal bias. I was not one of his pupils or of his followers. I never spoke to him ; I never heard him speak save with his official voice in the well-filled Theatre. And yet I am bound to honour him as a master in a sense in which I can honour no other. On one side I have learned more from him than I have learned even from my Right Reverend predecessor. For of Arnold I learned what history is and how it should be studied. It is with a special thrill of feeling that I remember that the chair which I hold is his chair, that I venture to hope that my work in that chair may be in some sort, at whatever distance, to go on waging a strife which he began to wage. It was from him that I learned a lesson, to set forth which, in season and out of season, I have taken as the true work of my life. It was from Arnold that I first learned the truth which ought to be the centre and life of all our historic studies, the truth of the Unity of History. If I am sent hither for any special object, it is, I hold, to proclaim that truth, but to proclaim it, not as my own thought, but as the thought of my great master. It is a responsibility indeed to be the successor, even after so many years, of one who united so many gifts. New light has been thrown on many things since his day; but it surely ill becomes any man of our time who, by climbing on Arnold's shoulders, has learned to see further than Arnold himself could see, to throw the slightest shade of scorn upon so venerable a name. Surely never did any man put forth truths so high and deep in words so artlessly and yet so happily chosen. If he were nothing more than the teller of a tale in the English tongue, he would take his place as one who has told a stirring tale as few could tell it. It was something to make us quiver at the awful vision of Hannibal, and to show us Marcellus lying dead on the nameless hill. It was a higher calling to show, as no other has shown, that history is a moral lesson. In every page of his story Arnold stands forth as the righteous judge, who, untaught by the more scientific historical philosophy of later days, still looked on crime as no less black because it was successful, and who could acknowledge the rights even of the weak against the strong. But more than all for my immediate purpose, Arnold was the man who taught that the political history of the world should be read as a single whole, who taught that the true life of the tale, the true profit of the teaching, should not be made void and of none effect by meaningless and unnatural divisions. It was he who taught us that what, in his own words, is "falsely called ancient history," is in truth the most truly modern, the most truly living, the most rich in practical lessons for every succeeding age. From him I learned that teaching; it will be my highest aim, in the place in which I am now set, to hand that teaching on to others. If I can do ought to break down the middle wall of partition that is against us—if I can do ought to make men feel more deeply that so-called "ancient" history without "modern" is a foundation useless for lack of a superstructure, that so-called "modern" history without "ancient" is a superstructure ready to fall for lack of a foundation—if I can bring home to men's minds that the patriarchs of our own folk, the Angul and Dan of the old legend, the mythical representatives of our speech, our laws, our whole historic being, are as such the equal brethren of Hellên and Latinus—if I can bring but one of you to work, as I have ever worked, with the kindred records side by side, with the fates of one branch of the house ever called in to throw the needful light on the fates of the other branch—if I can bring but one to trace out with me the work of Kleisthenês, of Licinius, of Simon of Montfort, as parts of one living whole, a whole of which every stage needs to be grasped by the same faculties, to be studied by the same methods—then indeed I shall have done the work that I have come to do ; but I shall have done it only as the loyal follower of the master who being dead yet speaketh, if only by the mouth of a distant successor.

I have paid my homage where homage from a holder of this chair is due chiefest and first of all. But there are others, others of whom I have already spoken, of whom, living though they are, I still feel that I have not yet said all that is their due. Arnold was taken from us too soon, taken in the fulness of his strength, when he had indeed done much, but when much more, above all in this place, might have been looked for from him. He was lost to us; but worthy successors were in time to fill his place. Again, after a season, his chair passed to a memorable man. It passed to one who had indeed drunk in the spirit of Arnold, to one who knew, as few have known, to grasp the truth that history is but past politics and that politics are but present history. It passed to a scholar, a thinker, a master of the English tongue, to one too who is something nobler still, to one whom we may truly call a prophet of righteousness. The name of Goldwin Smith is honoured in two hemispheres, honoured as his name should be who never feared the face of man, wherever there was truth to be asserted or wrong to be denounced. He went forth from us of his own will; but it was but to carry his light to another branch of our own folk, and it may be more graceful in us, if we do not so much regret our own loss as congratulate the kindred lands to which he is gone. And in absence he yet teaches us; some truths have perhaps become clearer to him on the other side of Ocean than they could ever have been in our elder world. Not the least among his many services to truth and to right reason has been done within this very year. He has taught us, in one of those flitting papers which, when they come from him, speak volumes, where to look for the true Expansion of England. His keen eye has seen it, not in the spread of "empire," but in the spread of that which is the opposite to empire —not in the mere widening of dominion—an Eastern despot could do that—but in that higher calling which free England in the later world has shared with free Hellas in the elder. He has taught us the meaning of words, the realities of things; he has taught us to see, if not a "Greater Britain," yet a newer England, in the growth of new lands of Englishmen, new homes of the tongue and law of England, lands which have become more truly colonies of the English folk because they have ceased to be provinces of the British Crown.

And one more tribute, not the last, I feel sure, by many, to him in whose immediate place I stand, my predecessor in the University and in one college, my successor in early days in another. In those early days I may, I think, fairly claim that I was the first to grasp more fully than others all that was in him, to see in him something more than the clever men whom we meet with daily, to pick him out as one with whom his first class and his fellowship were not the ending but the beginning of his career. It seems not so many years since I was often asked, sometimes by men who deemed themselves specially learned, who this Stubbs might be of whom I talked so much but of whom nobody else had heard. No one will ask that now of the historian of the English Constitution, the enlightening spirit of the Ecclesiastical Courts Commission, and beyond all these, the man who has drawn the life-like portrait of Henry the Second, and who has thereby shown that he has a call before other men to draw a life-like portrait of Henry the Eighth. I have had in my life the honour and advantage of knowing not a few wise and learned men, some who have passed away from us, some who are still among us. Among them two stand forth before all others ; one of my own time of life, the other of an older generation ; one an intimate friend of many years, the other a master at whose feet I deemed it a privilege to sit now and then as a humble listener. To those two I can honestly pay a special tribute which I can hardly pay to any other. Among many of whom I have learned, those two, the late Bishop of Saint David's and the present Bishop of Chester, Connop Thirlwall and William Stubbs, stand forth as the two from whom one might always learn without any need to doubt or stumble at what one learned of them. Others may know how to tell a more popular tale; others may indulge in more brilliant feats of the imagination ; of none other can I say, as I can say of each of them, that his minute accuracy never fails and his impartial judgement never swerves. In a long and careful study of the Bishop of Chester's writings, I will not say that I have always agreed with every inference that he has drawn from his evidence ; but I can say that I have never found a flaw in the statement of his evidence. If I have now and then lighted on something that looked like oversight, I have always found in the end that the oversight was mine and not his. After five-and-thirty years' knowledge of him and his works, I can say without fear that he is the one man among living scholars to whom one may most freely go as to an oracle, that we may feel more sure with him than with any other that in his answer we carry away words of truth which he must be rash indeed who calls in question.

Standing then in the place of such men as these, of predecessors whom we have not wholly lost but to whom I can still look as friends and fellow-workers, I feel the responsibility, the burthen of my new office the more keenly. It is no small matter, at an age when the best part of one's days is gone, to be carried away to a wholly new manner of life, to begin a career at a time when one who had begun it earlier might fairly think of withdrawing from it. To that work then I am the more bound to give the fulness of such powers as I have because I am likely to have a shorter time than others to do it in. In such a post as mine, each man will have his own way of doing things, and he will do his work the better, if he does it in his own way, the way which his own nature and his own studies lead him to. In this case, in defiance of Aristotle and Aristotle's teacher, I venture to think that there may be more good ways than one. . I feel sure that my two illustrious predecessors must have done their work, each admirably, but in utterly different ways. And I feel sure that each of them did his work the better for doing it in his own way, and not trying to follow the way of some other man. To them, as well as to our teachers of past days, I may apply the words which Cicero applies to the great orators whom he followed—" omnes inter se dissimiles fuerunt, sed ita tamen ut neminem sui velis esse dissimilem [1]." And I trust it is not presumptuous in me to say that I feel sure that my way of doing the work will also be different from that of any who have gone before me, and moreover that I shall do that work all the better if I do it in my own way and do not try to copy the way of any of those who have gone before me. I need not tell you that I come back to the University after many years, and those years full of great changes. I need not say that much in the present teaching and administration of this place is altogether new and strange to me. Of its examinations I once knew something, but even then I found the course of change to be so fast that, each time that I was appointed Examiner, I had to learn my trade afresh ; my experience from the former time had already become a matter of ancient history. Of teaching in the strict sense, in the University or out of it, I have had no experience whatever, unless any one chooses to count two terms' possession, eight-

---

[1] De Oratore, iii. 7.

and-thirty years back, of a lowly office in my own college, an office which the progress of reform has since swept away. In the art of preparing—I will not use the ugly word cramming—an undergraduate for his class or for his pass the last bachelor who has won his own class or his own pass is necessarily more skilful than I am. But I do not feel that my lack of experience of this kind is necessarily a disadvantage ; every man has his own line of duty, and it seems to me, strange as I believe the doctrine will sound in some ears, that to prepare men for examinations is no part of the duty of a Professor in such a subject as mine. Duties he has, and no small ones ; but they are, as I hold, duties of quite another kind from even the widest and most liberal form of teaching into which the thought of success or failure in an examination is ever allowed to enter.

There is surely a certain lurking fallacy in the word "Professor." The name surely means wholly different things according to the subjects to which it is applied. It surely implies a different relation to the Professor's subject, according to the nature of that subject, or rather perhaps according to the position of that subject among the studies of the University. When a subject, for whatever cause, is studied by a few only, when the Professor is perhaps the only teacher of the subject in the University, I should conceive that, while it is his duty to stand forth as a representative of the highest learning in his subject, it must also be his duty to bend himself, if need be, to the humblest form of its teaching. A

Professor of Arabic, while master of a mighty literature from which I daily mourn that I am shut out,
must also, I imagine, be ready to teach the Arabic
alphabet, even, if need be, to a brother-professor.
No such duty lies on a professor of that which is
alike the oldest and the newest speech of European
freedom; none such lies on a professor of the undying tongue of Empire, the tongue of the consuls,
the Cæsars, and the pontiffs. A professor of Greek
must, I assume, be master alike of every stage and
every phase of that still living speech, from the song
of Homer to the song of Rhêgas, from the prose of
Hekataios to the prose of Trikoupês. A professor of
Latin, I assume, must be alike at home in every
page of the long life of the Imperial tongue, from
the song of the Arval Brethren to the hymns of Ber-
nard of Clairvaux, from the sharp sayings exchanged
between Nævius and the Metelli to those yet more
memorable Saturnians in which the nameless poet of
the thirteenth century set forth the earliest platform
of Parliamentary Reform. Nay, it might hardly be
unreasonable if we even asked him to begin a fresh
journey from the oath of Strassburg, if we called on
him to trace the fates of the children as well as of
the parent, to trace them even to the most wayward
shapes which the speech of Latium has put on by
the springs of the Rhine or by the mouths of the
Danube. Each alike, he who represents Greek and
he who represents Latin, is surely set in his place to
be the representative of the widest and the deepest,
the oldest and the newest, learning that can bear on

the history of the undying tongue that forms his subject. But they are spared the lowlier duties which I conceive that a professor of Arabic or Chinese must combine with a learning no less deep and wide of the tongue that forms his subject. And so, I take it, it must be with the professor of every subject which has many followers in this place and of which there are many teachers besides himself. If I may so far magnify an office in which I am myself a sharer, I would say that a professor of any of the great branches of study in this place should hold a place something like that which the prince held in the view of Tiberius Cæsar[1]. The prince was not called on to discharge the duties of an ædile, a prætor, or a consul ; so the Professor is not called on to discharge the duties of a college tutor or a private tutor. " Majus aliquid et excelsius a professore postulatur." His business is, not to make men qualified for classes and fellowships, but to be the representative of that to which classes and fellowships, if they are not to be wholly useless and mischievous, are simply means. His place is to be the representative of learning. He should stand ready to be the helper, if need be, to be the guide, of any, old or young, be they freshmen or be they doctors, who, in days like these, between the frenzy of amusements and the frenzy of examinations, can still find a few stray hours to seek learning for its own sake. But before all other classes he will welcome the younger graduates, those who have already learned

[1] Tac. Ann. iii. 53.

something, but who still have much to learn, and among them he will specially welcome those who have undertaken the work of teaching in his own subject. He and they are alike teachers, though teachers of different kinds, and his experience in the art of teaching himself may make him of some use to them in the art of teaching others. But his own calling is different from theirs. He must be ready, in set discourses, to show forth whatever, in his own researches or in the researches of others, he may deem most fitting to suggest thoughts as well as to supply facts to his hearers. But he will not confine himself to this more easy, more showy, perhaps both to himself and to his hearers more taking work. He must not forget the most solid business of his calling. He must ever bear in mind himself, and he must ever strive to impress on the minds of others, that the most ingenious and the most eloquent of modern historical discourses can after all be nothing more than a comment on a text. All that he can say of his own thinking, even all that the newest German book can tell him, will after all be but illustrations of those original authorities without a sound and thorough knowledge of whose texts all our finest talk is but shadow without substance. To the law and to the testimony, to the charter and to the chronicle, to the abiding records of each succeeding age, writ on the parchment or graven on the stone— it is to these that he must go himself and must guide others. He must himself toil, and as far as in him lies, he must constrain or beguile others to toil with him, at that patient study of contemporary texts, of contemporary monuments, which to some minds seems a good deal less taking than the piling together of theories to be upset the next day by some other theory. He must work to lay the foundation; when the foundation is once laid on the rock of original research, a superstructure may be raised on it which may live through a good many blasts and storms of controversy. But he who without a foundation builds on the sands of theory, he who rushes at a difficult and controversial period with no knowledge of the periods that went before it or of the periods that came after it, he who conceives of events, not as they are reported by those who saw them, but as may be convenient for some favourite doctrine, political or theological, philosophical or artistic—against such as these our professor will hardly need to raise his voice of warning. He may spare himself the task ; he may leave events to take their course ; the house built on the sand will presently crumble of itself, without needing any special blasts and storms to sweep it away.

It is, as you will see, a somewhat lofty standard that I have formed to myself of the professor's office. But it is only by aiming at the highest standard of all, at a standard which may be far above our reach, that we shall ever attain to the highest standard that is within our reach. In other words, the professor should be one who has at least striven to be a master in that branch of knowledge which he is called on to represent, and he should be ready to devote himself heart and soul to the advancement of knowledge, of knowledge in the highest sense, in that branch. If he is not thus qualified, intellectually and morally, he is not fit to be professor at all. If he is thus qualified, he is surely fit to judge for himself how he can best promote the interests of that branch of knowledge. It is therefore surely a mistake to lay down a code of hard and unbending rules, not only for professors of this or that subject, but for all professors of all subjects. I cannot but think that my idea of a professor must be widely different from the idea which seems to have been entertained by the last reformers of the University. I can speak the more freely on this head, because the last reform was not a reform of our own making, but a reform which was thrust upon us from outside. I had passed my life in the belief that an University ought to be, before all things, a seat of learning, or, if the word be liked better, a seat of research. And I had thought that for some years past the great object of reformers had been to make learning or research less difficult, perhaps even to make it, in a meaner sense, less unprofitable to its followers. Whoever dictated the ordinances of the last set of Commissioners must have thought otherwise. It is indeed hard to believe that the object of the Commission really was to do all that could be done for the hindrance of learning and for the humiliation of its official representatives. But, if such had been their objects, no one could have denied that they had adapted means to ends very skilfully. The ordinance seems to look on a professor, not as a representative of learning, but as a mere teacher, as an usher, I might say, an usher too of a low moral standard, who will be likely to shirk his work unless he is bound down to it by minute and rigid rules. Nothing surely can be more likely than this to hinder the professor from giving full play to whatever powers he may have, nothing more likely to make him look on his work as a task and to keep him back from throwing himself into it heart and soul. It is, or lately was, the fashion to mock at the old founders of colleges for making strict and unbending statutes to control the discipline and manner of life of their members. Yet here, as the last instalment of reform, as the newest developement of enlightenment, we have a set of professorial ordinances, ordinances almost as minute as the statutes of any founder of past ages, designed for the guidance, not of lads and their immediate teachers, but of men who, if they are not masters of the several branches of learning, are altogether out of their places. For a man who is what a professor ought to be, what I am sure that not a few of the professors in this place are, it is not exactly encouraging to tell him that he must give so many lectures at such and such times, that he must announce them beforehand at such and such times, that he must hold himself responsible to one Board and that he must take counsel with another. Will the members of the Boards forgive me if I tell them that as yet I feel towards them much as Apollônios of Tyana felt when he had never seen a tyrant, when he did not know how many heads a tyrant had, or what kinds of necks and teeth those heads might be furnished with[1]? But I am told that the boards are much less terrible in real life than they seem in the bristling language of the ordinance. The good sense, no doubt, of their members hinders them from really being such thorns in the professor's side as it would seem that the authors of the ordinance meant them to be. But neither professor nor board can wipe out the ordinance, with all its petty and grotesque restrictions. Till some deliverer from outside steps in to undo the work of the invader from outside, we must bear our yoke as we can.

An Oxford professor then in these days must work in fetters, but he may still work. And a professor of what is called " Modern History " may feel himself bound by fetters which seem to be more firmly rivetted than those of any of his brethren. I need not tell you — I have already told you in this lecture—that I acknowledge no such distinction as that which is implied in the words " ancient " and "modern" history, " ancient " and " modern " languages, and the like. In the course of a life divided about equally between what are called " ancient " and what are called "modern " studies, I have never been able to find out the difference between the two. I have never been able to find out by my own wit when " ancient " history ends and when "modern " history begins. And when I have asked others, when I have searched into the writings of others, I

---

[1] Philostratos, Life of Apollônios, iv. 37.

have found so little agreement on the point that I
have been myself none the wiser. A living friend
once told me that modern history begins with the
French Revolution, and I fancy that a good many
people, at least in France, would gladly agree with
his doctrine. On the other hand, Baron Bunsen
held that modern history began with the Call of
Abraham. These, I think, are the two extremes;
but I have heard a good many intermediate points
suggested. Those perhaps are wisest who decline to
define at all; only the thought will follow that it
might be wiser still not to draw a distinction which
cannot be defined. At any rate the University has
never ruled the point. In all the controversies of
five-and-thirty years ago I never could get a definition of modern history. More than all, even the last
set of Commissioners have not taken on them to
define it. Even those who are so minute as to rule
that the Professor of Modern History is to give
exactly forty-two lectures in a year—they do not
say how they propose to compel him to give forty-
two good lectures—even they do not undertake to
tell him what he is to lecture about. They tell him
to lecture in "some part of modern history;" but
they do not tell him what "modern history" is. It
is surely open to him to accept either of the defini-
tions which I have quoted. I should, I conceive, be
strictly keeping within the four corners of the ordinance if I were to begin with the battle of four kings
against five, or again if I were to decline to touch
any matter older than A. D. 1789. In short out of the

very abundance of the Professor's fetters comes his
means of escape. As to my subjects, at least I am
free. But let no one fear that, because I am free, I am
likely to make any raids on the domains of other professors of which they might reasonably complain. It
is one of the dearest wishes of my heart to see this
vain distinction where no real distinction is utterly
wiped away from the legislation of the University of
Oxford, or even to see such promising approaches
towards wiping it away which have been actually
made in the University of Cambridge. At Cambridge
there is now a tripos where, at the bidding of
common sense, in the interest of sound learning, it is
possible to take up Thucydides and Lambert of Herz-
feld side by side. All honour then to our illustrious
sister, and may we soon have the wisdom to follow in
the track which she has opened. I will not at present
enter with any fulness on a subject on which I trust
to have other opportunities of speaking at greater
detail. But I cannot help pointing out, now at the
very beginning, that this unnatural division into
" ancient " and " modern " hinders the great central
fact of European history, the growth and the abiding
of the power of Rome, from being ever set forth in all
the fulness of its unity. The strange confusions
which prevail in many minds with regard to the
Empire in East and West, the utter blank which the
whole subject is in many minds, come largely of this
piecemeal way of looking at things which are simple
enough if looked at as a whole, but which are
utterly meaningless when this and that fragment of

the story is looked at apart from its fellows. No
man can ever understand how truly the last Constantine was the successor of the first, how truly
again the last Francis was the successor of the first
Charles, unless he has fully taken in in what sense
and through what stages Charles and Constantine
alike had stepped into the place of Gaius Julius Cæsar
Octavianus, consul, tribune, and pontiff of the commonwealth of Rome. Or, look at the history of one
of the noblest of the provinces of that commonwealth,
of that illustrious island whose story is in one of its
brilliant times so closely interwoven with our own.
Look at Sicily, the meeting-place of the nations, the
battle-field of creeds and races, where the strife
between Aryan and Semitic man has been since
fought out in all its fulness. That wonderful cycle
of events loses all its historic life, if we look at one
fragment of it only; the strife with the Phœnician and
the strife with the Saracen each loses half its meaning if either is parted from the other; Timoleôn cannot hold his full historic place apart from Roger, nor
can Roger hold his place apart from Timoleôn. But
the mischief of this unnatural division where no real
division is is not confined to any one of the subjects
of University study; it affects our whole system to
its very centre. We in the nineteenth century are
called on to do a work of the same kind as that which
was wrought by the scholars of the sixteenth century.
They brought to light a new learning, a learning
which seemed like the discovery of an elder world.
We have to put all worlds and all learning, old and

new, past and present, into their due relations
towards one another. The sixteenth century found
out the life and value of certain stages of the history
and the languages of Greece and Italy ; it is for
the nineteenth to put those stages into their due
relation to other stages in the history and the languages both of those lands and of other lands. The
question is one which does not touch the study
of political history only ; it touches no less the
study of language and the study of art. We
need here no "modern school," no "modern side ;"
we need no school of so-called "modern" languages
apart from "ancient," we need no chair of so-called
"classical" archæology apart from the archæology of
other times. The warning that is now needed is a
general one, and one which closely touches the very
existence of Oxford or of any other University as a seat
either of really sound learning or of really liberal teaching. Those studies which are the truest foundation of
all studies, studies without which we may as well shut
up our halls and schools and lecture-rooms altogether,
studies which are misapplied only when it is forgotten
that they are only the foundation and not the whole
building, are daily threatened, daily mocked at, it may
be by men who, as has been happily said, sometimes
dissemble, it may be by the ignorant and presumptuous who deem themselves philosophers, and who even
come to be so deemed by others. We ought to be
ready with our answer to the gainsayers, and, if we
think good, we may make ourselves ready with it. But
we shall never be ready with it as long as we remain

deaf to the teaching of the great discoveries of the
age, as long as we take no heed to the new life
thrown on all knowledge by the comparative method,
as long in short as we obstinately part asunder
"ancient" and "modern" history, "ancient" and
"modern" languages. We are told over and over
again that the time is wasted which we spend on the
teaching of what are called "dead" languages, that
the time is wasted which we spend on the political
communities of small physical extent in ages which
are far distant. Cavils like these are indeed only
the cavils of ignorance and shallowness, but, as the
world goes at present, they are cavils which need a
practical answer. And our answer will never be
so practical as it might be as long as we give an
advantage to the enemy by keeping up these
artificial barriers. We all, I trust, agree in holding
that there are no tongues more truly living, no
tongues which even now more deeply influence
the speech and thoughts of men, than those older
forms of the still abiding tongues of Greece and
Italy which the unlearned and unbelieving think
good to speak of as "dead.' If they are dead,
bury them; or at least leave them as a matter of
curious study for those whose tastes may lead their
studies in that direction. It is surely because they
are not dead, because they are the most living and
practical of all tongues, that we hold that they
must still abide, as the foundation, as the corner-
stone, as the crowning of the edifice, as the centre
of all that is worthy of the name of culture or

liberal education. But we make our ground less
strong than we should make it, we leave our
fortress more open to the assaults of ignorance,
if we part the elder from the younger, if we part
the parent from the children, if we fail to proclaim that our knowledge of any language is
imperfect, unless we know both whence words
come and whither they go. "Ancient languages,"
"modern languages," Latin to be learned with
no regard to its later fruit of French—French
to be learned without regard to its parent stock
of Latin—such a cruel severance as this is indeed
to betray one of our strongest outworks into the
hands of the besiegers. If the sixteenth century
made such a severance, it was neither wonderful
nor blameworthy; but it is blameworthy indeed
if we keep it on in the fuller light of the nineteenth. And as with language, so with political
history. We shall never be able to make such
answer as we ought to make to cavils about "small
states," about "battles fought two thousand years
ago," unless we boldly write on our banner the
golden words of Arnold, to which I have referred
already, when he speaks of "what is falsely called
ancient history, the really modern history of Greece
and Rome." One might think that the Roman
Empire was big enough even for a declaimer
against "petty states;" but we must take the
cavillers on their own ground; we must proclaim
aloud that the history of those small states of a far
distant age is, as the history of small states of a

far distant age, an essential part of the study of
man's progress, without which we shall never fully
understand the workings of greater states in later
times. We must proclaim that the real life of
the history of those times lies not in its separation
from the affairs of our own time, but in its close
connexion with them. But this we cannot do in
its fulness as long as we part asunder periods
of history each of which loses half its value if it
is looked at apart from the other. We cannot
make our full defence as long as we condemn so-
called "ancient" and so-called "modern" history
to be taken up in distinct schools as wholly unconnected subjects, to be taught and lectured on
by teachers and professors who stand in no kind
of relation to one another. If we wish to keep
our "ancient" history, our "ancient" languages,
as an essential part of any sound and liberal teaching, we can do it only by letting the gainsayers
know that the falsely called "ancient" studies
are, as Arnold taught us forty years ago, the
most truly "modern" of all.

To me then the very title of a Professor of
"Modern" History is in itself a fetter. It is be
sure made one degree less hard to bear because no
attempt is made to define "modern" history, because
it doubtless has been felt that it was impossible to
define it. There is indeed one definition of "modern"
history which I would gladly accept; there is one
point at which I would even be content to draw a
hard and fast line between "ancient" and "modern."

That point is one which is not quite so near to our own day as the French Revolution nor yet quite so far from it as the Call of Abraham. We may well agree to draw a line between "ancient" and "modern," if we hold our "modern" period to begin with the first beginnings of the recorded history of Aryan Europe, whether we place those beginnings at the first Olympiad or carry them back to any earlier time. There alone can we find a real starting-point; a line drawn at any later time is a mere artificial and unnatural break. It is then that for us, for the nations of Europe of our own day, the story of ourselves and of our kinsfolk begins. It is the beginning of our political being; it is the beginning of tongues kindred to our own, tongues which still happily form the groundwork of all our studies. Then begins that one great and unbroken drama which takes in the long political history of European man, the history of the Greek and the Italian, the history of the Celt, the Teuton, and the Slave. By "modern" history then I should understand our own history in the widest sense, as distinguished from certain branches of history which are older than our own, and from certain other branches which, though contemporary with our own, are not our own. We, students of modern history, of the European history of perhaps the last seven-and-twenty centuries, should be among the first to welcome the vast additions which our own days have made to the knowledge of history which is truly ancient, of languages which are truly dead. While we claim

the records of Athenian archons and Roman consuls
as essentially parts of the same tale as the records of
Venetian doges and English kings, we welcome the
recovered records of the Accadian, the Assyrian,
and the Hittite, as materials for a high and worthy
study, but for a study which is not our own. The
two studies are closely connected; each may give
good help to the other; but Accadian history is
helpful to English history, not as Latin or Hellenic
history is helpful, but as anthropology, as palæon-
tology, as geology—studies all of them which deserve plain Teutonic names—are constantly found
helpful. All these are helpful, indeed there is
hardly any branch of knowledge which is not helpful
to the true historian; but they are helpful as distinct,
though kindred, studies, not as parts of the same
study. There is then, beyond the first beginnings of
our "modern" history, a wide field of truly "ancient"
history, of history which does not directly influence
the political life of modern Europe, but which is
fully worthy of its place as a separate branch of
knowledge, with its distinct students, its distinct
teachers. And we, students and teachers of the
history of living Europe, must give a welcome yet
more brotherly to all that advances the knowledge
of those branches of history which are still living,
though not European. We do not fully understand
the history of the lands and nations which are our
own, unless we know at least their relations to the
lands, the nations, the tongues, the creeds, which
have supplied the men of Aryan Europe with their

immediate neighbours and rivals. The tale of
Greece, the tale of Italy, brings us at almost every
page across the records of the Hebrew, the Phœnician, and the Arab. When in the palaces of Palermo
we see the letters traced from right to left, traced at
the bidding of Norman kings but by the hands of
Saracenic craftsmen, when we see the sadder sight
of legends in the same world-wide alphabet blotting
out the mosaics of Justinian in the most glorious of
Christian temples, we must indeed acknowledge that
the teaching of Arabia has truly a history of its own,
a history parallel to our own history, a history in-
tertwined with our own history, but still distinct
from it. Semitic history, Arabian history above all,
must have its distinct students and distinct teachers,
yet it still is so closely connected with our own
studies that the votaries of either subject must at
least know the main outlines of the other. The
history of the Phœnician and the Arab and of those
who have adopted the creed of the Arab, must be
known as the history of mighty and abiding rivals,
not as part of the history of our own home and of
our own folk. For this last we can acknowledge but
one boundary either in space or in time. It spreads
wherever men have spread themselves who have
been brought under the political, the moral, or the
religious influence of Rome. For its beginning we
may not seek at any time more recent than our first
glimpses of Rome's own Hellenic teacher.

But in an imperfect world man must yield to
circumstances. Vain and mischievous as is the dis-

tinction, yet as long as it is formally acknowledged in
the University, as long as there are distinct schools,
distinct professors, of "ancient" and of "modern"
history, and as long as the accepted sphere of the
"ancient" professor takes in times much later than
the first Olympiad, a professor of "modern" history
must, if only under protest, try to put some meaning
upon his qualifying adjective, and to chalk out for
himself some special sphere which will not bring him
into any open clashing with his "ancient" colleagues.
And I think that a boundary may be drawn between
us which, better at least than some others, may serve
as a fair temporary shift till the whole arrangements
of the University as to the teaching of history and
language are thoroughly recast in accordance with
the advance of modern knowledge. The fifth century of our æra, the period of the settlement of the
Teutonic nations within the Empire, is one of the
most marked periods in the history of the world.
It is of equal importance with the earlier period
which in some sort balances it, the second century
before our æra. The earlier time ruled that Rome
should be the head of Europe ; it ruled what form
should be taken by her dominion ; the later time
ruled what form her abiding influence should take in
days when her political power was cut short and in
many of her western provinces broken in pieces.
The division is of course open to the objection that,
in any philosophical view of the course of events, the
age which saw the first sack of Carthage and the age
which saw the first sack of Rome answer to one

another and cannot be parted asunder. That strong
objections may be taken to this as to any other point
of division is indeed the essence of my whole case ;
but, if a distinction must be drawn at some point, the
point at which I propose to draw it seems open to
fewer objections than most others. It is a real
starting-point ; it is the time that saw the planting
of the germs of the great nations of Western Europe,
the age which saw the settlement of the Goth in
Spain, of the Burgundian and the Frank in Gaul, of
the Angle and the Saxon in Britain. I may admit
a secondary sense in which that age may be called
the beginning of "modern" history, if only it is
allowed that " ancient " history goes on alongside of
it for a thousand years. That thousand years the
professors of the two divisions will have in common,
but they will look at them from different points of
view. The "ancient" professor will look at them
with the eyes of one whose home is fixed within the
walls, first of the elder and then of the younger
Rome. His "modern " colleague will look at it with
the eyes of the younger nations, who have found
themselves dwellings on Roman soil, who in becoming conquerors have become disciples, who deem it
their highest boast to deck their princes with the
ensigns and the titles of the power whose political
greatness they have overthrown. In other words,
a Professor of Modern History, while he protests
against the name, will still have a definite and
intelligible function if he be understood to be a
professor of the history of the Teutonic and Slavonic

nations. He will do well to fix his ordinary limit at the point when Teutonic wandering changes into Teutonic settlement. Yet he may be forgiven if he is sometimes tempted to look back with yearning to that great day in the history of our race, in the history of the whole world, when it was ruled by the Teutoburg wood that there should be a free Germany to plant a free England, and a free England to plant a free America. Nay, he may even sometimes cast a backward glance to that premature wandering of our kinsfolk which was checked by the arm of the yeoman of Arpinum, when the eagle of Rome, the eagle of Marius, first spread her wings over the field of Aquæ Sextiæ. All that is purely Greek, all that is purely Roman, he will school himself to forego ; the historian of Teutonic nations and Teutonic laws cannot afford wholly to shut up his Tacitus, his Strabo, and his Cæsar ; but he must turn away, with however heavy a heart, from the widest and deepest teaching that ever came from the pen of one who set down the records of deeds in which he himself had played his part. To his " ancient " colleague he must give up the man of varied experience and varied thought, the man who looked at his own age with the eyes of an historian of all ages, the man who bore the urn of Philopoimên and who stood beside the flames of Carthage, Polybios surveyor and teacher of the world.

And now for a word as to the immediate choice and treatment of subjects and texts among all that fill the ages since the tremendous sound of the Gothic

D

trumpet was heard within the Salarian gate. Till
our whole system is recast, the best thing that can
be done for sound learning in the department in
which I am called to give my help will be to fix as
far as may be the energies of those who devote
themselves to the so-called "modern" school on those
periods which can be treated most nearly after the
sound fashion of the old school of *Literæ Humaniores.*
That school did not make a man a philosopher, a
philologer, or an historian, but it gave him the best
possible start towards making himself any one of the
three. In my long past character of Examiner in
the School of Modern History, I always noticed the
great advantage enjoyed by those who had gone
through the discipline of the elder school, not merely
in the amount of knowledge that they brought with
them, but in the habits of mind which they had
gained, habits which enabled them to do justice to
later periods as well as to earlier. Among the four-
teen centuries which we have just taken as our
special heritage, some times adapt themselves far
better than others to the acquisition of sound and
scholar-like habits of thought and judgement. I can
conceive nothing more utterly opposed to sound
learning, nothing which more thoroughly deserves
the name of building without a foundation, than the
fashion of rushing off at once to the most recent
times, to controversial times, to times for which
the original authorities are so endless that, for
ordinary University study, it comes to the same
thing as having no original authorities at all. For

it is quite certain that in nearly every case the professed study of very modern times will mean something other than the real and thorough study of original authorities. The last recorded event in the newspapers is indeed part of the history of the world. It may be, and it should be, studied in a truly historic spirit. We who have seen the union of Germany and Italy, who have seen the new birth of the nations of south-eastern Europe, have lived in an age almost as rich in great events and great changes as the age of Polybios or the age of Procopius. Only there is this objection to making our own age a direct subject of University study that there is as yet no Polybios or Procopius in whom to study it. Indeed the whole range of the last two or three centuries of European history is surely far better suited for private study, for the wider professorial teaching, than it is to be made a direct subject of enforced work to be tested by examination. Knowledge of those times may well be no less solid in itself than knowledge of any earlier time; but solid knowledge of them is not likely to be reached early in life, nor can it be so easily tested by examination as knowledge of earlier times. The excessive devotion to very modern periods which seems to have set in within the last ten years or so seems to me to be an evil in every way. It widens the partition which it should be our first work to break down; it is more likely than the study of earlier times to gender to shallowness and mere talk; it savours of the notion which was afloat a generation back that it was well

to bring in "modern" history as an "easier" study
than the severe labours of the elder school. As far as
I may have any influence, official or personal, that
influence will be given to attempting to show that
" modern" history is at least no more easy than
" ancient." I shall do all that in me lies to dis-
courage the delusive study of what are called " subjects " and " periods," and to do all that one man can
do to bring back the sound and old-fashioned study
of " books." The one foundation of learning is the
mastery of original texts. That must come first ;
there is much for the student himself, much for the
tutor and the professor, to add in the way of comment and illustration and comparison of text with
text. But knowledge of a man's books is the beginning, the foundation, the absolutely needful thing,
without which all the rest is vanity. The great
difficulty is to persuade people that there really are
original authorities for what are called " mediæval "
times, exactly in the same way that it is allowed that
there are original authorities for what are called
" classical" times. I remember well how hard a
saying this seemed in the days when " modern"
history was brought in as something which might be
learned in modern English and French books that
were pleasant to read, and needed no painful mastery
of writings in the Greek and Latin tongues—the yet
more terrible Old-French and Old-English were as yet
hardly thought of. By this time some at least
have found out that both Western and Eastern
Europe can show no lack of original writers for

the history of days since the fifth century, writers
who in their way deserve as much to be studied as
the original authorities of earlier days. By this
time it may not sound wholly a paradox to say that
the two cannot be studied so profitably as when they
are studied side by side, that the mind is far more
widened, that the historic judgement is far more
strengthened, by the study of the two side by side
than by the study of either singly.

It is now high time that I should tell you in what
way I propose to carry on the work which I have
this day begun, what shape I mean to give to my
first official contribution to historical learning. My
notion is, if I find support enough in the University
to carry out the scheme, to keep going, through at
least part of the year, two distinct courses of lectures
of different kinds. One course may well consist of
lectures of a more general kind, written or spoken,
lectures which I venture to hope may be interesting
and profitable even to those who have not specially
given themselves to minute historical study. Alongside of these I hope I may find encouragement enough
to enable me to carry on courses of lectures of a more
minute kind on the texts of original writers. These
will be for special students of history, and to them I
would bid any, of whatever standing, who may be
willing to try whether it is not possible to work in
the same solid and thorough way at a writer in the
Greek or Latin of a later age as it confessedly is to
work at writers in the earlier forms of the same
tongues. In the present term I propose, for the

more general course, to give a series of lectures
on the methods of historical study; in another term
I hope to follow this up with a general course on the
great periods of history. After these introductory
courses I trust to go on with others of a more special
kind, on the history of our own land, of the Empire
in East and West, of Sicily, of any other part of our
great subject which may be found expedient. As
the first stage in the more minute series, I propose
to begin during the present term with the Frankish
History of Gregory of Tours. He is, I find, the
earliest writer recommended for candidates in the
School of Modern History. I fear that he is not one
of those who are most commonly taken up. I was
tempted to begin with some earlier writers, with
some who not only recorded the events of the fifth
century, but who actually lived in it. Above all,
I was tempted to begin with Sidonius Apollinaris,
courtier, bishop, panegyrist, and saint. But the
writings of Sidonius, precious as they are as illustrations of history, are not themselves in strictness
historical writings. And if we are to make any
distinction, even under protest, we must reckon the
purely Roman Sidonius among the latest of ancient
writers, while Gregory, not Frankish certainly, but
yet not wholly Roman, may be fairly looked on as
opening the mediæval series. With him then I will
begin. I choose him for his own sake, and I choose
him for a further motive. When we have well
seen what the Frankish Conquest of Gaul was,
we shall be better able to understand by contrast

the true nature of the English Conquest of
Britain.

I have chalked out a scheme for the steady work
of at least a year. How and how far that scheme
can be carried out depends partly on the Professor
himself, partly on the University at large. My
object will be gained, my reward will be won, if
I can succeed in bringing any considerable number
of members of the University, of whatever standing,
to join with me in the study of those ages which
begin with the settlement of our own and of kindred
races in the lands which some of them still hold, as
a subject no less worthy than the study of the ages
that went before them, as a study which cannot be
worthily followed if it is kept wholly apart from the
study of the ages which went before them. To
fellowship with me in that attempt I bid any who
feel a call to learning as an object to be sought for
its own sake, and who feel a special call to research
in that particular branch of learning. But remember
that it is to the pursuit of learning for its own sake
that I would call them. I call them to the pursuit
of knowledge, the pursuit of truth, to that learning
which is said to be better than house and land, but
which perhaps is not the path best adapted for the
winning of house and land. And if it is better
than house and land, it is also, I presume, better
than classes and fellowships, though I presume also
that it will be found to be at least not a hindrance to
the winning of classes and fellowships. I only give
the warning that my work here will have no im-

mediate reference to the winning of classes and fellowships. I am put here to do what can be done by one man who cannot have many years to do it in, for the promotion of historic truth for its own sake. Or, if there is any object beyond, higher than the search after truth for its own sake, it will be the hope that our studies of the past may be found to have after all their use in the living present, that we may at least not play our part the worse in the public life of our own day if we carry about us a clear knowledge of those earlier forms of public life out of which our own has grown. We shall surely not be the less at home in our own generation, if we bear in mind that we are the heirs and scholars of the generations that went before us, if we now and then stop in our own course to thank the memory of those without whom our own course could not have been run, if we are ready, at every fitting moment, to " praise famous men and our fathers that begat us."

THE METHODS OF HISTORICAL STUDY.

LECTURE I.

HISTORY AND ITS KINDRED STUDIES.

I SAID somewhat in my Inaugural Lecture, it is not unlikely that I may find something to say in future lectures, on the difficulty of defining the exact range of our subject as implied in the title of the chair in which I am placed. It is truly hard to define "modern" history; in the sense indeed in which the phrase is commonly used, it is impossible to define it, because there is really nothing with any distinctive being of its own to define. But we may throw our difficulty further back; if it is hard to define "modern" history, it is equally hard, though not for the same reason, to define history at all. It is hard to draw the line between history in the stricter sense, history such as is the business of my own chair and of my brethren of the other chairs of history, and a crowd of other subjects for whose help historical research is always asking, and which in their turn are constantly asking for the help of historical research. It is indeed hard to conceive any kind of knowledge that is not purely abstract, any kind of knowledge which deals in any way with the affairs of men, with which the historian may not do wisely to enter into an alliance. It need not be an alliance offensive and defensive, but it may with great advantage be an alliance for mutual

society, help, and comfort. The historical inquirer
will feel so firm a conviction that his neighbours
will often be useful to him, he will entertain so
strong a suspicion that he may often be useful to
his neighbours, that he will not always be anxious
to draw any very hard and fast line between his
territories and theirs. There must be very few
studies which may not ever and anon, in some
incidental way, throw light on historical questions.
There are some indeed which I fancy hardly can.
A great mathematician among ourselves is said to
have made a discovery the great beauty of which was
that it could never be of the slightest use to anybody. Therein undoubtedly spoke the truest scientific
spirit, that genuine love of knowledge for its own
sake from which I trust that we too are not wholly
shut out. Still I feel sure that, whatever that discovery was, it will never give me the slightest help
towards any of my lectures from this chair. The fact
that it never could be of any use to anybody at once
puts it out of all fellowship with a branch of study
which we fondly hope may be of great use to many
people. If I am right in holding that history is past
politics and that politics are present history, that which
can never be of any use to anybody would seem to be
quite shut out from our range. But there are few
branches of knowledge, few forms of literature, few
forms of art, of which their own masters would thus,
with a kind of triumph, proclaim the utter useless-
ness. And any branch which deals in any way with
the affairs of mankind must be accepted by the

historical student as at least potentially useful for his own purposes. The historian may have incidentally to deal with any subject whatever, and the more branches of knowledge he is master of the better prepared he is for his own work. But we must make a distinction between branches of knowledge which may help him incidentally, but which will help him only incidentally, and other branches which stand in more direct connexion with his own subject. For instance, the science of chemistry may incidentally explain some point in an historical narrative which would otherwise be obscure; the historical student who is also a chemist will clearly have an advantage over one who is not. Still this kind of help from a pursuit of a wholly different kind is so purely incidental that we could hardly make it even a counsel of perfection to the historian to make himself an accomplished chemist on the chance of such occasion. It will commonly be enough to consult such a chemist whenever the case arises. It is otherwise with geology, and with a whole group of sciences which have a close connexion with geology. The historian will clearly do his own regular work better for being master of them. The method of study which is followed in those sciences has much in common with his own, and its matter will give him far more than merely incidental help. The physical construction of any country is no small part of its history; it is the key to not a little in the political destiny of the land and its folk. I know few things more instructive than a look at Mr. Dawkins' map of what we may call Eskimo Europe. We feel at once that the European history which we have to master could never have happened in such an Europe as that. There was no Greece, no Italy, no Denmark, no Netherlands, no Britain. The gulfs and straits and islands and peninsulas which have made Europe other than Africa and Asia were not yet. The Mediterranean was not yet; two huge lakes unconnected with one another and with the Ocean could have given no scope for the life of Sidon and Carthage, of Milêtos, Massalia, and Athens. The physical revolution which made the life of Greece possible, which called into being so many cradles of freedom on their islands, their promontories, their inland valleys, must be set down as more than a physical change; it was the greatest and the most healthful of moral and political changes. So, as I have often said and as others have doubtless often said before me, the geological process which called into being those hills by the Tiber, lower in height, nearer to each other, than the other hills of Latium, fixed the history of the world for ever. For that process made the life of Rome possible; it made the rule of Rome and all that came of that rule possible; the world could never have found its mistress on the single hill of Tusculum, apart alike from the sea and from the yellow river. The history of man is bound up in no slight measure with the history of man's dwelling-place, and we hail those who expound to us the history of man's dwelling-place, not merely as incidental helpers, but as abiding fellow-workers. And those who go on to tell us of the older occupiers of the dwelling-place, of races of beasts or of men which have vanished from the earth, or whose domain upon the earth has been cut short, come yet nearer to our subject than those who concern themselves with the dwelling-place only. The retreat of the lion from Mendip and from Nemea is at least as much a part of the tale of Britain and of Hellas as the retreat of those earlier races of men which held the soil of Britain and of Hellas before they came who were to give their soil a place among historic lands. The close connexion which used to be held to exist between those subjects and ours is shown in the name which, from the days of Pliny onwards, bound them together in one. In my younger days we still read our books of " Natural History," and I would not even blame the arrangements of the Scottish University which united "Natural and Civil History" under a single chair. The practical connexion which still exists between them is shown by the ease with which the students of those subjects pass to the study of ours. I have known at least two men of learning—and where I have known two there are doubtless others whom I do not know—whose studies began with the earth itself, and who thence steadily worked up their way, by an easy and natural ladder, through the several stages of extinct animal life, of existing animal life, of primitive and early man, to our own study of man as a political being. They made their way steadily up from lifeless matter to man as he has wrought the democracy of Athens and the Empire of Rome, the lawful kingship of an elder England and the federal union of a younger. It is indeed hard to draw the line between the study of the rock of Athênê itself and the study of all of which the rock of Athênê is the symbol. All the branches of knowledge of which I have been speaking, if not actually branches of our study, are its very closest allies. To my mind they are at least as near to us, students as we are before all things of the political life of Aryan man, as are those branches of man's recorded history which throw no light on that political life. The pursuits of which I have been speaking, geology and its kindred studies, have always seemed to me to be quite wrongly placed, when they are grouped far away from us, alongside of branches of knowledge which depend mainly on experiment or on theory. Like political history, their matter is the knowledge of facts drawn from records. The only difference is in the nature of the facts, in the nature of the records. And the intermediate branches, opening to us facts of so many kinds, recorded in so many ways, are quite enough to fill up the seeming gap between the two.

These then are kindred studies, distinct, though kindred. Either can stand apart, though either gains much by its connexion with the other. Of some of them indeed we must confess that we have more need than they have of us. A man may make out the geological history of a country quite thoroughly for purely geological purposes, without ever asking

what deeds of man were in after days wrought on its
soil, or indeed whether man ever set foot on its soil at
all. When we come to human life—I should be
almost inclined to add, when we come to existing
animal life—the temptation must surely be great to
go on from the ruder beginnings of the life and
works of man to those higher developements of them
which grow into art, literature, political history
itself. That the temptation is great I know from
the experience of those who have entered our own
hearth and home by that path. Still those studies
are distinct from ours, and they have objects apart
from ours. They are fully worthy of study for their
own sake, even if they never come into contact with
history at all. Alongside of them is a whole crowd
of other pursuits which it is impossible in this way
to separate from history. There are not a few
branches of knowledge which we may call satellites
of history; they are studies whose results are most
precious to the historian, but which, in themselves,
apart from their use to the historian, seem not
to rise above that kind of curious interest which
may be called forth by any inquiry to which a
man gives his mind. The study of coins and
weapons and antiquities of every kind, the study
of palæography as a special branch of knowledge
as distinguished from the study of inscriptions
directly as records of facts, the study of genealogy,
nay even the self-styled science of heraldry, each has
its place in the *comitatus* of our Lady Kleiô, and the
place of each is useful and honourable as long as that

E

place is kept.   All are branches of history; looked
on as branches of history, they all surely rise in
dignity; looked at each alone by itself without
reference to its fellows and to the centre of all, they
sink into little more than matters of curiosity.   None
of these secondary branches of history has thrown
more and more precious light on the main subject
than the study of coins; but the mere gathering of
the coins themselves, apart from the facts which the
coins prove or illustrate, hardly rises above the
gathering of postage-stamps, and in ages to come the
postage-stamps will prove something as well as the
coins.   When it comes to art in the higher sense, to
painting, sculpture, architecture, we have reached subjects which from one side are undoubtedly branches
of history, while from another side they claim
the rank of distinct branches of knowledge.   They
not only illustrate history, but are essential parts of
history; still they have a value of their own apart
from their strictly historical value.   A statue, a
painting, a building, has an artistic value in itself,
even if we have no knowledge of its date or author;
a coin, a vase, a weapon or implement of any kind, is
nothing apart from its historical value, except so far
as painting or sculpture or some other form of art
may claim it as belonging to its own province.
The architectural works of any nation are among the
most important of its monuments; they are among
those which throw the most valuable light on its
history; one side of them is indeed imperfectly
understood without the history of the folk that

reared them. Yet architecture has another side distinct from its historical side, while numismatics, purely as numismatics, without reference to either history or art, become simply the hobby of a collector. So again to the historical inquirer geography, as distinguished from geology, may well seem to be part and parcel of his own subject. Without political geography history has no being; or more truly, political geography, looked at simply in that special aspect, is simply one essential part of history. But political geography implies physical geography, and physical geography is parted by a very narrow line from geology, and we are thus again brought within the range of those subjects which are closely akin to history but which are still distinct. Geography and chronology have been called the two eyes of history, and assuredly without them history would be blind work indeed. But the two do not stand in exactly the same relation to the study which they in this sort enlighten. Chronology has to some extent its own method, and its perfect mastery implies a lore of its own of which the student of strictly political history has no direct need. Yet it is simply and purely a branch of history; except to make history clearer by putting events in their due order and distance from each other, it seems to have no object or meaning. Geography is more like the various forms of art; with one side that is strictly and purely historical, it has another which stands apart. It is plain that there is such a thing as a strictly geographical taste, that it is possible to take interest in geography for its own sake, whether it has any historical reference or not. To the strictly geographical inquirer a land where nothing is known to have happened may be as attractive as Greece or Gaul. But it is hard to conceive chronology as studied without some reference, even if an unconscious one, to the advancement of historical knowledge.

Of some of these subjects and of their relations to history and to one another I may have something to say in future lectures. The rest of the present lecture I wish to give to some remarks on two of the kindred subjects of history which are of even greater importance than any which we have named, whether in themselves or as holding a place among the studies of our University. They are two studies whose bearing on one another is comparatively rare and indirect, while both of them stand in the closest relation to those historical studies which in a manner stand between them. It is only incidentally that the study of language and the history of law do much to illustrate one another. It may often be well for the lawyer to learn of the philologer the original force of some word which he uses in a special sense, as a technical term of his own art. And the way in which words come to be used as technical terms of the lawyer's art will often supply the philologer with some of his most apt illustrations of the way in which words drop off old meanings and take to themselves new ones. But it is only incidentally that the two studies illustrate one another; the main body, so to speak, of each remains quite distinct from the other.

But it is impossible either to conceive law and language going on without reference to history, or to conceive history going on without reference to law and language. The connexion is constant; it is intimate; it is involved in the nature of the several subjects. But it is only of late years that the connexion of history with either subject has become so clear and so intimate. It is wholly owing to the great discoveries of our own time that either history itself or its two great allies on either side has been made worthy of the place which they all now hold. Law has ceased to be an empirical trade; language has ceased to be, sometimes an empirical trade, sometimes an elegant amusement; and both have taken their place among the sciences. They have risen as history has risen; it is hard to say whether, in actual amount, history owes most to them or they most to history. But in idea it is law and language which owe their scientific character to their connexion with history; history does not owe its scientific character to its connexion with law and language.

On the historical, in other words, the comparative, study of language in the wider sense it is not for me to enlarge. But it is surely the greatest of the many great discoveries of this century, or more truly of the century which went before it. It is only a few branches of that wide and wonderful subject which directly touches the business of the chair of Modern History. But those few branches touch the business of that chair very directly indeed. The first question which I am always inclined to ask, in reading the

history of any people, and one to which I often find
it very hard to get an answer, is, What language did
they speak? It is the question which goes further
than any other one question towards giving us an
idea of what we call the nationality of a people. It
is a question which comes before the questions that
must soon follow, about their mode of warfare, their
laws, their creed, their general condition, political,
religious, and moral. But it is a question to which
it is often hard to find an answer, because we have
commonly to put up with indirect and incidental
evidence. It is but seldom that those who record a
discourse or a dialogue think it needful to tell us in
what language that discourse or dialogue was carried
on. When only one tongue is spoken in a country,
that tongue is of course taken for granted as the
tongue of all that is said. When two or three languages are spoken in a country, we have a better
chance of some direct mention of them. But even in
this case it often happens that each language has its
own particular range within which it is almost as
much a matter of course as the one language is when
one only is used. Thus we know that, in the latter
half of the twelfth century, Latin, French, and English were all familiarly spoken in England. It is
said of particular men, as of Bishop Gilbert Foliot,
that they were eloquent in all three. Yet it is the
rarest thing for us to be told which of the three
Gilbert Foliot or any other man spoke at any particular moment. We are left to guess from the circumstances of the speaker and from the class of people

to whom he is speaking. So again, in the fifth
century, Latin—at least Roman—and the Frankish
form of German must both have been habitually
spoken side by side over a large part of Gaul. We
are constantly tempted to ask, In what tongue did
Roman bishops and Frankish kings speak to one
another? And this last question leads us to a fact
most important for our present purpose. Whatever
may have been the state of things while the two
languages were spoken side by side, we know what
was the result some ages later, when one of those
tongues had, under the influence of the other, grown
into what we may for practical purposes call a third
tongue different from either. Now I was reading not
long ago in a discourse by a master in his own branch
of knowledge, in nothing short of Lord Rayleigh's
opening discourse to the British Association at Mont-
real, a proposal, one not wholly new, to substitute, in
some cases, the study of French and German for the
study of Latin and Greek. This proposal could be
made only in utter forgetfulness of what the scientific
study of language is. No doubt it is true enough
that there are cases in which a lad who is dull at
his Latin and Greek grammar may easily be taught
to chatter French, as he might just as easily be
taught to chatter Greek, if Greek were in the same
sort set before him as matter for chattering. But
this is not all; we are told something very different
from this undoubted fact. We are told that French
and German might be made as useful for the discipline of the mind as Latin and Greek. Now it is

plain to every one who knows anything of the relations of languages that German in this matter stands on a wholly different ground from French; each language is instructive and profitable in its own way, but in quite different ways. I will here speak of French only. I would say here in the matter of language, as I have already said in the matter of political history, Break down the middle way of partition that is against us, and proclaim the unity of our studies in both branches alike. I would ask the old-fashioned tutor or schoolmaster, I would ask the innovating natural philosopher, how the one would teach Latin without French and the other teach French without Latin, so as to form any real discipline. The one no doubt may turn out an elegant scholar of a by-gone type, able to make elegiacs and quote tags of Horace a great deal faster than the historical philologer can. The other no doubt may turn out a practical man of business or society who can talk the latest form of polite French with a glibness which may astound the historical philologer. Of these two faculties the latter is undoubtedly a valuable practical gift, and the other may be an elegant accomplishment. But for discipline of the mind we must go somewhat deeper than either. If we are to study either Latin or French in any scientific, in any historical, way, in any way that is likely to give a discipline to the mind, we must study them, not as rival tongues, but as earlier and later stages of the same tongue. Our study of Latin is sadly cut short, if we do not look on to see how our

Latin passes away into French and the other Romance languages. And it is no study of French at all—it is mere empirical building without a foundation—if we do not look back to see how our French had its beginning in the Latin—at least the Roman—tongue which, for purposes of ordinary speech, lost itself in it. He who has mastered the process by which Latin changed into French or any other Romance language— though French is in some points the most instructive of all—has not only gained a mass of most curious and interesting knowledge, he has gone through a discipline of the mind which is surely to be called scientific. He has gone through a profitable practice in the art of making true analogies and rejecting false ones. He has learned to reduce certain phænomena which might at first seem capricious to rules not quite so certain, to be sure, as those of the geometer, but surely as certain as those inferences of daily life by which we direct our steps in public and private affairs. The probability that, in a word strictly and purely French—French within the needful bounds both of time and place—Latin *c* before *a* will change into French *ch* is not quite so certain as the eternal truth that every triangle will have its angles equal to two right angles, but it is surely as certain as the reasonable expectation, grounded on long experience, that the public creditor will receive his next half-year's dividends on his investments in the public funds.

Now wherein lies the difference between a scientific and an empirical treatment of language, between wild guesses at the origin and relations of words and a certainty as to their origin and relations second only to the certainty of the mathematician ?　It lies surely in the presence or absence of the historical treatment of language.　By this I do not mean merely the light which is thrown on the history of language by actual records ;　I mean a historical method of treatment, whether with or without records.　Much may be done without records which is truly historical in its method and spirit.　Among the masters of præ-historic history, the geologist fixes without records that such a formation is older than another.　The palæontologist fixes without records that such a species of extinct animal is older than another.　And, to come within the range of history itself, the architectural antiquary could, without records, without knowledge of the succession of styles, arrange the parts of a building in their right order by the evidence of the construction only. So it is with the history of institutions.　A man used to historical research, but who knew nothing of Roman history except that one functionary was called an *interrex*, another a *rex sacrorum*, that the house of a third was called the *regia* and that a feast was kept called the *regifugium*, would be able to infer, with a certainty second only to that of the geometer, that there had been a time when the Roman state had real kings.　In cases of this latter kind, though a sound historical inference may be made without records, yet records step in, not only to confirm the inference, but to make it more definite and minute.　The geologist and the palæontologist need no records; their time cannot be measured by kings or consuls; but their inferences are historical none the less. So it is with language. Let us suppose a philologer, practised in his art, but to whom Latin and French were as unknown as the tongues of Central Asia are to most of us. If the phænomena of those languages were laid before him in all their fulness as phænomena of language, but without dates, without names of countries or nations, he would still be able to put those phænomena in their proper order; he would be able to arrange in their due succession the stages by which the later forms of the language grew out of the earlier. He would be able of himself to report the true relation of language B to language A; what records only can tell him is what are the names of the languages concerned, what were the nations that spoke them, when, where, and how did the events take place which caused those languages to come into the relation in which he finds them. Leaving then the geologist and the palæontologist, who can get without records all the light that is to be thrown upon their subject, it is plain that the other three inquirers, the student of architecture, the student of institutions, the student of language, though they may make sound historic inferences by their unaided skill, can never by their unaided skill, without the help of history in the narrower sense, without the help of records, reach to the same complete and minute knowledge of their own subjects which they can reach with their help.

I say this, because in two of the cases of which I

have spoken it is hardly needful to be said. The studies of the architectural and the constitutional antiquary are in truth simply branches of history. An inquirer in either of those subjects is unusually lucky if he finds all that he wishes to know, all that he reasonably infers, set down anywhere in so many words ; but it is perfectly possible that every detail may be so set down. But by far the greater part of the discoveries and inferences of the philologer are of such a kind that they cannot be put on record till they are put on record by himself. The philologer notices that, in the change from Latin to French, *c* before *a* is turned into *ch* ; but it is certain that no one in the age of transition itself would be likely to record when and why men changed their utterance from *campus* to *champs* and *champ*. The philologer is thus in a stricter sense a discoverer than the student of antiquities or of constitutions ever can be. In short we have reached an essential point of difference between the science of language and such studies as the historical study of buildings. By this I mean the study of the buildings themselves, a study distinct from their value for the history of art, or which at least makes use of the history of art simply as part of the evidence to fix the date of the building. Such studies as those of which the late Professor Willis was the unrivalled master are in truth simply parts of history, just like the study of coins or of weapons or any other of those subsidiary branches of history of which we spoke some time back. But the science of language is something more than a mere branch of historical

study; it is one of the studies akin to history, one of
those which are most closely akin to it, a study from
which history is ever borrowing and which is ever
borrowing from history, but which still is a branch of
study distinct in itself. It follows a historical method
in its grand outlines; but it is itself historical and
something more; it makes its way into regions
whither the historic method cannot follow it. The
science of language is held by its votaries to be one
of the physical sciences; whether it be so or not I
will not presume to judge; but, if it is physical, it is
physical and something more, as I have just said that
it is historical and something more. The science of
language may well be looked on as one of the links
between the historical and the physical sciences. It
records and classifies, not only the workings of nature,
but the acts of man and his free will. For that mass
of unconscious, but still unconstrained, action, on the
part of countless individuals which goes to make up
what we call change, growth, developement, fashion,
in language or in any other matter, is in truth the
aggregation of endless acts of the human will. The
history of language is a record of physical facts, but
of physical facts controlled by human agency; it thus
becomes a record of human actions, a part of the
record of history. Even if the science of language
never drew, as for its fullest purposes it must constantly draw, upon the written records of history, it
would still remain, for one side of it at least, a historical science; its discoveries would still be set down
as part of the facts of history.

Now of these two studies, history strictly so called and language, each largely exercises the same faculties ; each largely employs the same methods ; the two have a vast field of inquiry common to both ; the master of the one must have gone no small way towards becoming a master of the other. No man can really understand history without a considerable knowledge of philology; no man can really understand philology without a considerable knowledge of history. Each will follow the other's study so far as it helps to illustrate his own, possibly a little further still. But if he goes no further than is needed to illustrate his own subject, that journey will carry him a good way. But we shall soon see the difference between studying with primary and with secondary objects, between studying a subject absolutely for its own sake and studying it only so far as it helps to illustrate another subject. The historian and the philologer have a wide field in common on which both will feel equally at home. But each has also a separate territory of his own on which the other feels no temptation to enter. A truly œcumenical historian, one who took the whole world as his subject and who felt equally at home in every age and country, might feel himself equally drawn to every stage and form of every language. But most of us have our special periods which we work in detail, while as to the others we think that we have done our part if we know enough of them to put them in their true relations to our own periods and to one another. As a rule then, while the true philologer will care for

the whole world of language—not necessarily as a
master of every language but as a master of some
and as knowing the general relations of all—so the
historical student who uses philology only as an
illustration of history will care only for those
languages which illustrate his own branches of
history; he may be indifferent even to the general
relations of those languages which throw no light
on his own studies. To most of us it may seem
enough if we have a mastery of some and a certain
knowledge of all, among the various forms of Greek,
Latin, and Teutonic, and if we add a general knowledge of the relations of the other European tongues
and of those non-European tongues which come into
historical connexion with them. At the same time
of course the more languages a man knows the
better; he who to his Greek, Latin, and Teutonic
can add Celtic, Slavonic, Lithuanian, the rival speech
of the Arab, even the more uncouth tongues of the
Turk and the Magyar, will certainly not regret
having added so many unusual weapons to his
historic armoury. On others whose work lies in
other fields of history than ours other tongues will
have the same claim that the tongues of Europe and
the neighbour lands have upon us. Still all whose
object is primarily history, and not language for its
own sake, will be likely to draw the line in every
department at those languages which have some
kind of history, some kind of literature. But I can
understand that to the philologer pure and simple
the tongue of some savage tribe of whom no acts

have been set down in writing, and whose speech has
never been brought within the fetters of any alphabet, may possess an interest and convey an instruc-
tion fully equal to that of Greek or Gothic. And
even with regard to the tongues which the historian
and the philologer may study in common, the two
will not look at them exactly from the same point
of view. To the philologer nothing is so precious as
the grammatical forms; the vocabulary is secondary;
the extant writings in the language are valuable
chiefly by way of evidence to illustrate the philological facts of the language itself. To the historical
student on the other hand the grammatical forms
are of comparatively little moment; they concern
him only when they illustrate some of the further
facts in the language itself or in its relations to other
languages. His main care is the vocabulary, and
specially when the words that form it are arranged
in the shape, not necessarily of literature in the
higher sense, but of compositions recorded or handed
down. In short, to the philologer every language is
precious as itself a possession for its own sake. To
the historian only this or that language is precious,
and that only as the possession—the chief and most
distinctive possession, he may be inclined to add—
of the particular nations with whose history he is
concerned. To the one in short every fact of language is valuable in itself; to the other only such
facts of language are valuable, a very large class
to be sure, as help to illustrate the more general
history of nations.

Thus, besides the large field common to the historian and philologer, a field in which both are alike at home though both do not use it exactly for the same purposes, there is another large field which the philologer keeps to himself and into which the historian does not penetrate. The historian in return has his own special plot also, which is not likely to have any charm for the philologer as such. As long as either is dealing with the migrations and relations of nations, each is on the ground common to both. But, as the historian is in no way concerned with large branches of philological research, so the philologer has no call to go into those details, political, military, and of other kinds, which form so large a part of our work. They concern him only when they throw some incidental light on his own subject. To him the chief interest of a *parliament* will lie in that remarkable train of verbal accidents which has made a *parliament* so nearly akin to a *parable.* He can throw light on the history of every technical term of every art which history has to borrow; but the history of the words will be to him of deeper interest than the history of the things.

Now we may further remark that it is only the more extended philology of recent times which can give this help to historical study. The antiquated style of classical learning, which was supposed to make a man a scholar and a gentleman, was of no great value for historical purposes. A strange devotion to the writers of a few arbitrarily chosen centuries gendered not a little to contempt, not only for the writings, but for everything else, belonging to other centuries. It would be amusing, if it were not provoking, to read the Greek and Italian travels of writers of the narrow classical school. It is curious to see how the smallest memory is cherished, how the most trifling relic is prized, if only it comes within the favoured period, while the scenes and memories of the most stirring events in the world's history are passed by without a thought, existing monuments are despised or their wanton destruction is rejoiced in, if they happen to be a little too late, or perhaps sometimes a little too early, to come within the artificially prescribed limit. The narrow classical scholar, who has ruled that certain languages are dead, seems sometimes to think it a presumption on their parts when they venture to show that they are alive. He stands amazed at the irrepressible life of the Greek and Latin tongues through long ages after he had doomed them to the grave. It is no less amusing to see the narrow classical antiquary standing amazed and shocked at the wonders of Spalato and Ravenna, to see him perplexed at the great works which cast aside all the narrow rules of his craft, and which opened the way for every true form of artistic growth in later times. It will indeed be a white day when the word " classical " no longer infests the nomenclature either of language or of art, and when both are allowed to be studied unhindered by worn-out and unmeaning barriers. The wider and more generous studies of the Comparative school hang together in all their branches. Be it language, be it art, be it political history, all alike draw new life from a method which does not shut itself up within arbitrary fetters, but which welcomes the witness of all times and of all places. While the narrow style of scholarship, like the narrow style of antiquarian research, can be looked on only as directly hostile to historical learning, in the wider philology of our own day, in the other kindred branches of study to which that wider philology has set the example, history welcomes allies without whose help she would find it hard indeed to do her own work as she is now called upon to do it.

In short, in the relations between history and philology we surely see the very best example of that kind of brotherhood which may exist between two branches of knowledge, distinct in their own nature, but which have much in common both in range and in method. It is hard to conceive how two studies which really are distinct can be more closely allied, and allied on more equal terms, than enlightened history and enlightened philology certainly are. Yet it is plain that, of the two, philology needs the help of history more largely than history needs the help of philology. Deprive history of the help of philology, and the gap would be frightful. If we were driven to study history without any knowledge of the languages and countries with which we have to deal, if we had nothing beyond a vague literary knowledge of some of those languages without any grasp of their scientific relations, we should indeed feel that one of the eyes of our subject was put out. We should lose one of the most instructive, perhaps the most instructive of all, of the particular branches of our own study, and we should be in danger of the grossest errors with regard to the great outlines of the history of the world. We see what confusions come of mistakes as to the history of language, as to the nature of the languages spoken in this or that time or place. I believe that there are still some who fancy that Charles the Great spoke French, just as there are still some who fancy that the earth is flat. I need not stop to show how the history of Europe must be turned upside down by such a belief; I will only point out that a merely literary knowledge of the languages concerned is no safeguard against such errors. What historical truth needs in such matters is something which may fairly come within the head of philology; that is, it needs a careful notice of every indication of language, a firm grasp of the meaning of every such indication. Addison conceived his Pharamond as speaking French ; at least if we may infer as much from his presiding over courtiers bearing very modern French names. And I can fancy that, if Addison had casually looked into Einhard, he would have taken the description of the great Emperor's speech, "lingua patria, id est Francica," as full proof—if it could ever have come into his head to doubt about the matter—that the *magnus et pacificus Romanorum Imperator* spoke in very much the same fashion as the *Rex Christianissimus* of his own day.

Into errors like this history might fall at any moment, if it had not the study of language to help it at every step in its passage through the field which the two studies have in common. And yet, as I just now said, language stands even more in need of history than history stands in need of language. Without language, history would indeed lose much; but it could still go on and discharge some of its functions. We might trace out political events and make political inferences, even while we practically knew nothing of the speech of those with whose institutions we were dealing. Our work would be very imperfect, often no doubt very inaccurate; but the essence of historical research might still go on. I once saw a History of Rome the writer of which knew so little of the Latin tongue that he thought that *plebs* was the plural of a singular *pleb*, that each particular plebeian was a *pleb*, while the whole body of plebeians formed the *plebs*. And yet this writer, so utterly in the dark in point of language, had grasped the political relations between patricians and plebeians with far greater power and clearness than many whose verbal scholarship is of a much higher kind. But it is hard to see how the study of language could go on without the help of recorded facts. At the very least it would put on altogether another character from that which it now has. It might withdraw to the position which it claims among the physical sciences; but it would, as far as I can venture to judge, stand under some disadvantages as compared with the other physical sciences. The difference would come in which exists between sciences which deal with the phænomena of nature and a science which deals with the acts of man. Philology, as a purely physical science, as a science without historical records, would surely be unable to marshal its facts in the same good order as the other physical sciences for whose perfect developement historical records are not needed.

Let us turn now to the other side, and see how history stands with regard to its other sister study of law. One point strikes us in which law differs from history and language, and from most of the kindred branches of knowledge. It is not merely a matter of learning followed for learning's sake or for the indirect results of learning; it is directly and immediately a matter of practical business, in which any man may be at any moment entangled, even against his will. Students of other branches of knowledge flatter themselves that their studies may ever and anon serve some practical object; they may even go so far as to flatter themselves that their studies may lead to their own private profit or advancement. But law, without its practical application, could have no existence at all; it is studied primarily for practical objects, among which the profit and advantage of those who study it is certainly not forgotten. Many branches of knowledge may incidentally become professions; but the law is primarily a profession; any other aspect is incidental. The side of law which makes it a branch of know-

ledge capable of scientific treatment is not its
primary and practical side. It is rather an esoteric
aspect of the study, whose pursuit is a kind of
counsel of perfection, a counsel which some of the
most successful masters of the law have certainly
not made it their business to follow. On the other
hand, it might be possible to define the study of law
from the other side, as one of the branches of history,
to define it as the study of institutions followed with
a practical object. But the practical object of law
makes it something more than a branch of history;
it causes a certain technical learning of its own to
gather round it ; it tends on the other hand to
connect the study of law as it is with questions as
to what law ought to be. But one side of law, the
knowledge of the actual enactments, of the time,
place, circumstances, motives, and results of those
enactments, is strictly a branch of history, to be
studied in a purely historic spirit and by a purely
historic method, just as much as any other branch of
history. Where the professional lawyer has, from our
point of view, so often gone wrong, is when he has
declined to look at his subject historically, when he
has declined to look at historic evidence, and has
preferred his own technical jargon to facts. But on
this side too we have to record an advance as marked
as the advance which we have had to record on the
side of language. In both cases the progress of the
last generation or two has been the progress of ages.
In the study of law we can now span the gap which
parts Blackstone from Maine and Pollock. If narrow

classical scholarship was a foe to history, narrow
professional law was a foe more deadly still. For
narrow classical scholarship was at worst narrow.
It was imperfect; it saw only a small part of its own
field; but what it did see it saw for the most part
accurately.   It refused to look at a whole range of
facts, but there was a smaller range which it mastered.
Its etymologies were wild; but that was the result
of living in a præ-scientific age; speaking generally,
it taught part of the truth; it did not pile up a
gigantic mass of error instead of the truth.   But
this last was just what a vast body of professional
lawyers for some generations did. Utter ignorance is
a hopeful state compared with that perverse ingenuity
with which the lawyer of a class which I hope is at
least dying out was wont to read through the main
facts of English history, and to read every one of
them backwards.   It is far better to know nothing
than to know everything wrong. The sheet of blank
paper may easily be written on; to turn out a palim-
psest is harder work.   I ventured to say some years
back that lawyers of this class believed that the
hereditary king had existed from all eternity, and
the hereditary lord of the manor from a time just so
far short of eternity as to give the king a moment or
two to make him a grant.   If so much serious error
had not sprung from it, there would be something
not a little amusing in the flounderings of Blackstone
when, starting from the à priori doctrine that the
English crown must always have been hereditary,
he comes across the evidence which shows that it

once was elective. He is honest, and does not shirk the facts; only in his eyes the sayings of the lawyers that went before him were much greater than the facts. The facts must be twisted and twirled into any kind of unnatural meaning rather than that he should dare to say a word against the infallible tradition of the very modern elders whom he was professionally bound to hold for oracles. As for the lord of the manor, I shall most likely have in some later lectures to say something about him and about some doctrines, yet stranger than those of the lawyers, which have lately been set forth about him. The lawyers have certainly read the lord of the manor's history backwards, but they have preserved at least one fact of his history. They have at least kept alive the truth that a manor implies free tenants; he who knows his law-books will not run after the last new craze, the craze which teaches that a manor necessarily implies bondmen and seemingly shuts out free tenants altogether.

Still on the whole I suppose that the temper of the mere professional lawyer is of all tempers that which is most alien to the true temper of the historian. It absolutely refuses to look at evidence; it deliberately, almost consciously, puts something else instead of the facts of the case. After a time not far short of thirty years I may reveal some of the secrets of old examination days. I once had a legal colleague, a gentleman I believe of repute in his profession, but who was hardly known in the University, and who is not now alive. He required the candidates for degrees to say that William the Conqueror "introduced the feudal system" at the great Gemót of Salisbury in 1086. I prayed him not to lay so heavy a yoke of falsehood on the neck of any man; I tried to put the case before him, and to show him that, so far as his words had any meaning, they meant the exact opposite of the facts. I would fain have shown him the passage in the Chronicle, and have explained that what William the Great really did in that assembly was—so far as we can talk of a " feudal system" at all—to keep the most important feature of the "feudal system" out of his kingdom. But my little lecture went for nothing; my colleague held himself bound to have nothing to do with the facts of history; he was Examiner in Law—an inaccurate description by the way; to Law facts were indifferent; facts might be found in Chronicles, but Law was to be found in Blackstone; it was to be found in Blackstone as an infallible source; what Blackstone said he, as a Law Examiner, could not dispute. Surely I was justified in thinking that such teaching of Law as this was fully entitled to the woe denounced against certain earlier lawyers, who, like my colleague, took away the key of knowledge, who, like him, refused to enter in themselves, and who hindered them that would have entered in. There surely never was such another case of making the simple truth of none effect by arbitrary traditions. Such a position has been laid down as law by such a judge or in such a law-book. Never mind how contrary it is to fact, never

mind that it rests neither on immemorial custom
nor on recorded enactment, never mind that its whole
authority comes from the fact that some man who
knew nothing of the matter in hand, who had perhaps never looked at an original record in his life,
chose to say this and that—when it was once written
down in a law-book, it becomes law, it becomes
something which, if not fact, is greater than fact,
something against which not only the judgement of
experts, but the plainest words of contemporary
writers cannot stand for a moment. Like a flock of
sheep, one writer of law-books follows another. One
sometimes wonders how my colleague who deemed
Blackstone infallible thought that Blackstone himself
came to know things. But it is a more curious
subject of inquiry by what supposed rule of professional duty Blackstone contrived to force himself
to copy down and to hand on the amazing things
that he did copy down and hand on. It is perfectly
plain that he could have done something much better.
Now and then he did think for himself; and, when
he thought for himself, his thoughts were to the
purpose. He has put on record a saying about game
laws which any reformer may be glad to quote. He
even saw through one of the strangest superstitions
which ever grew round a very simple matter, but one
of the superstitions which have most thoroughly bound
down men's minds. To say the least, he allowed
himself to wonder at the strange doctrine that a writ
of summons to Parliament does in some mysterious
way " ennoble " the blood, and that a bishop who

holds an almost immemorial see by what our fathers called *jus hæreditarium* is less a peer of the realm than his modern temporal brother created out of nothing but yesterday. At such passages as these he who deemed Blackstone infallible must have been sore puzzled ; if Blackstone was infallible, an act of Parliament, and even a standing order of the House of Lords, must be yet more infallible ; and the truth of history might have a chance when the two infallibles fall out.

Now this direct opposition between the facts of history and the imaginations of what within my own memory passed for law was the more wonderful because there had been an earlier time when assuredly law and history were no more enemies to one another than they are now. Law in the hands of Selden was indeed another matter from law in the hands of Blackstone. Whatever we say of the eighteenth century, the seventeenth was an age which no man can despise. But even in the age of Blackstone there were men who had kept on a far truer tradition of English history than Blackstone ever dreamed of. Perhaps indeed knowledge coming at all near to that of Selden was in that day more likely to be found among laymen than among lawyers. There was certainly one layman at a time a little later than Blackstone whose work on another branch of law does indeed carry on the natural connexion between law and history. The law of Rome was traced up to its sources by Gibbon in a way in which not many professional lawyers of his generation could have traced up the law of England. But in the seventeenth century at least the natural union of law and history was undisturbed. It was at all events not harder for a lawyer to grasp the true history of the institutions of his country than it was for another man.

That good estate of an earlier time has now more than come back to us. Law, as a generation younger than mine is used to it in the teaching of this University, is another matter indeed from law, as my colleague of eight-and-twenty years ago understood it. The step from longs and shorts and scraps of Latin verse to the comparative philology of our day is hardly wider than the step from the Commentaries on the Laws of England to that great series of volumes, partly springing, like the Commentaries themselves, out of lectures in this place, the first of which bears the emphatic title of "Ancient Law." Law has now become a mainstay of history, or rather a part of history, because the knowledge of history is coming to be received as part of the knowledge of law. The lawyer of the new school, at all events when he is out of court, is no longer bound to worship the ignorance of his predecessors ; it is lawful for him to read and to think, to compare and to infer. The experience of all times and of all nations is open to him ; he may trace the origin of some feature of our English common law through its kindred institutions among every branch of the Aryan family and even beyond the Aryan pale.

India and Ireland alike are pressed into the service of law as they have been already pressed into the service of language. The law of Rome herself puts on a new meaning and a new value when we see that the institutions of "the great group of village communities by the Tiber" were essentially the same as the institutions of less famous village communities in other lands. The help given to historical story by this enlarged treatment of law has been beyond words. And we laymen are bound to add that the professional lawyer, whenever he breaks his chains, has in some points the advantage of us. The habits of his calling give him a certain quickness and sharpness, a certain power of speedy discernment, which, when once put on the right track, are invaluable. A lawyer's argument, such as we find in our law-books, is for the most part a most ingenious and commonly unanswerable chain of reasoning from its own premisses. Each step in the argument is sound, it is only the premisses from which the whole starts that are good for nothing. We now have the same ingenuity set to work on sound premisses, and the result is the sister study which history must greet with thankfulness as the third member of a triple alliance. We have not yet defined history; but, on the principle of "noscitur a sociis," we have learned something about history. The very yoke-fellow of philology and law, the more distant ally of a whole crowd of branches of knowledge which deal with days before political history began, such is the study one branch at least of which I am called on to represent among you. If I claim a high place for our pursuit, I claim for it no exclusive place. But I may claim for it a pre-eminence of one kind. No study, except its ally philology, is so liable to be misunderstood, to be misapplied, to be taken up hastily and without fitting preparation. If any one still cleaves to the superstition that history or "modern history" or any branch of history is an "easy" study, easier than the other studies of this place, it will at least be my calling to deliver him from his error. Our work, if it is to be done at all, must be done by men of zeal who do not shrink from hard work. I seek as my companions, my *comitatus*, my δῖοι ἑταῖροι, the three hundred who lap, and none other. The next time we come together, it may be well to give an hour to the difficulties of our study, to the causes which make it and its fellow philology more commonly misunderstood, more commonly superficially treated, than any other branches of knowledge.

LECTURE II.

THE DIFFICULTIES OF HISTORICAL STUDY.

I HAVE referred once or twice in the lectures which I have already given to a doctrine which was largely in vogue some five-and-thirty years back, when the new arrangement of the Examinations of this University first came in, namely that History was a specially easy study. The saying was indeed not put quite so broadly as that; it was not History as a whole, but whatever was meant by the words Modern History, which was pronounced to be so remarkably easy. But as no definition of Modern History was given, as a high authority has ruled that Modern History may be carried back to a very early time indeed, as it is quite certain that whatever one part of History is another part is, I think that I am justified in leaving out the quali-fying adjective. "Ancient" history was allowed to be hard, perhaps because in those days it was still read in the original writers, and some of the original writers were confessedly hard. It was hard too, because it was taken up in common with certain other subjects which were confessedly not easy. "Modern" history was supposed to be easy, because it was to be read after a different fashion from "ancient." It was to be read without the trouble of turning to the authorities; it was to be read as a pleasant amusement in this or that modern French or English book. William of Malmesbury was the only original writer that was recommended—malicious folk said that he was the only original writer that the authors of the scheme had heard of—and I fear that William of Malmesbury was sometimes read in a crib. I dare say "modern" history would be easy, if read in such a fashion; but then "ancient" history, if read in the like fashion, would be just as easy. It was simply the happy union of language and history in one school which kept for "ancient" history its honourable character of hardness. We were told that "modern" history would be of great use in the University, because, as an easy study, it would enable rich men to get first classes without going through such a mass of puzzling Latin and Greek as was needed for first classes in the elder school. For all men knew that Thucydides and Tacitus wrote, the one in Greek, the other in Latin; nobody stopped to think whether the same was not equally true of Procopius and Hugo Falcandus. A study that might be got up in cribs and modern books without any great exertion was just what was wanted, an easy school for the rich. It reminded one of the way in which royal and princely persons seem to have sometimes won the honours of saint-ship on easier terms than meaner folk. It reminded one of the days when crusades were preached as an easy means for laymen to win salvation without the trouble of leading Christian lives. It was as an "easy" study that "modern" history was first given a place in the pursuits of our University, and it was matter of sheer accident, not of anything in the study itself, that "ancient" history was not coupled with it as an "easy" study too.

Now I believe that, after five-and-thirty years, I can look on those controversies, and the part which I myself played in them, very much as if it had been a part played by another man. "Modern" history was proposed as a new study in the University, and I was one of those who opposed its introduction. I can see now that I was wrong as regarded the general proposal. But I was right as regarded the particular shape which the proposal took, and the particular arguments by which it was supported. I was right in opposing a school in which "modern" history was parted from "ancient," and which was proposed on the ground that "modern" history was easier than "ancient." I was wrong in thinking that "modern" history was not a subject suited for academic study. But I was led to think so simply because I had not then fully taken in the dignity of the study of "modern" history. I had not then learned how thoroughly it stands on a level with the study of earlier times, and how thoroughly the two must be studied after the same method. I had learned that "modern" history was not an easy study; I had not fully taken in how very hard it is. Certainly I have for the space of forty years found whatever periods of history I have taken to, earlier

and later, hard work enough in all conscience. And
I do not believe that, if I had been born to the possession of a great estate, I should have found them
easier.

But this notion of "modern" history, and by im-
plication all history, being an easy study is one
which has great power in the world, and one which
well deserves that we should give it some thought.
In truth it helps to make real historical study still
harder than it need be. It causes the way of him
who would teach history to others, and even the way
of him who would teach it to himself, to be cumbered
with difficulties which are altogether needless, and
which I do not believe to exist in the study of any
other branch of knowledge. I ought perhaps to
except some branches of the kindred study of language. I do not think that the study of language
as a whole is looked on as an easy study; but some
branches of it certainly are. And so in truth with
regard to history, the notion of its easiness is often
oddly combined with something that might be called
an exaggerated notion of its hardness. The outer
world seems to waver to and fro between a belief that
original authorities either do not exist or are not
needed, and a belief that the original authorities are
something so strange and rare and out-of-the-way
that only a very few people can ever know anything
about them. And this is sometimes mixed up with
a notion that all our authorities are in manuscript,
or that they can be found only in the British Museum.
From this point of view "modern" history is clearly

looked on as being harder than "ancient." Most people must know that Thucydides has been printed; some may even know that he has been translated. But I was seriously asked not long ago whether any of the books which I had used in writing the History of the Norman Conquest were printed. How did I consult them? Where were they? Was there any key or any grammar to any of them? Above all, was Bæda printed? It is odd that a man should have heard of Bæda and should fancy that he still exists only in manuscript; but so it was. There is thus a notion afloat that the task of the professed historian is in some respects a good deal harder than it is. But this is balanced by the notion, acted on if not expressed, that the labours of the professed historian may be dispensed with, that anybody is qualified to understand history without an effort, seemingly that anybody is qualified to write it or teach it without any attempt to learn it. And what people think of history, they think also of certain branches of the study of language. Anybody, it is clearly the general belief, can deal with etymology, above all when etymology is applied to local nomenclature. Not very long ago some articles on that subject, whose authorship it is in this place not hard to guess at and whose authority no man can dispute, were published in the *Times* newspaper. But the words of wisdom were no sooner spoken than the flood-gates of folly were at once opened. Every one who had a craze on the subject thought the time was come to air it. Absurdity after absurdity was solemnly printed, down to the talk of a man who seemingly thought that the modern forms of the names of French cities were as eternal as the lord of the manor himself, and who quoted the name of *Evreux* as if it had been on a level with the name of *Eboracum.* It is quite inconceivable that the publication of three discourses by a master of astronomy, of chemistry, above all of geometry, would have been followed by the publication of a like torrent of nonsense on any of those subjects. Most likely no one would write to prove that Jupiter was the smallest of the planets, or that some triangles had all their angles not equal to two right angles. It is pretty certain that, if he did so write, his letters would not appear in the *Times*, or that they would appear only by way of a cruel joke. Those who hold that the earth is flat and that the sun is only three miles from it do, I believe, form a sect; but it is a sect which, if it is not everywhere spoken against, it is because on such subjects it is hardly worth while to speak against the crazes of men who are past reasoning. It is quite certain that a man who took to astronomy because he had nothing else to do, and the result of whose astronomical studies was the belief that the sun went round the earth, would nowhere be looked upon as a great astronomer. Yet a man who gives the same reason for taking to history, and the result of whose historical studies is the belief that a Prince of the Empire means something in France, may come to be looked on as a great historian. Now to any one who knows European history, to fancy that a Prince of the Empire means something in France implies an ignorance of the great central fact of history which is exactly on a level with that ignorance of the great central fact of astronomy which is implied in the belief that the sun goes round the earth.   Or we might add that he who holds this last belief has by far the better case of the two.   Every one, till he was taught better, would naturally think that the sun did go round the earth ; not only the mass of mankind, but astronomers of great merit, once thought so ; but there does not seem to be any such natural temptation to turn the whole course of history upside down by quartering the Princes of the Holy Roman Empire in France.   Yet, while everybody sees the absurdity of the one proposition, comparatively few people, we may be sure, saw the absurdity of the other.   It would be hardly worth the while of an astronomer to answer the silly talk in his department, but, if he did, he would assuredly have all hearers and readers with him.   But if the historian exposes equally silly talk in his department, it is thought to be some eccentric fancy of his own ; he is charged with pedantry, with hypercriticism ; he is happy if he is not charged with anything worse.   At any rate the question between knowledge and ignorance is looked on as a " controversy," in which the votaries of each have an equal "right to their own opinion."   It is plain that the studies of history and language have not, as far as any sound knowledge or them is concerned, made the same progress as certain other studies.   And this is not because history and language are unpopular studies with which few

people are disposed to meddle. It is rather because they are highly popular, because too many
people are disposed to meddle with them. It is because they are studies on which it is held that every
one may talk and write without any preparation, and
that such talking and writing has just as good a right
to be listened to as the talking and writing which is
the result of a life's work.

I think that this is not too hard a judgement, when
we look at the way in which matters of history, and
indeed matters of language also, commonly fare in
the casual writings and casual talkings of the day.
I am naturally not versed in those periodical writings
which are devoted to the natural sciences, nor have
I any great experience of meetings devoted to those
purposes. But though I am aware that sheer nonsense is sometimes talked on those subjects as well
as on ours, I cannot believe that it is talked in
anything like the same proportion. There is in truth
hardly the same opportunity. A large amount of the
nonsense talked on subjects of history and language
is local talk, talk on local subjects, often put forth at
local meetings or in local publications. Now local
study of this kind is absolutely necessary for our
purposes. General history, and the history of
language as one part of it, is largely made up of
local history, and it constantly needs local research for
its full mastery. But of course local study can never
bear any real fruit as long as it is purely local ; to
be of any value, the local objects, the buildings, the
institutions, must be dealt with, not as standing

alone, but as contributions to their several branches of historical knowledge. Now I imagine that it is only in some special branches of natural science, in those which I have claimed as having, to say the least, a close connexion with the historical sciences, that the local difficulty can come in. Geology, natural history, botany, are in their own nature local studies, exactly in the same way as the study of antiquities is local; local researches, local examples, largely supply the means for more general inferences. But I imagine that the truths of chemistry and astronomy, to say nothing of pure mathematics, must be the same all over the world. The field which lies most temptingly open for nonsense would therefore seem to be narrower in the case of the natural sciences than it is in the case of our own pursuits. But nonsense, in our pursuits at least, is very far from being wholly local; it attacks every branch of our studies, and there are few quarters from which it is possible to keep it out. There are those who write nonsense because they write in simple ignorance of the subject on which they write; they have not taken the most obvious steps to learn anything about those subjects. About them the simple question is, Why do they write at all? People who had never learned anything at all of this or that branch of natural science would hardly venture to write about it; at any rate their writings would not be admitted into periodicals of some pretension devoted to the objects of those sciences. And there are those who are not wholly ignorant,

men who have read something, who have read
enough to make them know better, who have not
only read good modern writers, but who have even
some glimmering of the original authorities, who
write, and are allowed to publish in respectable
quarters, even greater nonsense than those who have
read nothing at all. I lately read, in a publication
devoted to antiquarian research, a discourse on the
Salic Law, which the writer, in the year 1884,
evidently still believed to be a law settling the
succession to the crown of France on males only.
Of the text of the Salic Law itself, of Waitz and of
editors and commentators earlier and later than
Waitz, he had clearly never seen or heard anything.
Instead of Waitz, he quoted Voltaire. He had seen
the words "Salic Law" in some popular, perhaps
in some comic, reference, and, with this amount of
knowledge, he sat down and wrote a discourse on the
Salic Law, and found an antiquarian editor to publish it. I tremble as I draw my illustrations from
subjects of which I know hardly more than this
daring man knew of the Salic Law; but I conceive
that his state of mind is very much like that of one
who should sit down and write on the sun, moon, and
planets, without having ever heard of Newton or
Copernicus or of anything that Newton or Copernicus
found out. Yet in making this comparison we may
perhaps do some injustice to Claudius Ptolemy, and
we may perhaps be letting off our commentator on
the *Lex Salica* too easily. Or again, I have before
me a number of papers published by a very respect-

able local society, whose writer goes about to prove, not only that there is a large Celtic element in the present English people—a proposition with which, in its truth and in its falsehood, I may have to deal in some later set of lectures—but that the Angles themselves were a Celtic people, speaking a Celtic tongue. And this doctrine is thought to be established by finding Celtic derivations for the plainest of English words. And this is the work of a man who has read something, a man who not only knows that Bæda is printed, but who knows something of the contents of his works. Only he will not believe in Bæda ; he denounces him and his followers, old and new, as blind guides. The parallel surely would be a man who should know the discoveries of Copernicus and Newton and of philosophers later than Newton, but should look on their discoveries as mere delusions. And such, I believe, there are. I have seen a publication called " The Bible Earth," devoted to the refutation of that class of heresies which Galileo had to retract. Only I fancy that the writers of " The Bible Earth " keep pretty much to themselves, and that their theories would find no admission in any publication laying any claim to a scientific character. But the kind of nonsense of which I speak on matters of history and language does find a place in publications of considerable pretensions, publications which contain other papers which are by no means on the same level of absurdity. Here is a sign of the different position which is held in the world in general by our studies and by those of some of our neighbours. To write about history or language is supposed to be within the reach of every man. To write about natural science is allowed to be within the reach only of those who have mastered the subjects on which they write.

Let me give one illustration more. I spoke of local research as an essential part of general history. And something has been done towards putting local research on a more scientific footing. But on those who cater for the information of the general public all efforts of the kind seem to be thrown away. When any particular town or district comes into notice, when some great meeting is to be held in it, when it is to be honoured with what is called a "royal visit"—that is commonly a visit from some of our fellow-subjects—it is commonly thought becoming that a sketch of the history of the place should appear in the newspapers. The sketch is invariably præ-scientific; the characteristic points in the history of the place are always left out; the old wives' fables are always told again. I can even believe that, the next time that the affairs of the English Universities come to be discussed in Parliament, we shall again listen to noble lords and honourable gentlemen who believe that the city of Oxford and borough of Cambridge grew up around those Universities which in truth gradually arose in them some centuries after the towns themselves had begun to play a part in English history. The grandest case to be sure lies beyond the four seas of Britain. Does any one remember the "naval de-

monstration" of four years back on the eastern shores
of the Hadriatic? Our daily papers then were full
of Spalato and Ragusa and the neighbour cities
thereof. Strange tales to be sure they told of them.
But the greatest exploit of all was that of an ingenious correspondent of the *Times*, who chanced to
visit the isle of Curzola, who found that its ancient
name was Black Korkyra, who accordingly got up
the history of the greater and more famous Korkyra,
and carried it off bodily, the seditions of the fifth
century B.C. among the rest, and set it all up again
in the Dalmatian island. I do not expect to see in
the same columns a description of the planet Mars,
in which some daring astronomer has transferred to
our own heavenly neighbour the belts and satellites
of distant Jupiter.

Now all these things are examples in different
ways of the notion that history is an easy study,
that it is a subject within any man's reach, without
that kind of preparation which he would think it
necessary to give to other branches of knowledge.
They are examples of the notion that it is a subject
about which anybody has a right to talk, and about
which every man, learned and unlearned, has an
equal "right to his opinion." Perhaps no one would
accept this description, put into such plain words as
I have put it, as a true picture of his own notions of
historical study; but it is one of the thousand cases in
which men practically believe, that is, they act upon,
some principle or assumption which they would not, on

examination, confess that they believed. The mass of people do practically believe that history, and language too in its historical aspect, is a matter within the reach of every man without very much trouble. And matters are not mended when the real historical student is credited with work perhaps much harder, certainly much further removed from ordinary human concerns, than his work really is. For this notion is simply another side of the other; men think, though they would not allow that they think, that they can dispense with the help of a guide in historical matters in a way that they certainly would not think that they could dispense with a guide in any branch of natural science. Now all this is very mischievous and very annoying; but there must be some cause for it. A popular error is never pure and unmixed error; it is always the distortion of some truth. Some aspect of the case, perfectly true as far as it goes, is looked at so exclusively, so wholly out of its proper relation to other aspects of the case, that it practically ceases to be true. There must be some real ground for these mistaken beliefs, and a little thought will show us what the facts are which give our studies a superficial look of being so much easier than any others.

Now one foremost cause, perhaps the foremost cause, of the mistake is that there is a certain sense in which the proposition is true, a certain sense in which history is an easier study than most others, and one whose students stand less in need of the guidance of teachers. History is the least technical of all studies; it is absolutely without technical terms. Let a wholly uninstructed person take up a book of chemistry, and he finds it utterly unintelligible. He cannot tell what the book is about. He sees sentence after sentence which does not contain a single word which gives him any meaning, save only those absolutely necessary words without which a sentence cannot be put together. For the words are in truth not words; they are not the natural words of any language; they never formed part of the ordinary speech of mankind in any time or place. They are words invented by scientific men to express purely scientific ideas. Let no one think that I am blaming the use of such words for purely scientific purposes. The professors of any branch of knowledge have a perfect right to use among themselves whatever kind of language they may find best suits their purpose, whatever words will best convey their ideas to one another. They are to be blamed only when they come out of their inner recesses, and use their own special language to those—they sometimes call them the vulgar public—to whom that language conveys no idea at all. Only one is tempted to think it a little hard when one is driven away from a study for which one once had a certain liking purely by the never-ending invasion of technicalities. The books of natural history of my youth were interesting books, books that told us something about the creatures and their ways. Whenever I have opened a book of natural history in later years, it has commonly seemed to be simply a string of

hard words conveying no meaning save to those who
are initiated in the seventh or the seventy-seventh degree. Now historical study has the advantage or
disadvantage of being altogether free from words of
this kind. History has no technical terms of its
own, though it often has to use the technical terms
of other branches of knowledge. An uninstructed
man opens a book of history, and he finds little or no
difficulty in understanding it as far as the mere
words go. There may be references to things and
persons that he never heard of; there may be particular words which he does not understand, but if
the book is decently written in English or any other
language, it is hardly possible that there shall be
any sentence which shall give the reader no meaning
whatever. He may mistake the meaning; he may
go away with a dim and imperfect meaning; this or
that word may be strange; but there can hardly be
a sentence so made up of strange words as to carry
with it no sense at all even to the unlearned. And
the words which are strange will not be technicalities
of history; that is, they will not be words invented
by the historian himself, coined in Greek or in some
other foreign language, to express ideas or facts
which students of history have all to themselves.
They may likely enough be technicalities of some
other subject with which the historian has to deal
in its historical aspect, technicalities of theology,
technicalities of warfare, above all, technicalities of
law, perhaps even, from some incidental cause, technicalities of natural science itself. History, which

has no technicalities of its own, is constantly called on to make use of the technicalities of all these subjects. And there are other words which may possibly seem to be technicalities of history, but which are not really such. The historian has constantly to use, in a fixed and definite meaning, words which are no longer in common use, or which, if they are in common use, have in common use lost that fixed and definite meaning. He may have to use the words *patrician, plebeian, ovation, triumph, demagogue, tyrant, ostracism, decimate, metropolis, province,* and a crowd of others, in senses widely different from those which they commonly bear in the newspapers. But the words are none of his coining; the meanings are none of his inventing; he simply, when recording the events of certain times and places, uses words belonging to those times and places in the meanings which they bore on the lips of those of whose native tongue and daily speech they formed part. He may even have to use words altogether belonging to some foreign tongue or to stages of our own tongue which no longer convey their meaning to all hearers. He may have to distinguish *bookland* and *folkland* ; he may have to speak of the *imperium* of the consul, the *potestas* of the tribune, the *auctoritas* of the senate. The Latin words of course convey no meaning save to those who have learned Latin, and among those who have learned Latin they convey their correct meaning only to those who have also mastered the forms of the Roman constitution. The English words, compounded as they are of the simplest words in our tongue, will still convey no accurate meaning except to those who know something of the tenure of land in England in early times. But none of these are really technical terms; there was a time and a place when they were words of daily speech. A Roman of the days of the commonwealth could distinguish *imperium* and *potestas* as naturally as a modern Englishman can distinguish Lords and Commons; an Englishman of the ninth century could distinguish *bookland* and *folkland* as naturally as an Englishman of the nineteenth can distinguish freehold and leasehold. Words of this kind are the nearest approach to technicalities that history has to deal with, and they are not technicalities in the same sense as the technicalities of natural science. They are not arbitrary words invented yesterday; they are words called back to their proper meaning; they are at most old words called back to new life. And their use in historical writing is rare compared with the use of technical terms in other branches of knowledge. One may write page upon page without using any of them, without using any but every-day words in their every-day sense. And we are never called on to write sentences so full of such words that they do not convey some meaning, even to the unlearned. The reader of a page of history should never find himself in any position of greater difficulty than that in which he can say, " I shall fully understand this saying as soon as I find out the meaning of this particular word that puzzles me."

In this way history seems to be easier than other

H

subjects; it seems to be so because in a certain sense it is so. It stands to reason that historical statements made in untechnical language must be easier to understand than the statements of other studies which have to be made in technical language. The mistake lies in thinking that, because the mere statements are easier to understand, therefore the subject itself is easier to master. A subject whose statements are so easy to understand seems as if it could not need the same judgement, the same application, the same general training of the mind, as subjects whose statements are harder. And this difference at once leads to another. No other branch of knowledge has so close a connexion with mere literature as history has. Some branches of knowledge stand wholly apart from literature ; by some literature is looked on as an enemy. The geometer needs no graces of style ; he altogether eschews them. I well remember how in my boyhood, when proving a proposition in Euclid, I said, not simply "much more," but "how much more, is AB greater than CD." I was told, and I have never forgotten the telling, that geometry knows no emotions. So with other branches of knowledge ; there may be a literature about them, but their actual propositions are not literary. If they are accurate and intelligible, it is enough ; if they are anything further, it is more than enough. A book on a subject of natural science may easily and rightly contain much of stirring narrative and picturesque description ; but the pages which contain it are likely to be those which set forth the way

in which the scientific knowledge was gained rather
than the scientific knowledge itself. But in historical
writing, narrative and description, though very far
from being the whole of the matter, are no small
part of it. And description, if it gets beyond
definition, narrative, if it gets beyond annals, are
both in their own nature literary. For the narrative historian then it is not enough that his statements shall be accurate and intelligible ; the annals
of the Pontiffs or the *Anonymus Cuspiniani* may be
that. He cannot help having some kind of style,
good or bad ; and, being placed under this necessity,
he had better have a good style than a bad one. To
take no other view, if he tells his story attractively,
people will be more likely to listen to what he says
and to profit by it. But this unavoidable connexion
between history and literary style brings with it
further difficulties and temptations. There are
temptations which beset the writer himself and
temptations which beset his readers. There is the
constant danger that he himself may sacrifice
accuracy to effect, that he may exaggerate something, that he may leave out something, that he may
throw in some epithet or give his sentence some
turn, which may depart from simple truth of statement, which will no longer set forth facts as they
really happened, but which may make the tale more
attractive in the eyes of those who read for pleasure
or amusement and not from true love of knowledge.
For as soon as any composition assumes a literary
form, such readers will, or at least may, follow; and

the temptation arises to give them, not the food which may be best for them, but the food which will most please their palates. In this way false reputations are formed, false views of history are spread abroad; let the tale be prettily told, let it be told in any way which pleases the taste of any class of readers, and that class of readers will accept it, true or false.

Let us pause and see more narrowly how some reputations are formed. A man shall sit down and profess to write the history of a period chosen at random, without the needful knowledge of times before and after the time chosen; he shall show in every page, perhaps actual indifference to truth, perhaps only a kind of physical incapacity to make an accurate statement; he shall go wrong on every opportunity of going wrong; if a man bore one name or title, he shall give him another; if a thing happened in one place, he shall say that it happened in another; he shall show in every page an ignorance absolutely grotesque of the laws, the customs, the language, of the times of which he is writing, of the geography of his own country and of every other; words, phrases, allusions, which are the daily bread of the true student shall for him have no meaning; with his manuscript before him, he shall be followed with a judicial incapacity for copying it; with his printed book before him, he shall be followed with the like judicial incapacity for construing it; yet, if he be master of a style which pleases some tastes, the tastes which delight in sneers and metaphors, in

scraps of strange tongues and in the newest improve-
ments that the newspapers have given to the language—above all, if he uses his gifts, such as they are,
to set forth paradoxes at which common sense and
morality revolt—then he shall be hailed as a master
of history; volume after volume shall be received
with the applause of raptured admirers, and even
honest searchers after truth, if they have no means at
their disposal for testing the accuracy of statements,
shall be led away—and small blame to them—into
the evil fortune of mistaking falsehood for truth.
And there shall be another man who, with an honest
and good heart, shall give himself to record the tale
of one of the great periods of his country's history;
he shall choose a yet later time, a time whose understanding implies no slight knowledge of every century that went before it, and he shall not shrink
from the long, perhaps weary, preparation which is
needed for his immediate work; he shall not venture
to grapple with the details of his chosen age till he
has fully mastered its relation to the ages before it
and the ages after it; he shall make himself master
of all points of law and custom and language which
may illustrate the work which he has in hand;
and when he draws near to his immediate work, he
shall never shrink from labour, from searching, from
journeying, from poring one day over a forgotten
record and the next day tracing a forgotten field
of battle; he shall choose a controversial time, a time
beset with disputes and prejudices on every side,
and he shall so deal with it, perhaps not so as to

satisfy every zealous disputant, but so that none can charge him with letting indolence or caprice or prejudice ever stand in the way of a honest desire to set forth the truth at any price. He shall, it may be, forbear to deck his tale, or feel no call to deck it, with the metaphors or the smartnesses of the novelist; but he shall tell it in clear and manly English, perhaps not tickling the fancies of his readers, but being satisfied with appealing to their reason; and he shall do all this with but scant encouragement save from the few who are like-minded with himself; his volumes shall come forth, pair after pair, growing in value as he feels himself surer on his ground, but drawing to himself only a small share of the applause and incense which wait on the steps of his rival. To the one with whom truth is nothing, or rather to whom truth is simply unattainable, fame shall come as to a favoured and spoiled child of fortune; to the other, to whom truth is everything, fame shall come only slowly and painfully, as he toils on with undaunted heart till men's eyes are at last taught to know the true light of day from the *ignis fatuus* that guides only to darkness. Nor is the injustice done to particular men the worst thing, nor yet the particular errors and delusions which must follow if men prefer mere prettiness and startling paradox to sound sense and sound learning. It is an evil greater still that history, as a branch of knowledge, is lowered from its true place, that it is judged by a false standard. Silently, almost openly, it is accepted that truth, accuracy, careful and honest

dealing with authorities, are matters of less account
than a way of writing which tickles the popular
fancy. We are told, almost in so many words, that
the story is so pleasant to read that it matters nothing
whether it be accurate or not ; it is almost deemed a
crime to give a warning against so pleasant a delusion. The champion of truth against falsehood has
indeed an uphill fight to wage, when truth has come
to be so little cared for that love of truth for its own
sake has become a motive which not a few seem to
have lost the power of understanding.

Here we have perhaps reached the fullest developement of the notion that history is an easy business
on both sides, that any man with a fluent pen is
qualified to write it, and that any man to whom the
work of a fluent pen gives pleasure is qualified to
judge of it. And this degradation of our subject is
a direct result, by no means a necessary result, but a
result against which we must always be on our guard,
of that literary character of our work which cannot
be avoided. We must take things as we find them ;
we cannot help being judged, partly at least, not
only by the inherent value of what we have to say,
but by the kind of shape in which we are able to say
it. The sternest seeker after truth will welcome
truth more gladly if it comes in a pleasing than if it
comes in a repulsive shape. How much more they
to whom truth is a secondary object compared with
the amusement of a moment, or even they who in
their hearts really wish for truth, but who have not
gone through the schooling which might enable them

to discern truth from falsehood. Style then and form are not to be scorned; a narrative that is true and dull is better than one that is false and lively; but best of all is the narrative which unites accuracy of matter with vigour and eloquence of style. English historical literature can boast of at least three great writers, each of whom knew how to tell his tale, though they told it in three ways as unlike one another as if the later in each case had striven to avoid the manner of the earlier. The mighty work of Gibbon, alone among the works of his age, still keeps its place. Now and then, mainly by help of lights that he had not, we can give a truer picture than he gave of this or that part of his story; after a hundred years we can put some things in proportions and relations different from those in which he put them; but none of us can dream of displacing that vast and wonderful and unrivalled whole. And all this is largely by dint of a style which our reason often condemns but which we admire in spite of our reason, a style which sometimes misleads by its gorgeousness, but which none the less tells its tale in such a way that we do not blindly admire but understand and remember. Whatever else we read, we must read Gibbon too. I leap to times within the memory of some of us, to the lord and predecessor as whose man I am proud to bear myself. No style can be more unlike the artistic pomp of Gibbon than the native, unstudied, diction of Arnold, rising and falling with every turn of his subject, simple even in its highest flights of eloquence, but

akin to Gibbon in the main point, that of telling his
tale so that we can understand and remember. At
my third name I am prepared for an outcry; I know
that to run down Lord Macaulay is the fashion of the
day. I have heard some speak against him who
have a right to speak; I have heard many more who
have none. I at least feel that I have none; I do
not see how any man can have the right who has not
gone through the same work through which Macaulay went, or at least through some no less thorough
work of a kindred sort. I can see Macaulay's great
and obvious faults as well as any man; I know as
well as any man the cautions with which his brilliant
pictures must be studied; but I cannot feel that I
have any right to speak lightly of one to whom I
owe so much in the matter of actual knowledge, and
to whom I owe more than to any man as the master
of historical narrative. Read a page of Macaulay;
scan well his minute accuracy in every name and
phrase and title; contrast his English undefiled with
the slipshod jargon which from our newspapers has
run over into our books; dwell on the style which
finds a fitting phrase in our own tongue to set forth
every thought, the style which never uses a single
word out of its true and honest meaning; turn the
pages of the book in which no man ever read a sentence a second time because he failed to catch its
meaning the first time, but in which all of us must
have read many sentences a second or a twentieth
time for the sheer pleasure of dwelling on the clearness, the combined fulness and terseness, on the just

relation of every word to every other, on the happily chosen epithet, on the sharply pointed sarcasm. These are indeed books which it is dangerous to take down to look at for any single fact or picture. Begin at any random page, and it is hard to put the volume again in its place till the rest of its pages have been read for the hundredth time.

There is then no real opposition between excellence of style and excellence of matter. The only question that can ever arise is as to which shall have the preference when they are unhappily divorced. The earnest student will always make one choice; it may be that the general reader—though I believe that the intelligence of that mysterious personage is a good deal underrated by his patrons and caterers —will make another. The danger may sometimes make us almost lament the unavoidable partnership between history and literature. We may be tempted to envy the lot of the geometer or the chemist in whose way are no such pitfalls. The most winning style, the choicest metaphors, the neatest phrases from foreign tongues, would all be thrown away if they were devoted to proving that any two sides of a triangle are not always greater than the third side. When they are devoted to prove that a man cut off his wife's head one day and married her maid the next morning, out of sheer love for his country, they win believers for the paradox.

But the danger of deeming history an easy business comes earlier in the life-time of most of us. It comes

before the stage when we are called on to eschew the
evil and choose the good among writers who tell the
tale of long periods of history in many volumes. We all
learn something of history from the very beginning;
it would seem impossible that any one should know
absolutely no history. Now I conceive that it is possible to know absolutely nothing of many forms of
natural science; at least my own knowledge of many
of them comes so near to absolute nothingness that
the slight gap does not seem impassable. We all learn
some history from our cradles; we hear something
about the place in which we live, something about
our own families, something about Cæsar or Alfred or
Oliver Cromwell, something about Romans, Saxons,
and Danes, all which is history or something that
passes for history. We go on learning history, or
something that passes for history, every time we look
into a newspaper; we hear it or we discuss it almost
every time that we enter into common conversation.
In this way, though we are commonly set very early in
life to read something that professes to be a formal
book of history, yet our earliest notions of history are
not so much drawn from any book, good or bad, as they
are picked up at random from all manner of chance
sources. I believe that I was exceptionally lucky. I
was told by my nurse that "an Emperor has a great
many kings under him." That saying was not strictly
true at the time when it was uttered; but it had been
true only a few years before, and it was going to be
true again not very many years after. It is not impossible that that childish piece of teaching may have

helped my way to a notion of the Roman Empire in East and West clearer than that of some other people. But I fear that I did not get such helpful teaching as to the relations of Romans, Celts, and Teutons in our own island. It is this history picked up anyhow from the beginning of our lives which really makes the deepest impression on us, and which, if the impression unluckily happens to be wrong, it is the hardest to get rid of in after life. But while we are thus picking up a little history, we are most of us also learning a little natural science in a graver way. Everybody, I imagine, knows a little astronomy. He knows at least that the earth is a sphere and that it goes round the sun. Those who deny those doctrines do not deny them for want of knowledge; they have heard of them, and have rejected them. Every one then knows at once a little history and a little astronomy. But how different is the astronomy of most of us from our history. Our astronomy may be of the very smallest in point of quantity, but it is right as far as it goes; it is so far sound knowledge, and it may at some later time be made the path to wider knowledge. But while our rudimentary astronomy is thus true and wholesome, our rudimentary history is commonly the exact opposite. One never comes across a man who has a knowledge of history answering to that man's knowledge of astronomy who knows the old solar system and no more. He has commonly learned a great deal more, but he has commonly learned it in such a way that his first business in after life ought to be to unlearn it. It is just in the simplest points of history, in the truths which answer to such truths as that the earth goes round the sun, one might almost say to such truths as that two straight lines cannot enclose a space, that men's ideas get most hopelessly astray. And, if I may speak as a pedant, a confused nomenclature does no small part of the mischief. Vague ideas of geography, a superstitious carrying back of the modern map into all past ages, also do a good deal. Or rather they are the same thing ; geographical confusion is one of the most marked and one of the most mischievous instances of confused nomenclature. It is the greatest and broadest facts, alike in the general history of the world and in the special history of our own people, about which the mass of mankind, including many who can be acute and well-informed on particular points, have most to unlearn. The madness of Anglo-Israel is not to be touched by argument; it must be dealt with as any other form of madness. And the Anglo-Israelite at least knows that there is another teaching, just as the man who holds that the earth is flat knows that there is another teaching. I will rather choose a case of simple ignorance, ignorance of a kind which implies that the great leading facts of the world's history have been never heard of—I say never heard of, for, if they had been heard of, they could hardly have been read so utterly wrong. It is ignorance such as I can hardly conceive existing in the case of any other branch of knowledge, at all events on the part of any one who undertakes to write even casually about that branch of knowledge. It was not in the book of a dull man, but in the book of a man not lacking intelligence, not lacking knowledge on some other matters, that I read the statement that in the ninth and tenth centuries the Russians attacked Constantinople, but found the Turks too strong for them.

That such a saying as this is possible shows indeed the difficulties of historical study; it shows the kind of hindrances against which we have to strive. The union of knowledge and ignorance which it implies is really remarkable. To know that there was a Russian power in the ninth and tenth centuries, and to know that the Russians of those days made more than one attack on Constantinople, is a kind of feat which we do not expect from everybody. It is a piece of knowledge which might almost be taken as a sign that its possessor had made his way into the inner circle of historic lore. But as we find it in this case, it simply illustrates the danger of picked up knowledge—for the process of picking up, which begins in childhood, assuredly goes on in after life. The writer had lighted somewhere or other on a statement, seemingly quite accurate as far as it went, about the early enterprises of those Scandinavian adventurers from whom the Russian name has passed on to one of the great branches of the Slavonic family. The fact was striking ; to him it was probably new; it looked as if it might be given a convenient turn in a bit of political rhetoric. But the man who thus picked up this isolated and rather out-of-the-way piece of knowledge had no notion of its right place in the history of the world. It is in truth part of a very long series of facts, a series which has not yet come to an end, part of that rivalry between Greek and Slave which is the great inherent difficulty of South-Eastern Europe. But our writer mistook it for part of another series of facts which also has not come to an end, but whose beginning is a good deal later. To him Constantinople was simply the city of the Turk, and nothing else. Those who attacked Constantinople must have found Turks, and not any other people, ready to withstand them. In short to his mind the whole history of the Eastern Rome was a blank. So it is to not a few minds, even to many who show plenty of acuteness, plenty of knowledge, on other subjects, even on other branches of history. Yet without the history of the Eastern Empire of Rome the main story of the world becomes an insoluble riddle. If there had been Turks at Constantinople in the ninth and tenth centuries, the names Europe and Christendom could never have had so nearly the same meaning as they have had for ages. And one thing is more certain still ; if the Latin and English tongues, if the Christian religion and European civilization, had continued to live on or to come into being, one object at least of the most enlightened modern reformers would have been fully secured. With the barbarian on the throne of Constantine instead of the Macedonian defenders of the laws and creed of Europe, there would have been no danger of the tongue and literature of Greece forming a part of any man's studies in the islands of the Northern Ocean.

In all these ways we have to struggle with difficulties which surely do not beset other pursuits in anything like the same measure. Nowhere else is half knowledge so likely to be mistaken for real knowledge. Nowhere else is it so large a part of the work of him who would really understand his subject, first of all to unlearn a vast proportion of all that he has learned. The work of unlearning must have its turn in all studies whenever a new light shows the old doctrines to be mistaken. In historical study it is needful, not only because new light is often thrown on this or that point, but because so many directly prefer darkness to light, old or new. The seeming ease of the subject, its freedom from technicalities, the way in which it connects itself with all other studies and pursuits, the necessity which is laid on all of learning, or at least of picking up, some scraps of it, all help to make history the special sport of the unlearned. It becomes the field where every one, prepared or unprepared, has a right to speak his mind, where one man has as good a right to be listened to as another, and where a man commonly gains or fails to gain a hearing on grounds altogether foreign to the real matter of what he says. These are our difficulties, difficulties which, as being in the nature of things, we shall never wholly get rid of, and which we must strive against how we can. And in a place like this, we have the best remedy in our own hands, if we only choose to use it. Here we have the means of learning to distinguish good and evil in this as in other matters.

Our old time-honoured studies will help us in this as in other things. He who had mastered the books that were read in the old Literæ Humaniores School of Oxford had made the best of beginnings ; he had made the best preparation for doing justice to historical study or to any other study. He had taken in the training of the mind ; he had sharpened his faculties as no other process could sharpen them ; he had learned what thought is, what study is ; he had only to go on, to use the intellectual habits which he had gained, to use them for any studies to which he might have a call. I remember what an epoch in my life it was when I read the Ethics of Aristotle. I should be sorry to be examined in them now ; but from reading them I seemed to gain a new power which I had not before, a power of discerning and distinguishing, which was ready for use on subjects which had little to do with the matter of the book which thus endowed me with a fresh faculty. He who has cleared his brain by the study of the Ethics, above all if he obeys the precept given in its last sentence and goes on from the Ethics to the matchless Politics—if he grasps the full force of every distinction and definition set forth with all the clearness of that perfect speech, the attempt to represent which in any other tongue must ever be a mockery—he has swept away not a few of the difficulties of historical study from his path. If he still has to unlearn, he has been working in the best school for unlearning as well as for learning. To some parts of history he has, in the

I

kindred studies of the elder school been already taught to apply the mental training which he has gained; he has only to leap over the fatal wall of partition, and to apply the same training to other parts of history. He has only to grasp the truth on which, in season, out of season, I must insist as long as I hold this chair, that facts on one side of some arbitrary line, drawn or not drawn, are as worthy of his attention as facts on the other side, and that the same process of thought which is needful for one is needful for the other. Let him who has made himself master of a century or two of the history of Greece and a century or two of the history of Italy only stoop to believe that that century or two does not take in the whole history of those two illustrious peninsulas, and that beyond the bounds of those peninsulas there is the history of the Teutonic and the Gaulish mainland, of the lesser England in an European island and of the wider England in the world beyond the Ocean. Let him convince himself that he who, in his Thucydides, his Aristotle, and his Tacitus, has learned how history should be read has advantages above all men in carrying on his work to later times. Let him further convince himself that, unless he does carry it on to later times, his own work is utterly imperfect, a means without an object, a beginning without an ending, a foundation without a superstructure. It is strange indeed to see and hear men who have mastered in the minutest detail some little chosen spot in the wide field of history and language turn aside with scorn from the records of their own land, their own speech, and their own folk. Stranger still is it to see men turn away with the like scorn from all the ages of the lands and the tongues to which they deem themselves specially devoted, save some small fragments here and there which would seem to have been picked out by the chances of the lot or the dice-box. I do not say that even to them the history of the European world, that long tale which gathers around the fortunes of the elder and the younger Rome, will be wholly free from difficulty. But with them the chief difficulty is of their own making. It is the strange prejudice which parts asunder two things either of which loses half its value without the other, the strange unwillingness to acknowledge the near kindred, the equal worthiness, of studies whose essential unity is the life of both; it is this which forms the main difficulty which keeps so many who have made a good beginning from going on to its natural ending, and leads them rather to look on the ending as the natural work of those who have made no beginning. Is there any one here fresh from mastering his Spartan ephors and Athenian generals, his Roman kings and consuls, and who has perhaps even followed his Roman Cæsars for a little space? He has made a good beginning; let him not deem that he has made an ending; he has shown himself a worthy learner; let him not deem that he is as yet fit to be a teacher. Let him come and walk in the path which lies naturally open to him, a path which will not be free from difficulties even for him, but which if any man has a right to call easy, it is he. The speech of one age of Rome is fresh on his lips, the deeds of the great men of one age of Rome are fresh on his memory ; let him not halt where there is no halting-place ; let him come on and see what Rome did when she at last came to fulfil her mission, when she truly became the mistress and teacher of the world. Let him come and stand on that narrow threshold of the ages, when the victorious Goth, our kinsman in blood and speech, debated in his own mind whether Romania should be swept from the earth to make room for Gothia, and when he ruled that Romania without Gothia and Gothia without Romania was alike unable to do the work which the world needed. That decision of Ataulf the West-Goth made it possible that the world that now is should come into being, but it made it possible only by proclaiming the necessary fellowship of that world's older and younger elements. You, men of Romania, men of a world older than Romania, men of Hellas itself—we, men of Gothia, men, that is, of Germany, of England, and of America, call on you to join us, to help us, in a work which will be at least less hard for you than it is for others. We bid you, as elder brethren, to join our fellowship ; apart, the work of either is lame and imperfect ; our studies apart from yours rest on no sound foundation ; your studies apart from ours lie open to the reproach of those who begin to build, but who, being able to finish, are not willing.

LECTURE III.

THE NATURE OF HISTORICAL EVIDENCE.

WE have not as yet defined history, perhaps after all we shall be wise if we do not try very rigidly to define it. If I were called on so to do, I should be most inclined to give some such definition as this ; to say that history is the science of man in his character as a political being. And yet such a definition would hardly be satisfactory; we must at least attach some adjective to the word "science." Indeed I use the word *science* at all simply to assert our right to use it, if we please ; for our own use I far better like such plain English words as *knowledge* and *learning*. But if any one likes better to talk of Latin *science* than of English *knowledge*, we have a right to remind him that the two words are simply English and Latin for one another, and that whatever has a right to be called *knowledge* has an equal right to be called *science*. When I was young, *science* in this place meant chiefly the knowledge of man's moral faculties, the lore which we learned from Aristotle and Butler. It has now taken to itself other meanings, sometimes rather strange ones. But students of our branch of science and of other kindred branches have assuredly never denied the right of other branches of science, of all branches that can be pursued by lawful means, to rank fully on a level with our own. All that we have ever spoken against is the strange way in which the name of *science* is often confined to certain branches of knowledge, and the yet stranger way in which some special merit and dignity is often claimed for those branches on the strength of this unfair monopoly of a name. We have too deep a regard alike for the English and the Latin tongue to wish to be called *scientists*; but we do claim for our studies a place among the sciences. We claim no superiority; we claim simple equality; the various branches of knowledge should be content to stand side by side as brethren in a free democracy; yearnings after oligarchic or tyrannical precedence on the part of any one branch of knowledge over another simply show that the votaries of that branch have some little lurking doubt of the soundness of their own position. Asserting then our right to the name of *science* whenever we choose to use it, we shall hardly care to make much use of it. Teutonic *knowledge* comes more kindly to English lips, and, when we have learned to distinguish false knowledge from true, we shall assuredly allow nothing to claim the name of knowledge to which we should not, were we in a Latinizing fit, be ready to apply the other name. If Polybios and Tacitus, if Waitz and Stubbs, are not allowed to be men of science, the name may even go to any that may choose to take it up.

But we must go back to our attempted definition. I said that we were tempted to define history as the science or knowledge of man in his political character, and yet that that definition was not altogether satisfactory. That definition is perhaps a description of the highest aims of history, of the highest objects to which history can lead, rather than a strict definition of history itself. We cannot conceive such a science of man independent of history; for its teaching must be grounded on history; its conclusions must be deductions from the facts of history; an abstract science of political man, founded on theory and not on experience, would be little worth indeed. Yet we can conceive such a science distinct from history; for use has attached to the word *history* the sense of narrative, and political science, though founded on the results of narratives, is not bound itself to put on a narrative shape. And again, to such a science many things will seem altogether secondary, almost incidental, which must hold a foremost place in a narrative history. The science of man in his political character would hardly deal directly with the character and actions of particular men. Battles, negotiations, debates in ruling assemblies, a great deal else which must necessarily fill a large space in a historical narrative, will come within the range of such a science, but they will come only incidentally. They will come only as illustrative examples, showing what course, whether of true growth or of backsliding, the mind of man was taking at the particular time spoken of. And again, even if we accept the establishment of such a political science as the highest aim of our historical researches, we cannot deny the fact that much, and very good, historical work may be done and has been done, by men who have thought very little about any such science. Much work indeed that was doubtless agreeable and interesting to themselves, much which certainly has been profitable to others, has been done by men who have had a distinct unwillingness to be looked at as working for any such purpose. And certainly so much manifest nonsense has been talked about the "philosophy of history," so much too which may possibly be sense but which comes in a garb which gives it the air of nonsense, that one does not wonder at sensible men sometimes shrinking from applying the words "philosophy," "science," or any other terms of the kind, to their historical studies. And it is plain that history has both its pleasures and its uses without looking beyond them to the establishment of any general teaching of any kind. If we do set up our scientific object as something which it is well, if possible, to seek for, we set it up rather as a counsel of perfection for a few, than as a rule to be necessarily followed by every disciple. On the whole perhaps we gain most real knowledge in a kind of irregular way, and we use it in a kind of irregular way, without ever putting it into very accurate scientific shape. And, when we do try to put things into an accurate scientific shape, to arrange them, that is, under neat formulæ and well-defined classes, we only find ourselves beset with new difficulties and dangers besides those with which we had to struggle in the process of gaining our knowledge. If we define our classes too rigidly, if we lay down our general formulæ with too much confidence, we shall run the chance of being mistaken. We must at least so word everything as to allow for the possibility of exceptions. We cannot affirm the cause of a past political event with the same certainty with which a natural philosopher can affirm the cause of a past event in his department. We cannot foretell a coming political event with the same certainty with which the astronomer can foretell a coming eclipse. Sometimes indeed we can come very near to such certainty. There is one rule to which in my own experience I have never known an exception; but I am far from asserting even that rule so positively as to deny that there may be either past or future exceptions. When statesmen who pride themselves chiefly on common sense, when newspapers which pride themselves on a certain air of dignified infallibility, make light of a question or a movement, when they scorn it, when they snub it, when they call it "sentimental," when they rule it to be "beyond the range of practical politics," we know, almost as certainly as we know the next eclipse of the moon, that that question will be the most practical of all questions before long.

If then we establish a science of man in his political character, it must be a science which does not pretend to reach absolute certainty, which does not pretend to come so near to absolute certainty as some other sciences come. And this is true, not only when we look forward to the future, but when

we look back to the past. Such a science depends
on the facts of history, and we must confess, without
trying to blink the truth, that the facts of history
are not so nearly certain as the facts of some other
branches of knowledge. One does not like to refer
to one's own writings, but I believe it is only false
shame that makes one not like to do so. I have
therefore summoned up courage to tell you that I
have gone into this matter, in a somewhat more
minute and abstract way than I can venture to do in
a spoken lecture, in the paper headed Race and Language in the third series of my Historical Essays.
But a very little thought will bring any of you to see
that absolute certainty is unattainable by the very
best historical evidence. Be the witness who he
may, there is always the possibility both of error and
of falsehood. We are worse off in this matter than
our fellows in some of the studies which I claim as
most nearly akin to our own. The geologist may
err in interpreting the witness of the rocks; but the
rocks themselves can neither err nor lie. Now not
only may the historian err in interpreting the witness of records, but the records themselves may
either err or lie. Even when we reach what we
think a nearer approach to a certainty than that of
any written records, we still are a long way from
absolute certainty. Let any man take his own personal experience. Let him begin at the beginning.
Every man fancies that he knows who he is; but he
does not really know it for certain. He knows it
only as he knows a fact of past history. No man

can say of his own knowledge that he is really the
son of those whom he believes to be his parents; he
believes that he is so only as he believes that William
the Conqueror landed at Pevensey; he believes it
because he has been told it on what he believes to
be trustworthy evidence. When we go on to things
which do come within our own knowledge, to things
which we have ourselves heard and seen, each man
may seem to himself to have reached absolute certainty. Yet, first of all, he cannot pass on that
absolute certainty to anybody else; however certain
he may feel in his own mind, others will accept
his statement only so far as he is deemed to be
trustworthy. And besides this, he cannot be absolutely certain even in his own mind; he has been
at a certain place; he has seen a certain action; he
has listened to a certain speech; but he has to trust
others as to the identity of the place, the actor, the
speaker. Error or falsehood, though often very unlikely, is always possible. Men have often made very
strange mistakes of themselves, they have often been
very strangely deluded by others, on matters about
which they might seem to have reached that approach to certainty which is implied in their own
personal presence. It has become almost a proverb
that no two eye-witnesses describe the same event in
exactly the same way. For, in describing an event
on a great scale, say a battle, they will often not
really have the same thing to describe. They have
seen different parts of the main action; though
therefore there may be no actual contradiction in the

two stories, each will put things in quite different
relations from those in which they are put by the
other. But even if exactly the same things are put
before their eyes, it does not follow that they will
see exactly the same things. This may be even
physically true, according to a difference of eyesight
or according to even a very slight difference of physical position. But it is true in another sense also.
According to the different turns of men's minds, one
man will be most struck by one aspect of what he
sees and another by another; in their reports therefore, though again there may be no real contradiction,
yet there is likely to be a wide difference in the
relations and proportions in which things are put.
All this is so fully acknowledged that it is understood that slight differences in the accounts of the
same event are a sign of trustworthiness in those
who describe it, while exact agreement in every
minute detail is held to be a little suspicious. But if
several narrators of the same event, while telling
other points of the story in different ways, all tell
some one point in the same way, that is accepted as
one of the very highest forms of testimony. The
thing which struck every witness in the same way we
set down as pretty certain to have happened in that
way and in no other. Yet even this witness does
not amount to absolute certainty; it is possible that
even independent witnesses may all be lying; it is
also possible that all of them may severally have
been deceived. All these are very familiar facts,
which must, one would think, come into the head of

every one for himself. Yet it is not useless to
enlarge upon them, in order to show what kind of evidence it is with which in our own studies we have to
deal, how far removed it is, not only from the absolute
certainty of the geometer, but from various degrees of
assurance which come at different stages of the region
which lies between his measure of conviction and ours.

Some curious illustrations of the uncertainty of
even the best evidence often come out if we compare
the kind of evidence which we often accept in a
historical inquiry with our experience of the same
kind of evidence in real life. In our researches we
are often set upon questions of nomenclature and
family relations; it is often important, or at any
rate interesting, to make out in what degree of
kindred, if any, people stood to one another, and
we often have no guide towards fixing the degree of
kindred except by the names. And the customs of
nomenclature in different times and places often
enable us to fix it with a high degree of probability,
but still only with a high degree of probability, by
no means with absolute certainty. I read the remark of a writer on Roman history the other day,
that, as it was the custom at Rome for the eldest
son to bear the *prænomen* of his father, we may
infer that Tiberius Gracchus, famous as tribune, was
the eldest of the many sons of the elder Tiberius
Gracchus, tribune also and hardly less famous. But
we cannot be certain about it. The elder Tiberius
might have departed from usage, as Sulla departed
from usage when he gave one of his sons the *præ-*

nomen of Faustus, which no man is known to have borne before him. It was not more usual for an Athenian eldest son to take the name of his grandfather, and for a Roman eldest son to take the name of his father, than it is for an English peer to be succeeded by his eldest son. Yet, by virtue of a special patent, the dukedom of Edward Duke of Somerset passed first to the descendants of his second son, a singularity which afforded room for a remarkable dialogue between the Prince of Orange and the representative of the elder branch. " I believe, Sir Edward, you are of the Duke of Somerset's family." "Pardon me, your Highness, the Duke of Somerset is of my family." The Prince here made a very natural inference, but it happened to be a wrong one. In my work in the eleventh and twelfth centuries I have found the study of personal nomenclature a matter of no small importance, and I have often had to make inferences as to the descent and even the nationality of various persons from their names only. The custom of taking the name of a godfather was so common that, when I have found a Norman, in the days of the Confessor or in the early days of the Conqueror, bearing an English or Danish name, the name of some leading Englishman of the time, I have inferred with some confidence that that Englishman was his godfather. To take two cases out of many, it looks as if Harold son of King Edward's nephew Earl Ralph of Hereford was a godson of Harold Earl and King, and as if Edith daughter of William of Warren was the god-daughter of Edith

the Lady. One feels pretty sure of such an inference, one feels rather pleased with it ; but how far
it is from real certainty may be judged from an instance in my own personal experience. Many of
you, I hope, know well the name of my late friend
Mr. Dimock, editor of several volumes of the Chronicles and Memorials, of some of the works of Giral-
dus and of the Life of Saint Hugh—the real Life, the
real text, not the grotesque attempt at reproducing
it which some may have seen in a more popular book.
Now if you read in a chronicle that I was godfather to
a son of Mr. Dimock, and if you read in another chronicle that Mr. Dimock had a son baptized by the
name of Edward Freeman, I think you would infer,
and that you would think that you were inferring
with certainty, that Edward Freeman Dimock was
my godson. In making that inference you have
reached a much higher degree of probability than
was reached in my cases from the eleventh century.
You seem to have reached the stage of that argument from undesigned coincidences which we may call
the very highest degree of probability. Yet in this
case the argument from undesigned coincidences
would be mistaken. Edward Freeman Dimock is
not my godson ; he was called after another Edward
and another Freeman, and his brother who is my
godson bears the name of Hugh Percival.

This little bit of modern nomenclature is, I believe,
one of the most unlikely things that could have happened. I do not understand the doctrine of chances ;
but I should like to know how those who do under-

stand it would reckon the odds on either side. But it helps us to one of our most useful canons in weighing of evidence. " Credo, quia impossibile est," is a rule which we should always bear in mind, though it is a rule which needs much caution in its application. A thing which is really physically impossible—though even about physical impossibility I may have something to say before I have done— we do not, under ordinary circumstances, believe. But those things which we often loosely call impossible merely because they are very unlikely, are often the more likely to be true because they are so very unlikely. That is to say, they are so unlikely that no one is likely to have said that they happened unless they really did happen. And when we can say this, it amounts to a very high degree of probability indeed. Let us suppose that one who had read my two imaginary chronicles, one of which recorded the existence of Edward Freeman Dimock and the other recorded my gossipred to one of his father's sons, had gone on and found a third chronicle which recorded the seemingly very unlikely fact that Edward Freeman Dimock was not my godson but the godson of somebody else. Such an one would have done utterly wrong if he looked on this third statement as set aside by the undersigned coincidence of the other two. For there would be no real contradiction, no real impossibility; the third statement would have the force of an explanatory comment on the other two ; its very unlikelihood when compared with the natural inference from the other two would be the best reason for accepting it. But this is because, in my imaginary case, as in many real ones, it is hard to conceive any one making a wilful misstatement about the matter. A man might indeed blunder, but, with any man who is not physically incapable of making an accurate statement, the very oddness of the story would be likely to keep him from blundering, while for wilful misstatement there is no room for any motive.

It is another case when motives can be supposed to come in. Yet people who invent a story with a motive, unless they are very subtle indeed, will commonly invent a story that is likely, or at least one which they think is likely, not one which is manifestly unlikely. A made-up story, like that of the false Ingulf, is commonly not unlikely in itself. The Ingulf legend reads very much as if it were true ; it did not seem unlikely to its author, and it has not seemed unlikely to many of his readers. It is proved to be false, not by inherent unlikelihood, but by mistakes in the dates, by the introduction of words, customs, details of every kind, at a certain period which are known not to have been in use at that period. That Ingulf, if he went to Constantinople, should be presented to the Emperor was likely enough ; but it is not only unlikely but impossible that he should have been presented to the Emperor Alexios twenty years before Alexios began to reign. We find him out by this kind of blunder; we find him out when he talks of a certain canon holding "pinguissimam præbendam," at a time before capitular revenues were divided into prebends. The false Ingulf broke down because, though he was an ingenious inventor of a tale, he had not antiquarian knowledge enough to invent a possible tale of a time three or four centuries before his own day. Otherwise a forger, if only to make men believe in his forgery, will commonly be accurate in all points which do not touch the matter of his invention. A false charter therefore is often, on incidental points which do not concern the object of the forgery, as good evidence as a true one. Therefore, even where there is a motive for invention, the range of invention is limited; a forger who knows how to compass his own purposes will not venture on anything which he knows can be at once exposed. Where to draw the line is hard, as it depends so much on the amount of knowledge to be reckoned on in such and such an age, and among such and such classes of people. But it certainly was going a long way when the burgesses of Barnstaple in the time of Edward the Third brought forward a charter of Æthelstan, which not only gave them the right of sending two burgesses to Parliament, but further—such was the Glorious King's eagerness to be enlightened by the advice of the representatives of Barnstaple—relieved them from divers services and payments on condition of their sending those burgesses. The power of shameless fiction could hardly go further; but we learn something from the story. We not only learn how shameless forgers can be, and how great sometimes is the public ignorance on which they think they can reckon. The

notion about Æthelstan's favour to Barnstaple is not
a whit more monstrous, it reckons on not a whit
more of ignorance, than the equally shameless fiction
which used to tell us that Ælfred founded this University or some college in it.   Yet we know that
not many years ago eminent statesmen and popular
writers dined in honour of this last fiction.   But our
Barnstaple fiction teaches us more than this.   It
surely shows that in Edward the Third's day the
burgesses of Barnstaple had already come to see that
the right of sending two of their number to Parliament was a privilege, a privilege to be sure out of
which they hoped to gain something, but not, as
many boroughs looked on it, a mere burthen.

Now in the Barnstaple case, the motive is plain
enough; but it is hard to see on what ground the
forgers could have gone.   Some circumstance of which
we know nothing must have suggested the fiction.
Let us take another case of local assertion from another land, where the pretension is at any rate the
exaggeration of something real.   The local annals of
Monza record coronations of several kings in the
church of Monza of which no record is to be found
elsewhere.   They assert the right of the Archpriest
of Monza, the head of the collegiate chapter, to crown
the King of Italy, if the Archbishop of Milan refused
to do so.   In all this there is some falsehood, but
there is a groundwork of truth.   There is the undoubted fact that the Italian crown was kept at
Monza and had to be taken to Milan—once to
Bologna—for each coronation.   This certainly looks

as if Monza was the original crowning-place, and, though some of the alleged coronations are certainly fictitious, it might make us shrink from saying that they all are. The claim of the archpriest we may be inclined to dismiss. Our kings are crowned at Westminster, not at Canterbury, but they are not crowned by the abbots or deans of Westminster. Yet this is not proof; the use of Monza may have been different. Let us take one case more, a case of which I have said something in the fourth volume of the Norman Conquest. There is no evidence at all, nothing but what is called local tradition, for the story that Henry the First was born at Selby. Now we know what local tradition is. It is one of the most precious things in the world when we can get it; only we never can get it. What passes for it is as a rule the guess of some antiquary of the seventeenth or eighteenth century which has won for itself local belief. But the guess of the antiquary, though commonly wrong, goes on some kind of ground; it stands in some kind of relation to the facts. But what should make anybody say that Henry the First was born at Selby? One is inclined to say again, "Credo quia impossibile est;" what could put the thought into anybody's head if it were not so? And when we think a moment, we see that, besides this argument, a kind of likelihood comes out of the very unlikelihood. Selby was certainly a most unlikely place to be chosen for the birth of an ætheling. But York, or any convenient spot in Yorkshire, was a most likely place to be chosen for the birth of that particular ætheling, the English-born son of the Norman Conqueror. The policy would be the same as that which caused a son of the conqueror of North Wales to be Edward of Caernarvon, born beyond doubt at Caernarvon, though assuredly not in the tower of his own building. And some unforeseen accident might cause Henry to be born at Selby, especially if Selby was, as one form of the story implies, already drawing notice to itself as the dwelling-place of a holy man, though hardly as yet the site of a great abbey. That a building far later than his time was shown as Henry's actual birth-place is only the common run of such stories. It no more proves that Henry was not born at Selby than the fact that the Eagle tower is, I believe, still shown as the birth-place of Edward the Second proves that Edward the Second was not born at Caernarvon. Only we have distinct evidence that Edward was born at Caernarvon ; we have no evidence that Henry was born at Selby. All that we know is that he was born in England ; when we come to think, we see that it is very likely that he was born in Yorkshire ; if he was born in Yorkshire, it is not at all likely in itself, but it is made likely by the very unlikelihood, that he was born at Selby.

Here we have looked into a legend, and we have left mere likelihood in its slenderest form. We have not got so far as believing, and so far as we have looked in the direction of believing, it has been wholly " quia impossibile est." Now, if we rule that the unlikely is, in some sort, likely by dint of very unlikelihood, we can hardly go so far on the other side ; we cannot rule that a story is unlikely because it is likely. This would be going too far ; yet short of direct disproof, there is no argument so strong against any story as the argument that it is too obvious, that it is the kind of story that is sure to arise under the circumstances, that it is, with the needful change of names, really the same story which has arisen over and over again in the like case. Yet even here we are followed by a difficulty. We see plainly that stories of this kind do, as I have said before now, go about the world with blanks for the names, and get fitted with different names in different times and places. We feel sure that in most cases these stories are sheer fiction devised after the pattern of some other stories. But the question always thrusts itself in, Are all these tales fiction ? Was the very first story of the kind an invention ? Or did something of the kind once really happen somewhere, and so set the pattern for all the false stories ? You all know the almost invariable legend of an underground passage wherever two ancient buildings stand within perhaps several miles of one another. The notion is so very general, and yet so very strange, that I have sometimes been tempted to stop and think whether there must not be somewhere or other a real underground passage which has set the pattern for all the imaginary ones. With the oldest story of all, if we knew which that was, the rule " Credo quia impossibile est" would again come in ; but it could come in only with the oldest story of all. In all these cases therefore of current stories with blanks for the names it is quite possible that all may have arisen out of one true story. And now and then, though not often, we can see what that story was. When we cannot do so, though on the whole we do wisely in rejecting the whole mass of stories, yet it is always possible that, in casting aside many fictions, we may be casting aside one truth. We often cast a story aside because it seems to be a mere repetition of another; we specially do this in the history of the Roman commonwealth. And there is no doubt that we often act quite soundly in so doing. The Roman stories are so very often evident repetitions of one another, sometimes perhaps through sheer invention, sometimes perhaps through that process whereby two versions of the same event, differing in some small point, are mistaken for accounts of two different events. But there is however in some quarters a tendency to take for granted that any story which seems to repeat another must necessarily be a repetition of it, a repetition of it in the sense which implies that the second story never happened. I have read a German writer who holds that the devotion of the second Publius Decius at Sentinum is simply the devotion of the first Publius Decius by Vesuvius over again. Now, setting aside whatever amount of evidence we may think that we have for the second story, if we bring it to a question of likelihood, there is certainly the likelihood that the exploit of the father should be told again as an

exploit of the son ; but there is also the likelihood
that the son, finding himself in the like case with his
father, should be stirred up to follow the example of
his father. Most people, I fancy, accept the story of the
second Decius ; very few, I fancy, accept the story of
the devotion of yet a third Decius in the war with
Pyrrhos. And we act rightly, as it seems to me, in
accepting the second and rejecting the third. For
against the second there is really nothing to be said
except the suspicion that it may be a repeated story,
while against the third there is the existence of another version which bears the distinct stamp of truth.
This is the story that the third Decius thought of
renewing the exploit of his father and grandfather,
but was hindered from so doing by a proclamation of
Pyrrhos, which ordered that, if any Roman was seen
attempting to perform any such ceremony, he should
not be killed in the battle, but should be taken alive
and put to death as an impostor. It is hard to say
how this story could have arisen if a real act of self-
devotion had been carried out. We are here led to
that well-known law of criticism which applies to
judgements in our study and in many others. Critics
of texts prefer the more difficult reading; they
prefer the reading which the copyist would be
likely to alter into something else. So it is with
historical criticism. We have two stories of an
event. They stand in this relation to one another
that, if version A is true, we at once understand how
version B arose, while, if version B is true, we cannot
understand how A arose. This is one of the strongest

possible arguments in favour of A. If the third
Decius had really devoted himself, no one would
have invented the story of the proclamation of
Pyrrhos; but to many the story of a third devotion
would be so taking that they would not scruple to
tell it even in the teeth of the fact which upset
it. And I should be half-inclined to carry on the
same argument to another detail of the story. I fear
that many will cry out if I suggest the possibility,
the bare possibility, that, instead of the grand picture of the devoted consul riding to seek death in
the ranks of the enemy, the devotion was in truth a
human sacrifice. John Zônaras at least says that
the first Decius, when he had devoted himself, was
put to death by one of his own soldiers. Now
neither Zônaras nor Dio Cassius, whom he commonly
follows, was likely to invent this; he must surely
have found it in some early record; and we can
well believe that the splendid story in Livy is a
softening of an ugly truth. On the other hand,
the formula and ritual in Livy must be genuine;
those are things which may be trusted, even when
the event is purely fictitious. Tullus Hostilius
may be an imaginary king; but his "lex horrendi
carminis" is quite trustworthy. It is open to any
one to suggest that, as the gladiator-fights were a
softening of the original human sacrifice, so the riding
of the devoted general into the ranks of the enemy
may be a softening of the same kind; he may even suggest that this softening took place in the time between
the devotion of the first Decius and that of the second.

It may be so; but a wary critic will hardly build much on so slender a foundation of possibility.

At every step of this argument we are reminded of the uncertainty of historical evidence; and yet at every step we meet with something which warns us that the practice of rejecting a story merely because something very like it happened once before, is one that must be used with great caution. As a matter of fact, events often do repeat one another; it is likely that they should repeat one another; not only are like causes likely to produce like results, but in events that depend on the human will it is often likely that one man will act in a certain way simply because another man acted in the same way before him. I have often thought how easily two important reigns in our own history might be dealt with in the way that I have spoken of, how easily the later reign might be judged to be a mere repetition of the former, if we knew no more of them than we know of some other parts of history. Let us suppose that the reigns of Henry the First and Henry the Second were known to us only in the same meagre way that we know the reigns of some of the ancient potentates of the East. In short and dry annals they might easily be told so as to look like the same story. Each king bears the same name; each reigns the same number of years; each comes to the crown in a way other than succession from father to son; each restores order after a time of confusion; each improves his political position by his marriage; each is hailed as a restorer of the old native kingship; each loses his eldest son;

each gives his daughter Matilda to a Henry in Germany; each has a controversy with his archbishop; each wages war with France; each dies in his continental dominions; each, if our supposed meagre annals can be supposed to tell us of such points, shows himself a great lawgiver and administrator, and each, to some extent, displays the same personal qualities, good and bad. Now when we come really to study the two reigns, we see that the details of all these supposed points of likeness are utterly different; but I am supposing very meagre annals, such as very often are all that we can get, and, in such annals, the two tales would very likely be so told that a master of the higher criticism might cast aside Henry the Second and his acts as a mere double of his grandfather and his acts. We know how very far wrong such a judgement would be; and this should make us be cautious in applying a rule which, though often very useful, is always dangerous in cases where we may get utterly wrong without knowing it.

When I suggested the possibility that the noble tale of the death of Publius Decius may have grown out of an ugly story of human sacrifice, I did no more than suggest a possibility. But we have often to apply the same kind of process with much greater confidence. I need not tell you that the result of historical criticism constantly is to tear away all shreds of likelihood, all shreds of possibility, from the choicest, the most beautiful, the most cherished, legends. And this often makes our studies un-

popular ; people quarrel with us because we rob
them of their beloved fables, and they turn round
and say that they will believe the fables in spite
of us and our evidence. When it comes to this,
there is of course no more to be said ; we have led
the horse to the water, but we cannot make him
drink. One may doubt whether the same direct
refusal to accept truth is encountered in the same
way, or at least to the same extent, by the teachers
of other branches of knowledge. Something like it
doubtless comes in when a strong theological or
political conviction is touched ; that is, a man
declines to listen to arguments which he fears
might, if they were allowed a full and fair hearing,
compel him to give up that conviction. And in such
cases we must remember that, if a man does wrong
to refuse a fair hearing to arguments which tell
against his conviction, he does a worse wrong if he
gives up his conviction lightly, without that stress of
argument which is really needed to upset it. But
I am speaking, not of serious convictions of this kind,
but of the ten thousand cases in which people cleave
to a mere legend, simply because it is the story that
they have always heard, or because they think it
prettier than the true story. Surely the astronomer,
to turn to him again, does not meet with this particular form of opposition. There is something very
pretty in the old superstition that the sun dances for
joy on Easter-day; but I cannot fancy that anybody
rejects the truths of astronomy on the ground of its
prettiness. The votaries of the Bible Earth do not

cleave to their errors because they are pretty, but out
of a solemn conviction that they are true and good
for their souls. But the argument from prettiness is
one which he who acts at all as a missionary of sound
historic knowledge comes across daily. It comes into
play even when it is possible actually to disprove the
legend, much more does it come into play in those
many cases where positive proof and disproof cannot
come in. Many people seem to think that a proposition
is proved, if it cannot be disproved. It is a deep
saying of Grote that, if a man chooses to say that
rain fell on the site of New York on the day of the
battle of Plataia, no one can prove that it did not ;
only he cannot prove that it did. In a case like this,
where it must be clear to every one that no one can
know anything about the matter, perhaps every one
would allow the lawfulness of ignorance. But where
the case is not so clear, where knowledge may
possibly be reached, but where it does not happen to
have been reached, he who affirms has with many
minds a great advantage over him who simply denies;
he who professes knowledge has a great advantage
over him who confesses ignorance. Very few see with
Sir George Lewis—though Sir George Lewis perhaps
carried his own doctrine a little too far—that in a
great many cases we ought to be satisfied with a
negative result, that we must often put up with
knowing that a thing did not happen in a particular
way or did not happen at all, without being furnished
with any counter-statement to put in the place of
that which we reject. Nothing is more common, but

nothing is more unreasonable, than, when a man has shown that a favourite legend is a mere legend without a scrap of evidence for it, to ask him what he puts in its place. If he has nothing to put in its place, many will think that his case has broken down. Yet he has done all that he undertook to do ; all that he undertook was to show that the legend was a mere legend resting on no evidence ; he did not undertake to put something else instead of the legend ; nay, he did not necessarily undertake to prove that the legend was false. If any hitherto unknown evidence should be found in favour of the popular story, he will at once withdraw his objection to it, and that without in the least damaging the position which he held when he made the objection.

Let us see how the case stands with regard to the most famous of all legends. As we have no right to say that rain did not fall on the site of New York on the day of the battle of Plataia, so neither have we any right to say that Rome was not founded by twins who had been suckled by a wolf. I speak on the supposition that certain modern stories from India of children suckled by wolves are trustworthy; if they are not, we may perhaps go a step further. If those Indian stories are trustworthy, we have no right to say that the legend of Romulus and Remus is false. All that we have a right to say is that there is no evidence for it ; to say that it is not proved by the Palatine being a likely place for a wolf's lair—for how should the story arise in an unlikely place?— to say that it is not proved by the existence of Fasti of the time of Augustus beginning with "Romulus filius Martis"—that it is not proved by the existence of certain pieces of very ancient masonry which do prove a great deal in other ways. We may go on to say that the story is simply one of countless stories of the foundation of Rome which has happened to become more famous than the others, but which has not a scrap more of real evidence in its favour. We may add, what the comparative method teaches us, that it is one of a whole class of legends of the foundation of cities, and that the legends of the foundation of Ardea and Tusculum, which no one cares to believe, are worth just as much and just as little as the more famous legend of the foundation of Rome. Therefore, while the story is most unlikely, its unlikelihood is not of the kind which grows into likelihood ; we see how it came into men's heads to imagine it. Rome must have its foundation-legend as well as other cities, and a legend that suited a wooded hill by the Tiber grew up. Nor is there even the desperate chance that the Roman story might be the one true story after the pattern of which other stories were invented. For the legend itself, backed up so far by every evidence of geography and nomenclature, points to Rome, not as the eldest city of Latium, but as the youngest. In the Roman legend we have perhaps reached the very highest degree of inherent unlikelihood ; and it does seem absolutely impossible that any external evidence should ever be found to confirm it. It is the highest degree of unlikelihood ;

still it is mere unlikelihood. We are not inclined
to believe that Rome was founded by a king who
was suckled by a wolf and who killed his brother;
but we cannot deny that position with the same
undoubting confidence with which we can deny the
position that University College was founded by a
king who let the girdle-cake burn when it was his
business to turn it.

Now in all these various ways which we have
been speaking of, it may be said that, if we have
established anything, it has been the uncertainty of
all historical evidence of every kind. It may be said
that, if there is such a thing as the science that I
hinted at, the science which, if not the same thing as
history, must take history as its ground-work, the
science of man in his political character, that science
must be a science of a very uncertain kind. It must
be very unlike other sciences, sciences whose propositions may be made with certainty, where, given
such and such combinations, such and such results
may be looked for with perfect confidence. Such
a science, many will be tempted to say, is no science
at all; it is simple guess-work, following at its best
no higher law than the law of chances. Now it is
easy to make an answer which may lead us into
very deep questions indeed. We might ask whether
the difference between the nature of the evidence
with which we have to deal and the nature of the
evidence with which some of the sciences have to
deal is not sometimes exaggerated. We surely
sometimes over-rate the degree of certainty, perhaps

rather the approach to certainty, which is reached by
some of the natural sciences. It certainly seems to
me that their professors sometimes mistake for certainty something which is only the highest degree of
likelihood, and that they are apt to draw too wide a
line between their very high degree of likelihood
and the much lower degrees of likelihood with which
we have often to put up. The difference between
their evidence and ours is surely a difference only of
degree and not of kind. Complete certainty is the
possession of very few, some say of none. For I had
once gone on to say that no one is really certain except
the mathematician ; but I have since been warned
that even the mathematician is not really certain, that
even the truths of geometry are dependent on our
present conditions of being, and that there might be
a world, as Mill put it, in which two and two should
make five. Such speculations are rather beyond me ;
but there surely is at least a difference in kind between
the evidence of the geometer and the evidence of any
other of us. The geometer can not only say that a
thing is, but he can say why it is. I tremble when I
say it, but it seems to me that in most branches of
knowledge, in many of those whose results are
deemed to be most certain, their professors can after
all only tell us that a thing is so ; they cannot tell
us why it is so. I even venture to think, if it be not
a contradiction to say so, that, while the historian
must have less confidence than the natural philosopher has in saying that things are so, yet, granting
that they are so, he can come nearer than the natural

philosopher can to saying why things are so. The laws of natural science are after all only deductions from experience. As far as experience goes, things always do happen in a particular way; the philosopher cannot tell us why they happen in that way. He can give us immediate cause after immediate cause; but, if pressed to tell us the ultimate cause, he can only say it is Force. That is really only a philosophical way of saying that he does not know. Follow even the law of gravitation into all its endless and wonderful applications; still, after all, we cannot say why things gravitate; we can only say that they do. I may be saying something very old-fashioned, very unscientific, but surely, when we accept every fact and every classification of facts that modern science has brought to light, to say that those facts are the results of a personal will which rules that they shall happen in a certain way, is at least as philosophical as to say that they are the result of Force, when nobody can tell us what Force is. The truths of natural science are the result of experience; we feel sure that there must be an inherent connexion between the effect and the immediate cause, because, as far as experience goes, the effect always follows on the immediate cause. But, before experience, we could never see the connexion between the cause and the effect. We believe that the sun did rise on any past day that may be named, even millenniums before the beginning of recorded history. We believe that the sun will rise on any future day that may be named, be that day never so distant. That is to say,

we believe it both ways subject to the contingency—
for after all it is only a contingency—that the existing state of things was in being at the past date and
that it will remain in being at the future date. But
we believe it only because, within the whole range of
human experience, that process which in popular
language we call the rising of the sun always has
taken place once in twenty-four hours. The
astronomer can tell us the immediate causes why it
takes place; he can tell us the causes of those causes
through a long series; but he cannot reach the
ultimate cause. He cannot reach the certainty—if
I may call it certainty—of a proposition in Euclid.
He cannot show that there is not a cause beyond all
other causes which once set to work the causes which
he knows, a cause which may again cause them to
cease working. In other words, Omnipotence may
have called the solar system into being and Omnipotence may put an end to the solar system. So to hold
is at least as philosophical as any other theory on a
matter which is really beyond our faculties, faculties
which cannot understand either absolute beginning
or the absence of absolute beginning, which cannot
understand either the absence of an ultimate cause
or the nature of the ultimate cause. That is to say
once more, none but the mathematician is really
certain; in other matters we cannot get beyond
higher and lower degrees of likelihood. As to facts,
present and future, the natural philosopher, without
reaching the absolute certainty of the mathematician,
comes vastly nearer to it than the historian ever can

come. But when we have to do with the real causes
of the facts, I maintain that the historian comes
nearer to understanding their nature than the
natural philosopher can. We are often in doubt as
to our facts ; but we are never driven to explain our
facts by assigning as their cause a Force which is a
mere name, a decorous way of confessing ignorance.

Why are historical events uncertain, uncertain both
in themselves and in their evidence ? Because they
depend on things which are in their own nature
uncertain. The event itself depends on the human
will, a very uncertain thing ; the evidence for it
depends on human truthfulness, another very uncertain thing. When I say that the event depends
on the human will, I speak with all reverence, both
philosophical and religious. The Christian, the theist
of any kind, believes that man's will acts only in
subordination to a higher will. Nor would the
existence of that higher will be set aside, if it could
be shown, as some tell us, that we have no freedom
of the will, that we are all ingeniously constructed
machines, machines so ingeniously constructed as to
make us fancy that we have a free will when we
have none. Some of us may be unphilosophical
enough to say " Solvitur vellendo." It may be enough
to say that, if we have no free will, we live in a
world of sheer delusion, not only as to historical
knowledge, but as to all daily events, public or
private. In fact we are brought back to my favourite
proposition that history is past politics and politics
present history. Past history is uncertain, but so are

the things that go on under our own eyes. Everybody felt quite certain that Parliament would meet on
a certain Thursday [1]. Everybody who was concerned
acted as if its meeting was quite certain, as certain as
the rising of the sun on that Thursday morning. Yet
nobody could be really certain about the matter. So
far from having the certainty of the mathematician,
no one had the certainty of the chemist or the
astronomer. We do not, I venture to say it, know
why the sun rises, but no power within the range of
our faculties can stop it from rising. A thousand
things quite within the range of our faculties might
have hindered Parliament from meeting. The thought
that Parliament might not meet most likely did not
come into the head of any one on whom its expected
meeting imposed a certain course of action. Yet
after all it was only very likely that Parliament
would meet; it was very unlikely that anything
should hinder it from meeting; but something might
have hindered it, and that without any miracle,
without the world coming to an end before the
appointed day. Some moral or some physical cause,
some unexpected revolution in the world of matter or
in the world of man's will, might have made it
impossible for the Estates of the United Kingdom to
come together on the appointed day. The same uncertainty follows us as to all our schemes and engage-
ments, public or private; something may disappoint
all our expectations, and that without any change in
the ordinary course of nature. But the expectations

[1] [October, 1884].

of the natural philosopher that certain events will happen, that certain results will follow from certain causes, cannot be disappointed, except by a change in the ordinary course of things. But high above all is the position of the geometer, who has no expectations but certainties, to whom even the abiding of the ordinary course of nature is a slight matter. To him we may apply the old stock quotation,

> "Si fractus illabatur orbis,
> Impavidum ferient ruinæ;"

for the truths of his science will go on, untouched and unshaken, in boundless and empty space. We attain not to his heights; but we say that, if we do not attain to them, neither does the natural philosopher. Only the natural philosopher lies under a temptation from which we are free, the temptation of fancying that he has attained to them. He is tempted to think that, because nothing short of a change in the order to which we are accustomed can set aside his reckonings, therefore his reckonings can never be set aside. He comes so near to certainty that he is tempted to think that he has reached it; he is tempted to think that the order to which we are accustomed is eternal and unchangeable, of which there is not and cannot be any proof. He is tempted to forget that the laws, that is the deductions from experience, which he establishes may possibly be subordinate to higher laws, to laws which he has not yet found out, because the occasions when they come into play may be reckoned, not by days or years, but by countless millenniums. He is tempted in short to mistake high probability for certainty, to forget that the difference between him and us is only a matter of degree. For our own parts, we do not exercise ourselves in great matters which are too high for us. We freely admit that all our reckonings may be brought to naught without any change in the order of nature. For the order of nature in no way depends on that very uncertain thing, the human will. But that with which we have to deal, that course of human affairs which, when present, we call politics, and which, when past, we call history, does depend on the human will, and is therefore uncertain. We cannot be sure of the future; because, setting aside deeper contingencies, it depends on the human will to fix what shall happen. We cannot be sure of the past, because its evidence depends on human truthfulness; that is, because it depends on the human will to fix what shall be said to have happened.

We can then reach in our historical studies, as being studies of human affairs, the same kind of certainty which we reach in ordinary human affairs, public or private. We cannot reach mathematical certainty, we cannot reach a degree of certainty a good deal lower than mathematical certainty. But we can reach that high degree of likelihood which we call moral certainty, that approach to certainty on which reasonable men are content to act even in the gravest concerns of life. You believe that I am Regius Professor of Modern History; I believe it myself. But you have no proof of the fact, neither have I. Yet I did not decline to act because it is possible that what I believe to be Her Majesty's sign-manual appointing me may have been a forgery—for I certainly did not myself see Her Majesty sign it. You do not decline to come to my lectures because you have not seen the sign-manual, because you have no evidence for my appointment beyond my own word or common fame. And this kind of evidence, evidence on which we act every day, evidence on which we stake our fortunes, our honour, and our lives, is the kind of evidence which we get in our historical studies. Whether such evidence is enough to make history a science or the pathway to a science is really a question of words and nothing else. By this kind of evidence we can gain a vast mass of knowledge, of knowledge that is pleasant in itself, of knowledge that disciplines the mind, of knowledge that is of no small practical use. And I suppose that, if we had to speak of such knowledge in the Latin tongue, we should call it by no name but "scientia."

Our evidence then for the facts of our branch of knowledge or science is less strong than the evidence for the facts of some other branches. But do we not nevertheless know more than some of our neighbours as to the causes of the facts with which we deal? Surely we know more about the human will than we know about Force. Certainly we do so in that rough practical way which perhaps suits our rough practical subject, the affairs of men. And we can after all make some inferences from the course of those affairs, we can lay down some rules which may almost be called laws, and of which I venture to think that we can see the why and because more clearly than we can in the case of physical laws. Nothing is more morally certain, that is, nothing reaches a higher degree of likelihood, than the position at which I hinted at the beginning, that every worthy movement, be it on behalf of learning or of higher objects than learning, on behalf of freedom or humanity or right in any shape, will have to go through much opposition, much ridicule, that it will have to live through many adverse votes, through many scornful articles in newspapers, but that, if its promoters bear up stoutly, it will win in the end. To take an example from the history of natural science itself, how the *Times* jeered at the British Association fifty years back; how respectfully the *Times* speaks of it now. But it would never do to make the converse inference, and to hold that every movement that is spoken against and laughed at is necessarily a great and good movement, fated to be successful. All that we can say is that opposition and sneering prove nothing against a thing; they may be rightly applied or they may be utterly misapplied. Good is very likely, almost certain, to be evil spoken of; but we cannot say that whatever is evil spoken of is therefore good, or even likely to be good. It would be easy to put together a whole string of propositions which we might call axioms, except that they are deductions from experience, propositions which come very near to moral certainty, but to which it is still possible that there may be exceptions without any change in the

general order of nature. Some nation may find itself
in so unusual a set of circumstances, some one man's
will may be so strong or so capricious, as to baffle all
expectations and to belie all ordinary rules. The man
may be lacking to the hour, or the hour may be
lacking to the man. Compared with the fixity of
physical rules, human affairs may seem to be the
sport of chance ; the science which deals with them
may seem to lack the attributes of science. What
seems certain to one inquirer may seem wholly uncertain to another. We admit the charge, so far as it
is a charge. If it be an evil, it is an evil inherent in
our subject. Evil or not, it is something which we
cannot get rid of. And we may be inclined to think
that it is not an evil, that it is in truth a sign of the
worthiness and greatness of our subject. If mind is
higher than matter, if moral causes are higher than
physical, for that very reason they come less under
the dominion of rigid rules ; their details are, by
reason of the very height of the subject, less certain
than the details of those studies which deal with
lower subjects. Because we can come nearer than
the followers of some other studies to the real knowledge of the causes with which we deal, because we
can better understand the working of an intelligent
will than we can understand the working of an unexplained Force, for that very reason we cannot be so
sure, either in the past or in the future, as to results
which depend on an intelligent will. Thus each
pursuit has some advantages over its fellows. We
claim no superiority over other branches of know-

ledge ; only we confess no inferiority. If we proclaim the greater height of our subject, we allow with the same breath that our means for gaining an exact knowledge of it are smaller. But we do protest against the exclusive claim of any branch of know-ledge to boast itself as if itself and its fellows alone were knowledge. We protest specially against the attempt to support the boast by the mere legerde-main, the *prestige*—shall we say, the *præstigiæ diaboli*? —of calling certain studies exclusively by a Latin name, a name which simply translates the plain Teutonic word which should surely come with a more kindly sound to English ears.

LECTURE IV.

ORIGINAL AUTHORITIES.

THE kernel of all sound teaching in historical matters is the doctrine that no historical study is of any value which does not take in a knowledge of original authorities. Let no one mistake this saying, as if I were laying down a rule that no knowledge of any historical matter can be of any value which does not come straight from an original authority. If this were so, both I and many others, living and dead, must have spent a great deal of time to very little profit in cumbering the earth with not a few volumes which certainly have no claim to rank as original authorities. Such a doctrine would be at once confuted by the slightest thought. For it would not be a counsel of perfection, but a counsel of impossibility. If that be the duty of the historical inquirer, no man can do his duty. The field of history is so wide, even any one of its great branches is so wide, that no man can hope to master all history, or all mediæval history, or all English history, in the original authorities for every period. And, if he could master it all in the original authorities, he would hardly be wise if he looked at nothing

but the original authorities, and scorned to ask for
any help from those who had worked at the original
authorities before him. No; if any man ever dreamed
of mastering the original authorities for all history,
for all European history, for all English history, the
dream must have been dreamed very early in life,
when the dreamer had as yet no kind of notion of
the nature of the gigantic task which he was setting
himself. It must have been dreamed, one would
think, before any original authority whatever had
been grappled with. Yet such a dream would be
creditable compared with another dream which has
been dreamed in real life. I know of an ingenious
gentleman who put forth the first part—certain
circumstances hindered him from ever putting forth
the second part—of a Synopsis, or some name to that
effect, of Modern History, which was not to demand
any knowledge of any original authority whatever
on the part of the reader or even of the writer. The
enterprising author, a man not without some reputation in other walks, thought himself able to grapple
with Modern History as a whole, to master it
himself and to expound it to others, on the strength
of having read, I think it was two modern English
books and one French. Nor do I greatly blame him;
the attempt was a fair inference from the principles of
those who set up a School of Modern History as an
easy study. I do not know that his attempt was at
all more contrary to sound learning than the course of
those who run off themselves, and bid others to run off
with them, post-haste to the French Revolution,

without stopping to take a turn, if only to pick up habits of work, among the stiffer records of the Wandering of the Nations. On the whole, we are much more likely to be troubled with the error which deems either that there are no original authorities or that original authorities may safely be dispensed with, than with the more generous error of him to whom all original authorities shall seem so attractive that there is none which he can bring himself to forego the delight of mastering. The path of practical study lies between the two errors. Any knowledge of history which is good for anything must be founded on the mastery of original authorities; but it will not be founded on an attempt to master all original authorities. Every student must master some; no student can master all. Even he who makes historical study the main business of his life cannot expect to master more than the original authorities for a few specially chosen periods. As for other periods, he must be content to know only so much as will enable him to put them in their right relation to one another and to the periods of his own choice. And this he must largely do by the help, not of original authorities but of secondary writers. Yet, even when he is learning from secondary writers, he is in a sense making use of original authorities. He is at least making use of the habits of mind which he has gained from the use of original authorities. I should not counsel a man who is fresh from thoroughly getting up his Thucydides to rush straight at the French Revolution; but I will say this for him, that he will be far more likely to understand the French Revolution than the man who rushes straight at the French Revolution without thoroughly getting up his Thucydides or anything else.

But before we go on to try to establish any rules for the use of original authorities, it will be well to make sure that we have a clear notion what original authorities are. The very first business of the historical student is to clear his mind of any popular confusions on this head. It is wonderful how many people there are, often people who might know better, to whom a book is a book. Crowds of men who are not stupid, but who have never really thought on these matters, do not clearly see the difference between two wholly different classes of men. There is the man who writes a record of the events of his own age, often of events of which he was himself a spectator and very likely an actor, and there is the man who ages after sits down to put together, by comparing his evidence with other evidence, the best critical narrative he can of the times which to him are a far remote past, while to the other they were a living present. Both write about the same kind of subjects, and both are confounded under the common title of historians. Thucydides is a historian; so is Grote; Ammianus is a historian; so is Gibbon. And the matter is complicated by the existence of a large class of writers who are also called historians, but who hold a place intermediate between these two classes. What are we to say to the History of Livy, such parts of it as we have,

to the Annals of Tacitus, to the Lives of Plutarch ?
Their authors are clearly not writers of the same class
as Thucydides and Ammianus ; still less, most people
will say and will say quite rightly, are they writers of
the same class as Grote and Gibbon.   They did not
write down a record of things which they had themselves seen and heard.   But still less, it might seem,
did they sit down to write a critical history of things
which had happened long before their own day.
Yet this is eminently what Livy did, as far as he
knew how.   Some might be inclined cruelly to say
that Livy did not write a critical, but an uncritical history.   But if so, it is because he missed his
aim.   He tried to be critical, and now and then he
really was so.   He used various earlier writers, and
sometimes he really weighed their statements and
exercised a sound judgement between them.   The
unlucky thing was that Livy himself did not in the
least know what an original authority was.   He had
sense enough to kick at anything very monstrous,
like the lies of Valerius Antias ; but on the whole
one book was to him, as it is to many people now,
of just as great authority as another.   When he
speaks of " very ancient authors," he does not mean
authors contemporary with the alleged facts, but
men who lived at the outside three or four generations before himself.   When he comes to Polybios,
he seems hardly to feel the difference between the
great   master—in   his   eyes   only   " haudquaquam
spernendus auctor "—and this or that paltry compiler.   For far the greater part of his story Livy

is so far from being an original authority that he
had not himself any original authorities to make
use of. That is, he had no contemporary narrative.
He had *fasti* ; he had annals, and scraps of the
annals are always a relief. Cicero said truly of
the annals of the pontiffs that "nihil potest esse
jucundius." I cannot hearken to any criticism
that would change that word into "jejunius." It
is delightful, after pages of family panegyric, to
find oneself opposite to a line or two of real annals.
When the ox speaks, we may listen to his warn-
ings or not, though unluckily the matter of his
speech is revealed to us only now and then.
What concerns us is that the record of his speech
is surely contemporary. But if Livy had had
far better materials than he had, the fact that he
had to write from materials at all, that he put
together a story of times long before his own from
earlier accounts, parts him. off at once from writers
like Thucydides, writers who recorded the events
of their own time from their own knowledge as
spectators and actors, or from what spectators and
actors told them. The distinction is clear ; yet
there are a crowd of temptations, a crowd of
reasons good and bad, which lead us to forget it,
and which often make us, even against our wills,
put Livy more nearly than he ought to be put in
the same class with Thucydides. At any rate we
cannot help putting him nearer to Thucydides
than to Gibbon and Grote. A crowd of reasons,
good and bad, make us do so. First of all, Livy

M

writes Latin, "classical" Latin; he is one of
the "classics," the "ancients," the writers who are
read at school and college, the mysterious order of
men who stand all apart by themselves, altogether
aloof from men who lived in times not very far from
our own, and who wrote in our own tongue or
in some of the other tongues of modern Europe.
This fact makes some of us less alive than we should
be to the truth that Livy is no more an original
authority for any of the periods dealt with in his
extant books than Mommsen is.   Still in the case of
Livy any one who thinks for a moment cannot fail
to grasp this very simple truth.   In the case of
Tacitus it is harder.   It really needs an effort
practically to remember, that is to carry the remem-
brance about with us, that Tacitus was not a contemporary with Tiberius and Claudius.   It is just
the same with a writer so unlike Tacitus as
Herodotus.   It is very hard indeed to carry about
with us the truth that Herodotus was contemporary
with Thucydides and the Peloponnesian war, and not
with the men and the wars of which he writes.
And there is a real difference between the position
of Livy, in the books which have come down to us,
and the position of Herodotus and Tacitus.   These
last, though not contemporary, lived much nearer to
the time; Herodotus had largely talked with contemporaries; so might Tacitus for parts of his Annals.
Neither sat down, like Livy in the greater part of his
work, to compile wholly from earlier writers; Herodotus could have made very little use of earlier

writers at all. Livy, as far as we have to deal with him, comes far nearer to the position of a modern writer, and yet there are differences between the position of Livy and the position of a modern writer which are quite as great as the differences between the position of Livy and that of Thucydides. It is not merely that Livy is uncritical in the use of his materials ; many modern writers still are quite as uncritical as Livy; till two or three generations back, most of them were so. The difference is that Livy stands in a different relation to his materials and to the facts or fictions which were recorded in those materials. The fact that he is, at least that he would be, if his work were perfect, a really original authority for part of his story, that the parts for which he was and those for which he was not an original authority, all formed part of one whole, conceived according to one plan, makes a real difference in the way of feeling and looking at the matter on the part both of the writer and of his readers. He did not, like the modern critical historian, feel that he was living altogether in the past, in a remote past, cut off from the present. Between his two characters of critical examiner of the past and contemporary narrator of the present, between the facts with which he had to deal in those two characters, there was no very wide gap. He belongs in short to the same class as a crowd of writers, so-called classical and so-called mediæval, who wrote histories which begin long before their own times but which are continued into their own times. The chief of all, Polybios himself, belongs to this class, and it is by virtue of his belonging to this class that he is the chief of all. Had he written only the history of his own times or only the history of times before his own, in neither case could he have reached to that clear œcumenical view which makes him the teacher of all time. Ammianus again has undergone the exactly opposite fate to that of Livy. He too began before his own time, though not so far before his own time as Livy did ; but the part of his work which we have is that for which he is really an original authority. A crowd of later writers are in the same case as Livy and Ammianus ; take, as one out of many, Gregory of Tours. A meagre chronicle starting from the beginning of the world leads on, through a somewhat inaccurate account of the early history of the Frankish nation, to that minute and life-like picture of the events of Gregory's own day, events in which he was himself no small actor, which forms our chief source for any knowledge of Gaul in the sixth century. These books of Gregory rank with the lost later books of Livy, with the extant books of Ammianus, as an original authority in the highest sense. The early part of Gregory ranks with the extant part of Livy ; there is simply the immeasurable difference between the two as writers. Gregory could tell the tale of what he had himself seen with Herodotean life and simplicity ; he had no share in Livy's gift of calling up a real or imaginary picture of ages long since past. Or, five hundred years later, take Lambert of Hertzfeld. He begins with annals ; he gradually

enlarges and warms, till his tale grows into that
precious and admirable narrative of the great
struggle between Pope and Cæsar, that narrative so
clear, so full, so wisely treading the narrow path
between partisan writers on either side, that it has
won for a monk of the eleventh century his full right
to a place alongside of the foremost of the so-called
ancients. We may mark again that both Gregory
and Lambert, very unlike Livy, begin with mere
annals, very dry annals, which only gradually wake
to fulness and life as the writers draw near to their
own times. A nearer parallel to Livy will be
found in William of Malmesbury. He, like Livy,
took for his subject the history of a single nation ;
and from the beginning he writes, like Livy, as a
historian, and not, like Gregory and Lambert in
their early stages, as a mere annalist. Besides
his merits as a writer, he has his value as pre-
serving to us not a little from lost writers in prose
and verse ; but it is only towards quite the end of
his story, in the *Historia Novella* more thoroughly
than in the *Gesta Regum*, that he becomes a real
original authority for his own times. All these writers
then, Polybios, Livy, Gregory, Lambert, William, all
have something in common with the modern
critical writer ; but they have much more in
common with those writers who are original authorities pure and simple. The fact that they are
original authorities for part of their work makes
them come far nearer to those who are original
authorities and nothing else. And this is specially

true of those who, like Gregory and Lambert, begin with mere annals. Their value lies almost wholly in the parts where they are strictly original. Gregory and Lambert are beyond all things the living chroniclers of the days of Chilperic and Guntchramn, of the days of Henry and Hildebrand. And they are little else. William of Malmesbury, after all, gives us no such living picture of the days of Henry the First and Stephen; but then he has his use, no small use, if he is used warily, for days long before Henry the First.

But there is another class of writers, "ancient" writers, "classical" writers, who have no pretensions at all in any part of their writings to rank as original authorities in the strict sense, but who yet seem to have more in common with real original authorities than with modern critical writers. Take Plutarch, for instance. He can hardly be called an original authority, even in the one or two Lives for which he may have had some slight knowledge of his own. He is simply a compiler, though a compiler of a special kind, and a kind not to be despised. And yet, if we draw a hard and fast line, we can hardly help placing him along with the original writers rather than along with modern critics and commentators. The fact is that Livy, Plutarch, and a crowd of others, though they are not original authorities in themselves, are original authorities to us. That is to say, we can for the most part get no further than what they tell us. We know that they copied earlier writers; we often know what earlier writers they copied. But those earlier writers are for the most part lost; to us Livy and Plutarch are their representatives. For a large part of their story we have no appeal from them except either to internal evidence or to any fragmentary authorities of other kinds that may be left to us. There is no counter-narrative. Some of the earlier writers used by Livy have been called into new life by the ingenuity of German scholars; but it is out of Livy's own substance that they have been called into life. A writer of the last two or three centuries stands in altogether another position. In all but the rarest cases, we have an appeal; we can test him by the original writers whom he has used or whom he has failed to use. His whole purpose, his whole way of looking at and dealing with things, is altogether different from that of the writers who, after compiling a history of earlier times from earlier writers, went on to write the history of their own times from their own knowledge. But his position is also altogether different from that of those who seem to hold a place more like his own, those who did not touch their own times, who were simply compilers of past history, but who might be, if they chose, critical compilers, and who sometimes to some extent were so. On the whole, the old Greek and Roman writers, even when they were not really original authorities, have so much in common with those who are, that, wide as is the difference between Thucydides and Plutarch, we cannot help placing Plutarch nearer to Thucydides than to Curtius and Droysen. Whatever he

was in his own day, he is an original authority to us.
We yearn for the autobiographies of Aratos and
Sulla; but we yearn in vain. The kindly sage of
Chairôneia is the only substitute for them that we
are ever likely to have.

If then we are to define original authorities, we
might perhaps define them as those writers from
whom we have no appeal, except to other writers of
the same class. This distinguishes them from modern
critical writers, from whom we have an appeal to
writers of another class. And among the writers defined as we have just defined originals, we must at
once distinguish a primary and a secondary class, those
from whom there never was any appeal and those from
whom there once was an appeal, but from whom there
is an appeal no longer. That is, we distinguish between writers who wrote from their own knowledge
and who are original authorities in the strictest sense,
and writers who did not write from their own knowledge, but who are the only representatives of earlier
writers who did, and who therefore, though not original authorities in themselves, are original authorities to us. We are at this stage speaking of writers,
of men who have handed down to us a narrative of
some considerable part of the world's history. But
we must remember that even the best contemporary
writer is commonly a primary authority for a part
only of his subject. Though living at the time of
which he writes, though often an actor in the scenes
of which he writes, still he cannot always write from
personal knowledge; he cannot have seen everything

with his own eyes; he must constantly write only what he has been told by others; only he is able to judge of what is told him by others in a way that a later writer cannot do. And besides his narrative, there is often other contemporary evidence which for some purposes may be of higher authority than his narrative. The text of a proclamation or a treaty is, within its own range, of higher authority than the very best contemporary narrative. I say within its own range, because the official document, while it always proves a great deal, does not always prove everything. The doctrine that the history of England was to be studied in the statute-book had a large amount of truth in it. It was in some sort a needful warning. Yet it was rather one side of the truth than the whole truth, and it was a side that might be used in a misleading way. That the history of England cannot be rightly studied without a constant reference to the statute-book is a perfectly true proposition, provided only that the statute-book made use of begins at a time not later than the Dooms of Æthelberht.

The texts of documents then, along with inscriptions—which in some ages are the shape which the text of documents commonly takes — coins again, which in truth are one particular class of inscriptions, in short, contemporary monuments of any kind, are all of them in a sense original authorities; for some purposes they are original authorities in a higher sense than the narrative even of a contemporary writer. Still, though their authority is often higher in itself, we cannot help using the narrative as our primary authority and our other sources of knowledge as something subsidiary. The narrative is commonly continuous; if it does not tell us the whole tale, it at least tells us the tale as a whole. The documents and other sources of knowledge are for the most part not continuous; they come in only now and then; the knowledge that they give us is piecemeal. Or if, like our own rolls and records for many ages, they are chronologically continuous, still they only show certain sides and aspects of the time, and those mostly formal ones. We use evidence of this kind to illustrate, to explain, often to correct, our contemporary narratives; but it is only by the help of the contemporary narratives that we are able to use it in this way. The narrative without the documents, if imperfect, is at least intelligible; the documents would be hardly intelligible without some narrative. We can hardly be said to read the history in the documents; we read it in the narrative, but we keep the documents by us for constant reference. In short by original authorities we mean, first of all, contemporary narratives, or as near an approach to contemporary narratives as we can get. Sources of knowledge of other kinds, even if in themselves of higher authority than the narratives, are still, as we cannot help using them, something subsidiary, illustrative, corrective, to the narrative. In the present lecture therefore I purpose to treat mainly of writers of historical narratives, of the writers of those books which we do not merely keep by us to refer to on

occasion, but which we read steadily through from
one end to the other. I speak mainly of those writings, of whatever date, which have a good right to
count as "books" in the sense which the word
"books" bore in Oxford in my youthful days. In
the early stages of study, whether with view to examinations or not—though to be sure there is the
question whether mere reading for an examination is
worthy to be called study—it is well to draw a wider
distinction between books of this class and other
sources of knowledge than need be drawn at more
advanced periods of work. It is by thorough mastery of a few well chosen books that we gain those
habits of mind which enable us somewhat later to
make use of other authorities besides our books.
There may be in these favoured days royal roads to
knowledge of which I have had no experience. Wisdom may, for ought I know, come of the crib and the
summary; it may come of views and theories, brilliant
and taking, I dare say, which are reached by some
other path than the somewhat thorny one of grinding
at the texts of writers in strange tongues. I can only
say that for me it was a white day when I began
really to work at the history of Thucydides, not in
the glib English of the newspapers, but in the rough-
hewn sentences of his own tongue. For on that day
I assuredly took the first step towards one day writing the History of the Norman Conquest of England.
I suppose that, of all the books ever written, Thucydides, in his own text, is the best suited for this particular purpose, the purpose of teaching what history

really is.   The wider view of Polybios better suits a
later stage of intellectual growth, to say nothing of
his facts belonging to a later age.   Still Thucydides,
prince of original writers, is simply foremost in his
own class, a class taking in many other writers of
many ages and tongues.   My present object is to
speak mainly of those writers who may, like him,
each in his measure, be used as "books" in the special
sense, as texts, that is, to be mastered as centres, so
to speak, of historical knowledge for the times and
lands to which they belong.   Of some such I have
already incidentally spoken.   I will now go on with
a few words as to the way in which this primary
class of writers may be most profitably used.   Other
sources of knowledge, sources which are more or less
incidental, documents, even the most precious, among
them, will have another lecture to themselves.

It at once follows that, for this particular purpose,
that of choosing writers who may serve as " books "
in the old Oxford sense, as means of introduction to
historic study, we must make a careful selection
among the vast mass of those who may fairly rank
as original authorities.   Take the first class of all,
those who are original writers in the highest sense,
those who recorded the history of their own times
from their own knowledge.   I reckon here all who
did so for even part of their story, whether they
confined themselves to the history of their own times
or began their narrative at some earlier time.   The
authorities which come under this head vary not a
little in form and in value.   They range from writers

of meagre though contemporary annals, up to statesmen and soldiers describing in full the great events
of the world in which they themselves took a part.
It would be going too far to say that all are entitled
to equal credit ; for, as we see in daily life, the
degrees of credit due to this and that man even
as to contemporary matters are endless. A man
may record the events of his own time, and may yet
not record any of them from real personal knowledge. But on the other hand, as no man, hardly
the writer of an autobiography, can write wholly
from personal knowledge, the difference on this
head between one contemporary writer and another,
though in many cases a very great difference in
degree, is still only a difference in degree. All
form one great class, the class of men who do not
write from the records which others have given of
earlier times, but from their own knowledge, not
necessarily their personal knowledge, of things that
went on around them. They are all, in different
degrees, witnesses. Even those who are not in the
strictest sense witnesses to facts are witnesses to
reports as to the facts, and the reports are part of
the history. If even these writers cannot always
tell us how things happened, they can at least tell
us how things seemed to happen, both to themselves
and to others. And, if not actually in this class, yet
just alongside of it, we must place some writers
whose writings are contemporary in date and narrative in shape, but who wrote with some other purpose
than the mere handing down of historic truth. Those

purposes may be of many kinds. The reports of an
ambassador to his own sovereign are not written with
any strictly historical purpose. They are not written
to hand down the memory of facts to future ages,
but to let certain persons know, for purely practical
ends, what is going on at the moment. Yet the
reports of ambassadors are at least an undesigned
source of history, and they are often among our most
valuable historical materials. Dealing, as they do,
directly with current events, not only with the events
of the time, but with the passing events of the
moment, often recording things which the ambassador
himself had seen, heard, or done, they rank, as far as
their matter goes, among the original sources of
history in the very strictest sense. Yet we can
hardly call them actual history; we can hardly call
their writers historians. Another class of writers,
who are almost grotesquely unlike the ambassadors,
have still something in common with them, as being
like them narrative and not monumental, and yet
being only undesignedly historical. I mean those
writers of Lives of Saints, and even those collectors
of miracles, who deal with the events of their own
time. I do not mean writers like Eadmer and William
Fitz-Stephen; they belong to quite another class.
They are writers of real contemporary history in the
strictest sense, though the history that they write is
history of a special kind and written for a special
object. Eadmer and William are, in form, not professed historians of a kingdom, but biographers of
a particular man. But we place them in the same

class, and judge them by the same standard, as the professed historians of kingdoms. We only wish that we had narratives such as theirs for much larger portions of history. The ecclesiastical writers of whom I am now speaking are of quite another kind. I speak of those who write wholly for purposes of devotion and edification, often with very little heed to accuracy of mere statement. Yet they are writers who have a very special value of their own. Like forged charters, sometimes like real charters, their value is for incidental points about which they had no thought of conveying information to anybody. I mean points which the writers take for granted and about which their witness is quite unconscious. Such are points of custom and language, above all, illustrations of the customs and language of classes of men whom the historians of kingdoms are apt to pass by with very little mention. The main fact of the story may be true or false; but its details are sure to teach us something which is preeminently true. When stories of this kind are strictly contemporary, we may fairly reckon them among original authorities, though they are original authorities of a very secondary and incidental kind. It is indeed hard to draw the line between stories of this kind and mere anecdotes; and I suppose that the first shape of an anecdote, that which was given to it while it was still contemporary, may count as an original authority in some lower sense. As a statement of fact, even a contemporary anecdote is commonly of very little value. Many of you, I dare say, know that in your own persons; I certainly do. But a contemporary anecdote, when we really can get it in its contemporary shape, may give us the same kind of illustration of manners and the like which a contemporary legend gives us. And however untrue the anecdote may be as a statement of fact, however exaggerated as a picture of character, yet, if it be really contemporary, it has some value, even as a picture of the man of whom it is told. It will commonly exaggerate and distort the real features of his character; it will not often fasten on him attributes which are the exact opposite to the real ones. But we so seldom get anecdotes in their really contemporary shape, they are so largely improved in passing from hand to hand, the bright side of one man, the dark side of another, has its hue so carefully heightened, the probabilities of time and place are so utterly forgotten in the various stages of improvement, that a mere anecdote, as it commonly reaches us, is worth very little. In theory the anecdote is part of our contemporary materials; in practice it very seldom is so. Collections of anecdotes, like those of Plutarch and Valerius Maximus, are in their own nature not contemporary materials. And the work to which the name specially belongs, the Secret History of Procopius, chiefly shows us in this relation how widely the word *anecdote* has fallen away from its original meaning. The Secret History must rank among our contemporary authorities just as much as the Gothic War; the only question is whether it is equally trustworthy with the Gothic War. If its statements are false, they are not myths or legends or anecdotes in our sense, but deliberate lies.

Now what will be said if, among the original sources of history in this secondary sense, among writings which are narrative and not monumental, which are not written with the purpose of conveying historical knowledge, which are therefore, though original sources, yet undesigned sources, I place the great national poems of the chief European nations, the Homeric poems first of all? My subject is but little concerned with many of the disputes which have raged around the earliest memorials of Greek speech and Greek history. It matters a great deal in itself, but it matters very little for my purposes, whether the poems are the work of one gleeman or a hundred, provided only that gleeman or gleemen are allowed to have sung a good while earlier than the fifth century B.C. Nor does it greatly concern me whether the chief actors in the story were real men or mere creatures of the imagination. The historical value of the poems lies in the picture which they give us of one form of Aryan life, of the earliest Aryan life in Europe of which we have any record. Above all it lies in that map of præ-historic Hellas whose claim to belief does indeed rest on the argument that it is impossible. The Mykenaian empire, the position of the Bretwalda of Hellas, his under-kings, his ealdormen, his faithful thegns, the gatherings of his Witan and of his whole folk, the whole picture of a life so unlike that of democratic Athens or oligarchic Corinth, but a life so

N

thoroughly the same as the life of our own branch of
the great family, that at least is history. "Credo
quia impossibile." No man in later Greece would
have placed the chief of Hellas at Mykênê. No man
in later Greece would have conceived such a Thessaly,
such an Attica, such a Peloponnêsos, as we find in
the great Catalogue, the Domesday of the Pelopid
dominion. The instinct of our own Ælfred saw deeper
into the matter than many a laborious scholar, when he
said that Ulixes held two kingdoms under the Emperor, and that the Emperor's name was Agamemnôn.

The Homeric poems then must count among our
original authorities; so must in their measure the
great national poems of other nations. We have
still perhaps to learn the exact amount of the
historical element in the great Teutonic poems,
English, German, and Scandinavian; but there can
be no doubt or shrinking about the fact that some
poems, both English and Scandinavian, are among our
very best historical materials. In the saga of Harold
Hardrada it is clear that the part which is in verse
is far more ancient, far more trustworthy, than the
prose. Nowhere can we find such a living and
instructive picture of a fight between Englishman
and Northman as that which lives in our own song
of Maldon. It is a truly Homeric battle, but an
Homeric battle fought by men whose deeds were
sung on the morrow of the fight, and sung by a
gleeman who, we may well deem, had himself
wielded the sword of England among the immediate
following of the fallen Ealdorman.

Our original authorities then, not to go beyond those which are in the strictest sense entitled to that name, speaking for the present of narrative writings only, and reserving those which are documentary or monumental, are very various in kind, very various, I need hardly say, in strictly literary value. Now for strict purposes of evidence literary value goes for nothing. A picture wrought up by the master hand of Livy is of far higher literary value than a dry entry in the annals of the pontiffs. But, whatever the Greek Muses may have done, it is the annals of the pontiffs, and not the high-wrought romance, which the Camœnæ of Latin history did in truth dictate on the Alban mount. But when we come to the choice of authors for "books" in the technical sense, then literary value does come in. It comes in so far as this that, among writings of sterling historical value, we pick out those which are of literary value also. When I speak of literary value, I do not refer to mere style. Ammianus is the very prince of surviving Latin historians as an observant and thoughtful witness of the events of his own time. Of his style, perhaps rather the style of his age, it is unkind to speak. Now I not long ago came across the writings of one who thought himself a scholar, and who I fancy is a scholar in some of the narrower walks of scholarship, who went out of his way to sound a trumpet before him to announce that he at least was far above knowing anything of Ammianus. Students of the world's history, students especially of the great ruling ages of the world's history, will ven-

ture, in defiance of such a warning, to place him
who worthily recorded the death of Julian and
the Gothic passage of the Danube among the
great masters of history, among the great teachers
of all time. Ammianus is emphatically a " book,"
alongside of Thucydides and Lambert. But that
which is to be a book, must really be a book;
it must be a compact narrative, a literary work
in form, whatever it may be in mere style; mere
annals, mere connected scraps, precious it may be
in the highest degree as pieces of evidence, will not
discharge this particular function. We want a book
that can be read as a book, whose text can be mastered
as a text. We want a book whose text, thoroughly
mastered, may serve as a centre round which to
group whatever other knowledge of the period is to
be had, whether from other original writers less happy
in their form, or from other sources of knowledge,
documentary, monumental, or any other. The true
course of historical study is that for which the old
school of *Literæ Humaniores* in this place gave a
man so admirable a start. Let the student pick out
two or three well-chosen periods of history; one
man will be drawn to one, another to another, according to the turn of his mind, and any period that can
produce an author or authors fitted to serve as
"books" will serve the purpose. I will not recommend one period before another; I will only go so
far as to hint that the second century B.C. and the
fourth, fifth, and sixth centuries A.D. have the two-
fold merit of being at once specially instructive

and specially neglected. But whatever periods may be chosen, the full benefit of such study is not gained, unless more than one period is studied, and the further apart those periods are from one another the better. I have an American friend who has two tastes which seem to have little to do with one another. He studies everything that bears on the history of Iceland and everything that bears on the writings of Dante. His studies are of course of a more advanced kind than those which I am now speaking of; but his choice illustrates my principle. If only he does not make his Iceland and his Dante quite isolated, if he further masters in a sound general way all that lies between and around, before and after, Iceland and Dante, I maintain that his choice of subjects is a thoroughly sound one. But that very important proviso must come in. Besides the periods of his choice which he studies minutely, our historical scholar should know, according to a formula which I have used already, enough of the times which connect his chosen periods, of the times before them and of the times after them, to put those times into their true relations to his own periods and to one another. To apply to historical knowledge a saying which I remember being applied years ago to knowledge of all kinds, he should know something of everything and everything of something. Herein comes one great use of good modern writers ; and herein too comes no small help in the way of using them. He who has once gained the habit of using primary authorities, of comparing and

criticizing evidence, can trust himself among modern
guides in a way which is not safe for those who have
not gained that habit.   He knows how to deal with
them; he is not at their mercy.   His studies will
have given him a certain historic tact which will
largely enable him to discern between good and evil.
He will feel at once among modern writers who can
be trusted and who cannot.   From mastering certain
periods in minute detail, he will gain a certain power
of putting out his hand and grasping the main outlines, the leading facts, even of periods which he has
not mastered in detail.   And even for those periods
for which he has largely to trust to modern writers, he
will not wholly neglect original sources.   He will at
least learn what the original sources are and what is
their character ; he will verify many of the references
for important matters ; great and weighty documents
he will make a point of reading in the original.   No
man can read all history in original writers ; but in this
way a man may read—not all history, which is rather
too large a matter to be read anyhow by a single man
—but large parts of history, parts as large as any one
man can expect to master, not always directly from
the original writers, but in such a way that he is
never out of sight of them, never wholly out of reach
of their help.   I speak of those who are simply
teaching themselves.   On those who take on them
to teach others a heavier burthen is laid.   I cannot
believe that any man has a right to teach, at least
where teaching is supposed to have any kind of
thoroughness, any period of history which he has not

himself really mastered in the original sources. I cannot believe that any kind of historical teaching can be of any scientific value, that it can have any value among the higher studies of this place—the passman and his studies are things too mysterious for me to presume to pass any judgement upon them—if it be not grounded on reference to the original authorities at every step.

But while we pick out certain writers in various periods for our special study, while we make them the centres of our work for their several periods, we must beware of making idols of them. We must remember that they are after all not infallible ; we may sometimes correct them by the help of writers very inferior to themselves ; we may sometimes even correct them by our own inferences from their own statements. The very greatest of original writers, being after all only men, have sometimes passed judgements which their own statements did not bear out. Thucydides himself, who surely never perverted his statement of a fact, who seldom indeed allowed his feelings to pervert his judgement of facts, did yet allow himself to be unduly favourable to his master Antiphôn, to be unduly hard upon his enemy Kleôn. Yet how fierce a storm arose when a great modern historian dared to set forth this last manifest truth. Some of us may remember the Cambridge tutor who, because he could write clever imitative verses, thought himself fit to judge between what he called " Thucydides or Grote," and rejoiced that the great historian of Athenian democracy had not been brought up at

either of the ancient Universities of the land.   How
amusing it was, when Trôilos thus challenged Achil-
leus, to see the self-chosen champion of Thucydides
show his own incapacity to understand his Thucydides ; to see too how the little scholar, in a vulgar
attempt to sneer at the great one, let out the further
fact that he had not even read his Plutarch. So again
Polybios, calm master of the world's history, could not
look with calmness on those parts of the local history
of his own peninsula which were to him the immediate tradition of the elders,   He who could look at
the history of the world as a citizen of the world,
could look at Kleomenês only with the narrow prejudice of a citizen of Megalopolis.   Nor was he free
from the constant temptation of men who rise above
their own day; he was too apt to look on men as
either foolish or corrupt, simply because they had not,
like him, learned to look on their own age with the
eyes of all the ages.   This criticism may, I believe,
be safely ventured.   The class of scholars who might
be likely to write pamphlets like "Thucydides or
Grote" are likely to throw Polybios aside altogether, because his Greek is not exactly the Greek of
Thucydides, any more than the Greek of Thucydides
is exactly the Greek of Homer. We must avoid the
temptation of blind following; we must also avoid
the opposite temptation which delights in mere
paradox, which thinks it fine to upset established
beliefs, established reputations, simply because they
are established beliefs and established reputations.
The statement of Thucydides or Polybios is not an

infallible oracle ; it may be set aside by other evidence ; but it is a very strong presumption in favour of any position ; it needs very strong evidence indeed to set it aside. He who chooses a great writer of any age as his " book " does in some sort enroll himself in the *comitatus* of the writer of that book. He seeks him to lord ; he becomes his man ; he owes him the honourable duty of a faithful ἑταῖρος or *gesi*ð ; he does not owe him the cringing worship of the δοῦλος or the þeow.

Let us take a leap for one moment from the great writers of Greece to some of the original authorities for our own history. We should hardly be wise if we put any contemporary writer of English history on a level either with the undying masterpieces of Hellas or with some of the historians of Germany and Sicily in far later times. But we have two possessions, one narrative, one documentary, such as no other nation can boast of. We have our Chronicles from the beginning in our own tongue ; we have Domesday in the common tongue of Western Christendom. I will not again sing their praises ; emboldened by the example of my colleague of the Fine Arts, I will not scruple to refer to the volumes in which I have sung them already. And I will not scruple to refer to one particular point which I believe myself to have established. I do so both because I cannot see that anybody has ever taken the slightest notice of it, and because I nevertheless believe that it is both a discovery of some importance in itself and one that well illustrates the way in which, after some practice,

we come to use our authorities to throw light upon
one another.　If any one found it out before me—
and it is very hard to find out anything which some
German scholar has not found out before one—I both
mourn and rejoice ; I mourn because I have unwit-
tingly done him wrong.　Still I am not aware that any
one ever noticed before me, and I am pretty sure that
no one has noticed since me, the manifest connexion
between a few speaking words of that hurried narrative of the Peterborough Chronicle, in which, hurried
as it is, every word has the force of volumes, and a
few no less speaking words of the East-Anglian
Domesday which, in a casual mention of a single
private transaction, gives us a living picture of the fate
of all the lands of England.　The Chronicle tells us
how, after the Conqueror's crowning, men paid him
geld and gave him hostages and bought their land.
" Men guldon him gyld and gislas sealdon and *heora
land bohtan.*"　Domesday tells us how the Abbot of
Saint Edmundsbury held certain lands in pledge
which were given him on the day when the English
redeemed their lands.　" Quando Anglici *redimebant
terras suas.*"　Surely I am not wrong in putting
these two passages together as one of the best
examples of an undesigned coincidence.　The formal
and legal language of Domesday shows that the
words of the Chronicle are not used lightly or
casually, but that they are to be taken in their
strictest sense.　The words of the Chronicle tell us
the date and circumstances of the transaction which
Domesday records without a date.　These few words

in the great narrative and the great document explain
one another; they are the key to a thousand other
phrases in Domesday and elsewhere; they set before
us the whole legal theory of the Conquest. Duke
William, lawful heir of the English crown, is kept
out of his kingdom by an usurper and his followers ;
he is driven to assert his rights by force of arms ; a
disloyal people—see how William of Poitiers speaks
of us—withstands him; no man fights for him ; many
fight against him ; but God gives him the victory.
The whole land of a nation of traitors becomes his,
not by force but by law, forfeited by the active or
passive treason of their owners. But the mild and
merciful king will not press his rights to the utter-
most; to the less guilty—the more guilty had fallen
on the hill of slaughter—he will grant their lands
back again, but not without a reasonable payment for
so gracious an act. And so men, in the phrase of the
Chronicler, bought their lands; they bought their own
back again for a price ; they held them by a new
tenure, by the grant of King William, without whose
writ and seal or some evidence equivalent to his writ
and seal, no man's holding of land was henceforth to
be lawful. This legal fiction on a gigantic scale is the
key to the whole position of William in England, and
thereby, we may say, to the whole later history of
England, above all to the history of the law of
England. We see that the lawyers' doctrine about
all land being held of the Crown, though far indeed
from being an eternal truth, has yet a basis in historic
fact, a sounder basis in truth than the elder school of

lawyers thought for. And all this is made out, at least it is all put into a clear and consistent shape, by the simple process of putting together two independent statements, each found in an original authority, in original authorities which stand alone and without rival, precious possessions of English history to which the history of no other land can show the like.

Of these two great national records, Domesday, chief of documents, can hardly be called a book in the sense in which I have used the word *book* in this lecture. But I can conceive no human writing better suited for use as a book than large parts of our national Chronicles, above all the last hundred and twenty years or so of the Peterborough version, from the accession of Eadward the Confessor to the end. There is no human writing in which the text better deserves to be studied word by word; for every word has its meaning, every word teaches us its lesson. Nowhere surely is a tale told with more life than the tale of the banishment and return of Godwine; nowhere surely does human speech, applied to something between narrative, comment, and exhortation, reach a higher level than the tongue of Englishmen had reached when it told what manner of man was the Conqueror of England. And what life is there, what pent-up force, in the awful picture of the nineteen winters that we tholed for our sins, the tale of the anarchy, told in English well nigh as rude as the Latin of Gregory of Tours, but from which no man turns away because its grammar, if it can be said to have any, is not exactly the grammar of the days of Ælfred. Our own tongue, our own history, have drawn some advantages from their very neglect. Here at least men have not set up an arbitrary standard, as they have in the case of certain forms of the Greek and Latin tongues, with the effect of leading not a few to despise some of the most precious monuments of both those tongues. Lord Chatham said of three words in the Great Charter that they were "worth all the classics." I will make no such harsh comparison, as my calling is to assert, not the rivalry but the brotherhood, of all periods and all subjects, of all nations and all languages, at least within the pale of Aryan Europe. I would only again appeal, as I appealed once before, to those who are fresh from the mastery of other lands and of elder ages. They have done right well in what they have done; let them only come on further in the same path; let them not scorn the records of our own folk, written, as no other land can boast them written, in our own tongue in which we were born. Let them even learn what may be the harder lesson, not to scorn the later days of the tongues and the lands towards the knowledge of which they have made so good a beginning. It may seem a hard saying when I call on you to look to the bishop of a Gaulish city, speaking his native Latin almost with a stammering tongue, to look to the monk of an English or German cloister who comes a degree nearer to the rules of Priscian only because Latin was to him a strange tongue learned as we ourselves learn it, and to place them as original authorities side by side with the great master-pieces of earlier times, as texts to be studied with the same care and the same reverence. But so to do is the only way to grasp as a whole the truths of history and even the truths of language. It is on you who have already learned what work is, who have already gone through that sound training of the mind which is needed for the true mastery of any subject, that I call on for help in the work that is laid upon me, a help which you can give in a shape so much sounder than any can give it who have been unluckily led astray into the false hope that they can crown the edifice before they have laid its foundation-stone.

LECTURE V.

CLASSICAL AND MEDIÆVAL WRITERS.

I HAVE been told more than once, and in more shapes than one, since I began my work in this chair, that I have been waging a battle which there is no need to wage, seeing it is already won. Nobody, I am told, disputes my doctrine, let me rather say Arnold's doctrine, of the Unity of History. I should be very glad to believe this; but I cannot see the signs of it. A little time back that doctrine had certainly not won for itself universal acknowledgement either in Oxford or elsewhere, and I am not vain enough to think that a lecture or two here can have carried this general conviction even throughout Oxford, much less throughout the whole world. But those who tell me that my doctrine is universally accepted tell me further that it is accepted with a somewhat large reservation, namely that the doctrine cannot be carried out in practice. The distinction between "ancient" and "modern" can be defended by no reasonable argument; but it must be kept up on the grounds of practical convenience. That is to say, unreasonable as it is, it must be kept up because to put something more reasonable in its place would take a good deal of trouble. That I fully allow; it would take a good deal of trouble. But then I never heard that any great object ever was gained, that any great subject ever was mastered, without a good deal of trouble. Even the "easy" study of "modern" history needs some trouble. And to devise a practical scheme to put the study of "modern" history in this place into a good working relation with the study of other branches of history would take a great deal of trouble indeed. It would take so much trouble that I do not expect ever to see it done in my time; I certainly do not wish to see it even attempted just yet. If my doctrine, that is Arnold's doctrine, is so universally accepted as I am told it is, it will bear to wait awhile, to work itself into men's minds, to bring forth fruit gradually, till it is so truly and thoroughly accepted that the notion of keeping up an unreal distinction for practical convenience shall have passed away from men's minds. By that time it will be found that there is no real convenience in keeping up arrangements which, however much trouble they may save, have the slight inconvenience of being wholly inconsistent with any clear views of the history of the world.

Meanwhile there is nothing to be done but to show in every shape and at every opportunity how much is lost by a division which tempts the students of one period to try to begin where there is no beginning, and which tempts the students of another period to make an end where there is no ending.

Something may be done towards that object, as in other ways, so by showing how impossible it is, in any general view of the whole of Europe, to draw a hard line between the writers of the so-called "classical" and the so-called "mediæval" periods. I in no way deny that it is possible to attach meanings to those words, and to use them as the names of two classes of writers between which there is a real difference. It is clear that, in the so-called mediæval writers, as contrasted with those that went before them, some new elements are coming in and some old elements are dying out. All that is expressed by the words Christian and Teutonic is coming in; all that is expressed by the words Pagan and Roman is dying out. Or rather perhaps we might say that the older elements are living on, but living no independent life, surviving only as something to modify the elements which have now become at least their fellows. It had been at last ruled, in the spirit of Ataulf, that the dominion of Rome should not come to an end, but that, in the Western lands at least, it should go on as a dominion of influence. The Teuton rent away the provinces of the Empire; but, in rending them away, he accepted the faith, the tongue, and, to a great extent, the law, of the Empire. This was of a truth the greatest conquest that Rome ever made; if Greece had once led captive her Roman conqueror, far more thoroughly did Rome lead captive her Teutonic conqueror. Her tongue became for ages the tongue of government, of learning, and of religion, in all the Western lands. We speak in the West of "classical" and of "mediæval" writers; but both come under the head of Latin writers. From one point of view we may look on it as a great evil that it should be so; and doubtless the abiding of Latin as the accepted tongue for so many purposes in the Teutonic lands had an evil side. But, good or evil, it is the surest and most abiding side of the continued domination of Rome, as a power no longer ruling over men's bodies, but more than ever influencing their minds. In the Teutonic lands the conquest was never perfect; the native speech never died out on the tongues of the people; it even became a written speech as soon as Teutonic hands had learned to handle the pen of the writer. First and most venerable among the monuments of Teutonic prose is the Bible of Ulfilas. But the Gothic Scriptures, and the other small fragments of Gothic speech, stand by themselves. They had no influence on ought that was to come. The professor of an Arian or semi-Arian creed could not become the apostle of Teutonic Christendom, and the Goth, foremost and noblest branch of the great family, was too soon cut off by the sword of the East-Roman or trampled under the horse-hoofs of the Saracen to do ought abiding for the kinsfolk who lagged behind him in the race of history. It was among our own folk in our own land, the land and the folk which received the torch of the Gospel from Rome herself and handed it on to other Teutonic lands, that a lasting literature at once Teutonic and

Christian was first to arise. Heroic lays of heathen times had lived on on condition of putting on more or less of a Christian garb. A distinctively Christian poetry arose when Cædmon—if Cædmon we are still allowed to call him—sang the tale which Avitus had sung before him, and which Milton was to sing after him. At last came the great step of all. The English speech, still in its undefiled Teutonic purity, became, at a single step, at the bidding of a single man, the mother of a rich and varied literature of prose. Not only did it show itself a fit means for handing on the thoughts of the wise men of earlier days and of other tongues; the Bible of Ulfilas had been that and more than that. It arose to show itself fit for the greater work of handing on the contemporary record of a nation, the contemporary record of that nation's greatest king. What abiding life a Teutonic tongue could keep after ages of Roman influence we see in our national Chronicles, the worthy fellows of the Gothic Scriptures. In the history of the two great intellectual conquests, the Hellenic conquest of the Roman and the Roman conquest of the Teuton, all honour must be paid to two men, to two champions of national life and national speech, to whom, each in his own age, it is owing that there is a literature of prose either in the tongue of Latium or in the tongue of England. The yeoman from Tusculum and the king from Wantage must be bracketted together. The elder Cato taught the Roman, as Ælfred taught the Englishman, that his own tongue, the tongue of his fathers, was the best tongue in which at once to hand on the deeds of his fathers and to put forth a varied lore for the teaching of his children. Every writer of Latin prose, classical, mediæval, imitative modern, has been the intellectual child of Cato ; every writer of English prose, from the Chronicler whom he himself inspired to him who speaks before you this day, has failed in the duty of a man to his lord, if he bears himself as other than the intellectual child of Ælfred.

The independent Teutonic tongues, which no man could mistake for dialects or corruptions of Latin, were thus the first to spring up as rivals to the supremacy of Latin. The Romance tongues began their work later. It was only by slow steps that men found out that the *lingua Romana* which they spoke had parted off so widely from the *lingua Latina* which they wrote that they had practically become distinct tongues, and that it was possible to write in the *Roman* speech no less than in the Latin. Gaul, where the spoken tongue had gone through greater changes than it underwent in Italy, naturally awoke to this truth sooner than Italy. From the eleventh century onwards we must reckon among our original authorities a series of Old-French writers, beginning with Aimé's history of Norman warfare in southern Italy. Villehardouin and Joinville, Froissart and Monstrelet, and a crowd of others continue the tradition of French prose ; nor must we forget the gleemen of foreign speech to whom we have often to turn for large parts of our own history, Geoffrey Gaimar,

Master Wace of Bayeux, and Benoît of Sainte-More. Later, but rising to a far higher level, came the great writers of Italy, ushered in by their chief and captive ; for surely Dante, if any writer of any age and tongue, claims his place among the original authorities of history. He must indeed be reckoned among the foremost witnesses of an age of great men and great deeds, an age of many sides of which we learn more from him than we can learn from any other source.

Now the first aspect of the history of language for the space of seven or eight centuries is that each nation gradually learned to write in its own native tongue, Romance or Teutonic, and that this use of the native tongue gradually supplanted the elder use of Latin. I was going to say that the use of Latin prose had gone on uninterruptedly from the days of Cato the Censor. And it would be going too far on the other side to say that there was any time when the custom of Latin prose composition, and even of Latin historical composition, altogether died out. But it is well to remember how very nearly, at one stage of the history of the Empire, Latin gave way to Greek. For a season, even in the Western lands, Latin seemed to have passed away as the tongue of anything that claimed to be literature. A second Greek conquest of the Roman mind seems to mark the second and third centuries of our æra. When Marcus wrote his private meditations in Greek, it was a sign of the times ; he seems to be fast approaching the position of his successors in the East with whom for so long

Latin was the formal speech of government and warfare, but of nothing else. If the feeble thread of the Augustan History did not bind together the age of Trajan and the age of Diocletian, we might almost say that it was by the Christian writers of Roman Africa that the Latin tongue was kept alive. Then came the day of reaction. Under the great Illyrian Emperors, under Jovius greatest of them all, Rome, Roman Rome, rose to life again, not indeed on the seven hills of her birth, but wherever the needs of a Rome of which York and Antioch were outlying bulwarks might rule that her Augusti should dwell. With the power of Rome her speech again came to the front; the richness of the Latin literature of the fourth, fifth, and sixth centuries stands out in marked contrast to the barrenness of the third and the greater part of the second. Instead of the Roman writing Greek, the Greek now wrote Latin; Ammianus told his tale of war and statesmanship, Claudian sang the praises of Emperors and consuls, in a tongue which was not theirs by birth. It was indeed needful that Rome should again put on her old garb and her old life; for now she had to gird herself for her greatest work; it was not a Greek- but a Latin-speaking Rome which was to be the teacher of our kinsfolk and of ourselves. Now, from this great Latin reaction to any date that we may choose in the so-called middle ages, it is impossible to find any hard and fast line between " classical" and " mediæval" writers. There is really a greater gap between Tacitus and Ammianus than there is between Ammianus and

Hugo Falcandus. It is by a really sound instinct from their own point of view that those who are too superfinely classical to read Hugo Falcandus are commonly too superfinely classical to read Ammianus either. Indeed I am not sure that the Frenchman— for so I suppose he was—who raised his wail over the griefs of Sicily does not come nearer to the standard of Livy or Cicero than the Greek soldier who makes us at home with Constantius and Valentinian. I would venture to throw out the hint for the consideration of those among us to whom the history of language as such, and specially the history of the Latin language, is a matter of more immediate concern than it is to me, whether this Latin reaction was not largely the child of the rhetorical schools of Gaul. Certain it is that the new fashion seems to be ushered in by those wonderful discourses which panegyrists who had studied at Autun addressed to Emperors who reigned at Trier. From this time onwards Latin prose becomes artificial rhetoric, except when by good luck it drops into the simplicity of annals, meagre it may be but at least intelligible. Happy are we when we get to writings in which men who confessed their unskilfulness wrote as they spoke, and who thereby help us to see some of the steps by which the tongue of Latium changed into the tongues of Aquitaine and France. The grand style, in various forms, is the style of Ammianus, of Sidonius, and of Cassiodorus; the wonderful thing is how much of sound wisdom, what a mass of precious facts, could, by their inherent vigour, escape being utterly

smothered by the mass of fine writing out of
which they have to struggle.   And this artificial
and vicious taste lived on ; it affects most of those
writers of the middle ages who affect any prose style ;
Dudo of Saint-Quentin perhaps outdoes all who
went before or after him ; but our own Herbert of
Bosham could do a good deal in the way of the grand
style two centuries later.   It is relief when a writer
is content to have no style at all, when he simply
tells us what he has to say, in such Latin, better or
worse, as he can give us, but without any pretence
at rhetoric.   The point that concerns me now in all
of these writers is that, in this as in other matters,
no real line can be drawn between " ancient " and
" modern," " classical " and " mediæval," or that, if a
line is drawn, it must be drawn at some point earlier
or later, which may be a little unexpected.   There
is no real halting-place between the *Renaissance* of
the third century and the *Renaissance* of the fifteenth.
It is open to any man to class Eumenius of Autun
among the moderns, or to class the Crowland Continuator among the ancients.   I deny the right of
any man to cleave asunder the unbroken series of
writers to which both of them belong.

And, if this is true in the Latin West, how much
more palpably true is it in the Greek East.   In an
argument which some of you may have seen in another shape, I have insisted on the unbroken continuity of Greek literature and the impossibility of
dividing the indivisible, unless it be at a point which
would rank not only Polybios but Aristotle among

the moderns. In the fourth century B.C. began the unbroken series of writers of Greek prose who talked one kind of Greek and wrote another. They talked whatever was the natural dialect of their age and country; they wrote with as near an approach to the Attic standard of purity as they were lucky enough to attain to. That series takes in the whole line of Byzantine writers ; it would not be too much to extend it so far as to take in the literary Greek of our own day. The last attempt at reviving ancient forms, whatever we think of it, and I for one deeply regret it, is simply one of several cases of *Renaissance* in the history of the Greek tongue. One very clear case of such *Renaissance* marks the age of Lucian ; another marks the age of Anna Komnênê. Where are we to draw the line ? Plutarch, I presume, is an " ancient ;" so must be his contemporary Diôn Chrysostom. But what of his grandson the other Diôn, who assuredly knew some things about Roman history that Livy did not know ? Where are we to put the Christian Fathers and the pagan philosophers ? Where will come that great collection of historians, ecclesiastical and secular, Christian and pagan, who, some of them even in their fragments, set the history of the fifth century before us, many parts of it in no small fulness of detail ? The living picture which Priscus has given us of the court of Attila makes us yearn for more than fate has given us of a writer who could observe so well and so well record what he observed. In the next century we rise higher and we fall deeper. It is a fall indeed when, after

reading the Gothic war in Procopius the statesman,
we go on to read the Frankish war in Agathias the
rhetorician. But the change is in the matter and
not in the form, in the man and not in the
tongue which he writes. In language, as in everything else, the whole duration of the Eastern Empire of Rome continues the elder state of things
with a continuity which is absolutely unbroken. If
we are to distinguish " ancient" and " modern "—that
is, if the words are to have any meaning, Greek and
Italian as distinguished from Teutonic and Slavonic
—we must allow that "ancient" and "modern" went
on side by side for at least a thousand years. In all
that constitutes language in the strict sense, Laonikos
Chalkokondylês differs from Xenophôn far less than
Xenophôn differs from Homer, I believe one might say
less than he differs from Herodotus. All Byzantine
Greek, if not Attic to the literary critic, is certainly
Attic to the historical philologer. If we are to draw
a line, it must be drawn between Xenophôn who
wrote Attic because it was his natural dialect and
Aristotle who wrote Attic because Attic had in
those few years become the received shape of literary Greek prose. If Chalkokondylês is not allowed
to be an "ancient," we claim Aristotle as a modern.

There is another incidental feature in the Byzantine
writers which helps to make the continuity of ancient
and mediæval Greek yet more marked than the continuity of ancient and mediæval Latin. In both cases
the mediæval tongue is an artificial dialect, a dialect
which the man who writes it does not speak in his

familiar moments. But mediæval Latin is the language
of a class in a way in which mediæval Greek is not.
Speaking roughly, mediæval Latin is the language of
the clergy.   Such a statement must be taken with
many modifications and exceptions; but it has essential truth in it.   The fact that the word *clerk* could
ever come to mean a man who could write speaks
volumes. Latin, learning of any kind, was by no means
an exclusive possession of the clergy, but it was their
possession.   The educated layman drew near to the
nature of the man in holy orders.   Our first Henry,
master of three languages, perchance of four, is marked
off from his illiterate brothers as Henry the Clerk.
The writer of mediæval Latin is, as a rule, a clerk in
the strict sense, that is, if we may take *clerk* to include
monk. Einhard and Nithard belong to an exceptional
group in an exceptional age.   We in England have
nothing to set against them better than Fabius Patri-
cius Quæstor Ethelwardus. And we cannot deny that,
though no hard and fast line can be drawn, a marked
change comes over Latin literature from the time
that it passes mainly into the hands of the clergy.
And in the West this change followed very soon upon
the change from paganism to Christianity.   The last
doctrine is that Boetius was after all a Christian ; but
we cannot call the "Consolatio" a Christian writing.
Cassiodorus is the last of the unbroken succession of
great lay writers, and he in the end withdrew to a
monastery.   But in the East the succession of lay
writers goes on unbroken to the end. Our Byzantine
volumes are quite as often, oftener, I should think,

the works of generals, statesmen, Emperors, as they are the works of bishops or abbots. To be sure the Byzantine laity would now-a-days be looked on as a clerically-minded laity; the Emperor is commonly a theologian quite as learned and quite as zealous as the Patriarch. Still in the East history did continue to be written by men of the world, men of the court and the camp. There is no real break in the West any more than in the East, but there is one marked change in the West of which there is no trace in the East.

In the East then there is no time, no place, on which we can fasten as the birth-time and the birth-place of a mediæval as distinguished from a classical literature. There are no men on whom we can fasten as embodying the change in their own persons. In the West we can in a very remarkable way connect the change with one special land, with one special city of that land, with two men before all others among the inhabitants of that land and city. There are some spots on the earth which seem to have a mission of historic teaching, which seem to stand as beacons to remind us of great events, of greater combinations of effects, of cause steadily working in their effects. Such spots stand forth as the homes, sometimes of men whose strong will must be set down as not the least among historic causes, sometimes of men who seem sent as examples of the way in which their age worked upon them, but who had hardly received a mission to work upon their age. And among such spots, as some remind us of warriors and statesmen who fixed the history of the

world, others remind us of the men whose names mark
the stages of human culture and human speech. So
there is one land, there is above all one spot, where
we may not say that the classical Latin literature
died out and the mediæval Latin literature came to
life, but where, before all other spots, we may say
that the one changed into the other, without breach
of continuity, without change of personal being. It
changed by gentle and natural growth, or if you will by
gentle and natural decay, as the newly chosen scholar
may grow or decay by gentle and natural steps till he
finds himself changed into the newly named Professor,
fully qualified, as my Latin brother will tell you, for an
unwilling plunge from the Sublician bridge into the
yellow Tiber. The history of the later Roman literature was emphatically wrought on the soil of Gaul, and
there is one spot of Gaulish soil which, more nearly
than all others, beheld the great turning-point in that
history. There is a spot which was the home of two
men who, without willing it, almost without knowing
it, must rank as epoch-making men in the long story
of the tongue which they spoke and wrote. We are
among the peaks of the Arvernian land, where each
hill, great and small, rests, as Vesuvius rested when
Spartacus found shelter in his *crater*, from the
working of the fiery powers the signs of whose
strength meet us at every step. Let us stand on the
hill which later time called the Bright Mount, head
of all other *Clari montes* in the topography of Gaul.
There, from among churches and houses built, as at
Catania, of the dark lava—strange gift of the burning

hills for man's behoof—we look up at the long line of
the camp of old Gergovia, the hill where Cæsar,
baffled for once, left his sword as the prize of Arvernian
victory. We look up too at the loftiest height of all,
the mighty peak on whose crown modern science tells
the stars and tracks their courses amid the ruins
alike of older nature and of an older creed. On that
height, by the quenched furnace of a world that has
passed away, lie the shattered temple-stones of the
gods of a mythology that has passed away after it—
shall we speak of the familiar Mercury of Italy? shall
we speak of the mysterious Gaulish deity whose exact
description I leave to my Celtic brother?—and yet
further, may we deem that, when Crocus the heathen
Aleman shattered the stones, the carvings, the mosaics,
it was as an offering to our own Teutonic gods, and
that Woden and Thunder also have been worshipped
on the height of the Puy de Dôme? We look to the
hills, but we also look to the lower ground below the
Bright Mount itself, on that pleasant plain, that
wide *Limagne*, which a Frankish king yearned to see,
but saw not for the mists that shrouded it. Close at
our feet, hardly to be marked among other buildings,
we may trace out the castle of the princes, the *château*
of the bishops, the wall that bears the name of the
Saracen invader, the wall of nobler workmanship
where we trace the abiding craft of Rome. Above
all, we see, beneath the city walls, the plain where
Urban told his tale in the ears of a world at once
shuddering and admiring, where—truly indeed *vox
populi vox Dei*—assembled Christendom spake the

great answer of God's will, and not only spake, but forth-
with girded on its sword for the first and greatest Pil-
grimage of Grace.   There, in the city around which
nature and art and history seem to have piled
together their choicest memories, but within whose
walls, among goodly piles of later days, no temple,
no church, no tower, no gateway as at Autun, no
baptistery as at Poitiers, abides on which the eyes of
its most famous citizens can have ever rested—in the
Arvernian city, the Nemetum of one age, the Cler-
mont of another, two men did their work, who joined
the highest nobility of the elder day to the highest
priesthood of the newer, two men whose days and
the space between them mark better than all else
the change between the pagan and the Christian
stages of the Latin speech on Gaulish soil.   There
lived the last famous writer of its elder form, the
first famous writer of its newer form ; the prelate-
poet who felt ill at ease under the dominion of the
Goth, the prelate-historian who had learned to shape
himself to the dominion of the Frank ; within the
walls of the Arvernian city both were alike at home ;
there dwelled Sidonius ; there was born Gregory.

The difference between the two men is marked indeed ; the memorable century which passed between
them had, whether we deem it for good or for evil,
done no slight work.   The change alike in language
and in feeling between Sidonius and Gregory would
seem to be a change of several centuries.   Even the
name of each is significant.   The full style of the
earlier writer is Gaius Sollius Apollinaris Sidonius.

The personal nomenclature of the fifth century A. D. is not exactly that of the first century B.C., but the prænomen of Marius and Cæsar still lives on. When we come to his follower, we have not indeed come back to the single baptismal name out of which modern nomenclature rose again; but we have no Gaius or Marcus now; the *tria nomina* of the sena-torial-born Bishop are Georgius Florentius Gregorius. The four names of Sidonius do not show among them the slightest mark of Christianity. Of the three names of Gregory, Florentius indeed is colourless, but the other two belong to hagiography; Gregorius indeed is a name saintly in its very essence, invented to call men to the practice of a Christian virtue. So when we turn from the names to the men, Sidonius is a Christian, a bishop, even a saint, nor have we anything to say of him that is directly inconsistent with those characters. He is so far removed from paganism, the paganism that his grandfather threw aside, that he can afford to play with the subject, and can venture, like a modern poet, to use the worn-out mythology as a source of poetic ornament. Christian, bishop, and saint, he is before all things a Roman, a Roman of Gaul, a skilled poet and rhetorician, a master of the Latin tongue according to the taste of his own time, a taste which was certainly not that either of Horace or of a modern critic. In his varied life, he had seen the world from many sides, and had played many parts in it, before he put on that of Bishop of Auvergne. Præfect of Rome, son-in-law of an Emperor, panegyrist alike of his father-in-law and

of the prince who was exalted on his father-in-law's
overthrow, he had in his native Lyons, in his
adopted Auvergne, as well as in the eternal city
itself, good opportunities of studying his age, its men
and its events. And the outside at least of all
of them he had studied to some purpose. We have
to thank him for a clearer knowledge of the ordinary
life of Gaul in the fifth century than we have of the
ordinary life of most times and places. We know
how an Arvernian senator, yet more, we know how a
West-Gothic king, passed his daily life from morning
to evening. We thoroughly grasp the nature of the
society, refined, courtly, intellectual, if feeble and
lacking in political or military spirit, into which the
unpolished Germans suddenly burst. Sidonius did not
love his barbarian enemies ; he hardly loved even his
barbarian friends ; he was not at home with greasy-
haired Burgundians seven feet high, even when they
came as his kindly protectors. We turn to Gregory,
Roman, like Sidonius ; like Sidonius also, Christian,
bishop, and saint. But the tables are turned ;
Sidonius is a Christian and a bishop, although he
is a Roman ; Gregory is a Roman, although he is
a Christian and a bishop. His creed and his office
have taken possession of his whole soul; unlike
Sidonius, he had no long secular life before he took
to his sacred calling ; but we are sure that at no
time of his life would he have ventured to take the
names of the evil dæmons Jupiter and Diana into his
mouth as names of harmless sport. He was a statesman, because a bishop of his day was forced to be

a statesman ; he had to curb the fierce passions of
rival kings, to correct unworthy and to shelter
unlucky brethren, as he might find occasion.   He
writes no sportive epigrams, no courtly panegyrics,
no rhetorical letters ; history, as he understood it,
history written for the confirmation of the faith, the
record of the worthy deeds of good men and the
unworthy deeds of evil men, the tale of the wonders
wrought by the saint, of the discomfiture brought
upon the heretic, form his grave and solemn task.   To
graces of style he makes no claim ; by his own confession, perhaps going a little too far in the way
of self-depreciation, he knew not the commonest
rules of grammar.   All the better for the purposes
of history; there is very little profit to be got from
writers who live under the rod of Donatus ; it is
when we get to false concords and false spellings that
we begin to learn something.   The Latin of Gregory
teaches us what the Latin of Sidonius does not,
it shows us how Latin looked in the first stage of its
slow change into Provençal and French.   Gregory is
a Roman ; but, if not thoroughly satisfied with Mero-
wingian rule, he at least accepts it as the inevitable
order of things ; he no more thinks of constructing
a world without Chlotachars and Chilperics than he
thinks of constructing a world without earthquakes
and pestilences.   We feel that, in passing from
Sidonius to Gregory, we are passing into another
world, into another region of thought and feeling.
But there is no sudden break ; old elements are
weakened, new elements are strengthened; that is all.

The change is great; but it is hardly greater than the change between Nævius and Ennius, assuredly not greater than the change which parted Ennius from Appius the Blind. The change from Herodotus to Aristotle, one might almost say from Herodotus to his contemporary Thucydides, is a change in the opposite direction to the change from Sidonius to Gregory; but it is assuredly a change as wide.

If then we are to draw a line between classical and mediæval Latin anywhere, we are tempted to draw it at a point that would make Sidonius the last of the classical, and Gregory the first of the mediæval writers. Yet such a division would be utterly deceptive, even in Gaul. Between Sidonius and Gregory comes Alcimus Avitus ; contemporary with Gregory comes Venantius Fortunatus. Both of them are bishops and poets ; Avitus was also a busy theologian, and a very clever and intriguing politician who had, in the cause of orthodoxy, a good deal to do with pulling the Burgundian down and setting the Frank up. Both in point of language belong to the fellowship of Sidonius rather than to the fellowship of Gregory; in spirit and objects Avitus belongs to the fellowship of Gregory rather than to that of Sidonius ; he is before all things the churchman. And it is needless to say that, long before Gregory or Avitus, we find strong signs of the spirit of Gregory ; the change from Orosius to Sidonius is in some sort a step back from the Christian Roman to the Roman Christian ; so Venantius, contemporary and friend of Gregory, seems to belong to quite an earlier stage,

His chief business is to sing the hireling praises of Frankish kings and great men, to enlarge on the merits of Chilperic and Fredegun, to tell the more honest tale of the fall of Thuringia and of the virtues of his life-long friend the holy Radegund. But he sings them in true Roman style; no forms of composition can be more unlike than the verse of Venantius and the prose of Gregory. It may of course be said that Venantius, a man of Italian birth, would naturally write in a purer style than the man of Gaul, in an age when, as Gregory himself tells us, learning had died out in the Gaulish cities. And so it may be; still we have side by side Venantius, who aims, not unsuccessfully, at being classical, and Gregory who makes no such claim, but confessedly writes the rustic speech which he spoke. And Gregory stands almost alone. When letters awake again under Charles the Great, men wrote both in verse and prose far more in the language of Sidonius and Venantius than in that of Gregory.

Sidonius then cannot be set down as chronologically the last of classical writers with anything like the same approach to truth with which we can call Gregory the first of mediæval writers. And yet he may be well said to close the period. He was the last eminent writer the main part of whose life was spent as a subject of the West-Roman Empire beyond the Alps. Boetius and Cassiodorus wrote after him, but they wrote in Italy as subjects of the Goth, and the first aspect of Cassiodorus is that he was minister of the Goth. But Sidonius is simply and purely Roman;

it was only in the last years of his life that, deeply
against his will, he became a West-Gothic subject.
Those who came after him are survivals carried on
into a later state of things ; Sidonius is the last of
the old series, the last who grew up and flourished
and spent the best years of his life under the elder
state of things.   The peculiar interest of his position,
the deeply instructive character of his writings, writings not in form historical but among the most important materials for history, have drawn to Sidonius
the careful attention of every student either of history or of language who has learned how great a
place in the history of the world is filled by the fifth
century after Christ.   Guizot in one land, Hodgkin
in another, have gone to him—how could they fail to
go to him ? — as the chief interpreter of his age.
From the appreciation of scholars such as these, it is
curious, and if provoking, it is also both amusing and
instructive, to turn and see how a writer who has so
much to teach, who has taught so much to so many,
looks in the eyes of those who, walking round and
round in their narrow orbit, are so unlucky as to think
that they know everything already.   I heard the other
day a story which, whether true or false, is illustrative, a story which, if any one disbelieves, it
will not be *quia impossibile*, but because it is almost
too obvious to have really happened.   It is said that
a student, not of history but of language in the
strictest sense, but a student of language of the more
enlightened kind, one whose eyes had been opened
to see the need of knowing, not only whence his

favourite tongues came, but whither they went, had, in the course of a long study of Latin literature, made his way at last to the pages of Sidonius. What could be more natural? what could be a surer sign of the deep and genuine nature of his Latin learning? Then, so the tale goes, a scholar of a narrower type, finding him so employed, jeered at him for wasting his time on "the smallest points in the smallest writers." As a specimen of self-satisfied ignorance, the tale is perfect. But the type of character which it reveals to us is worth dissecting a little further. It is self-satisfied ignorance, but it is not merely self-satisfied ignorance. An element of a more respectable kind steps in. This narrow kind of scholarship, which positively refuses to look beyond a few arbitrarily chosen centuries, is to some extent grounded on a mistaken theory of the duty of a man to his lord. Scholars of this type are the sworn votaries of certain special authors, of certain special periods. I can understand that an editor or translator of Virgil might feel it a breach of loyalty, a failure to maintain his lord's honour, if he thought Sidonius worthy of so much as a glance. Such is not the feeling of the historian; it is not the feeling of the philologer; but it is a feeling by no means unnatural, by no means unusual, among men whose whole line of study has gone in one narrow groove. The meaner feeling of jealousy towards knowledge which one does not oneself share, the feeling which sometimes even denies the name of knowledge to that which it does not itself know, may doubtless come in in its measure, but I believe the comparatively worthy feeling to come first. Certain writers are set up to be worshipped with an exclusive worship; honour, even thought, bestowed on others, is treason against their divinity.

Be this as it may, this exclusive feeling on the part of the narrower scholarship undoubtedly exists; it forms one of the difficulties of our work; it is one of the enemies that have to be striven against by every one who gives himself to any wider and more enlightened study either of history or of language. It sometimes shows itself in yet more remarkable forms than that of looking on Sidonius Apollinaris as one of the smallest of writers. The line drawn is not always chronological; the ban is sometimes put forth, not only against writers of what are held to be inferior periods, but also against writers of the periods which are most held in honour, if these do not themselves belong to the very chosen few. I remember reading some years ago, in a book which I have not now by me, a warning against bringing Thucydides —he is so completely the chief and captain of original authorities that we cannot help coming back to him again and again—against bringing Thucydides into any kind of fellowship, even with writers of his own age, even with the great orator Lysias. The doctrine was set forth in a metaphorical strain; but it came to something like this; Thucydides is so great that he must stand by himself; we must take his narrative as we find it; we must not eke it out by any other. Now, if any one had proposed to put forth an edition of Thucydides, patched up with scraps from Lysias or Plutarch or any other writer, as Croker patched up Boswell with scraps from a score of other writers about Johnson, no warning could have been more in place. But the warning, if I rightly understood it, was not against corrupting the text of Thucydides, but against treating the narrative of Thucydides as amenable to the common laws of historical criticism. That narrative must be taken as something altogether by itself; no other witness must be brought either to confirm or to confute the statements of the great master. This, it will be seen, is exactly the spirit which dictated the outcry against the free criticism of Mr. Grote. No spirit can be more directly opposed to any method of sound historical study than one which puts any writer, however illustrious, beyond the reach of that process of comparison and criticism, which is the very life of all historical research. Be he never so great, he cannot bar us from the right and duty of weighing every statement against some other statement, of filling up the gaps in one narrative by statements and notices in another. And the narrative of Thucydides, of all narratives, needs filling up from other sources. His subject is not the whole history of his times, but only one aspect of it. He writes the story of the Peloponnesian War; he does not write the full story even of Athens during the time of the Peloponnesian War. To grasp that whole story in all its bearings, we must turn to many sources of knowledge besides the head one. We must eke Thucydides out with patchwork from many quarters, even from quarters very inferior to himself. And Lysias, a younger contemporary, a careful spectator, indeed an actor in events only a few years later, one of the greatest masters of one of the greatest of arts, a witness who is inferior to Thucydides only because the craft of the orator does not bind a man to truth so strictly as the craft of the historian—if he may not be referred to for events within his own knowledge, our means of understanding the days in which he lived are cruelly shortened indeed.

I have referred to this last case, because it illustrates two opposite sources of danger which affect the treatment of different periods of history. In my last lecture I insisted on the necessity of choosing in every period some special book as the centre of study, of mastering its text minutely, and making all other sources of knowledge for that period gather round that one book as their chief. I applied this rule alike to so-called classical and so-called mediæval studies. Now in dealing with writers and materials which are to be looked on as on any ground secondary, I find that the danger on the classical side is exactly opposite to the danger on the mediæval side. In the earlier time the danger is lest the inferior writers should be thought too little of; in the later time the danger is lest they should be thought too much of. Real masters of the earlier Greek and Latin learning —and not a few such real masters we have in this place—of course know full well how to put the different authors in their own walks of learning in their true relations to each other ; and they do so with no small effect. But the smaller sort are constantly tempted to confine their studies, not only to a very small range in point of time, but to a very few authors within that range. They show a feeling of surprise, almost a feeling of resentment, at the hint that there are writers even in their favourite tongues who are well worth studying, but of whom they know nothing. The man who almost boasted that he knew nothing of Ammianus, as if to know something of Ammianus would be to lose caste among Latin scholars, may pass as the most fully developed specimen of the class. This feeling is a curious reaction from the way of thinking of a past age ; in the sixteenth and seventeenth centuries men seem hardly to have grasped the fact that Thucydides was a writer altogether different in kind from Diodôros and Plutarch. The delusion, not unnatural in the days of the Renaissance, of thinking that " the ancients " were another species of men, altogether apart from ourselves, and further of practically thinking that these "ancients" lived all at the same time, hindered men from seeing the wide difference in value and authority between one old Greek or Latin writer and another. It is perhaps partly the habit of looking at things too much according to a purely literary standard which has led many to think that those Greek and Latin writers who are not picked out as models are not worthy of any attention at all. Diodôros is a dull writer enough ; but he is our main authority for some of the most stirring and instructive times of

Greek history, for the larger part of the history of his own island. The traveller in Sicily, if he remembers his Thucydides on the shore of the Great Harbour, should not forget his Diodôros on the heights of Tauromenion. Diôn Cassius wrote at a very late time, and, what is worse, he rejoices in finding fault with everybody; but the senator and consul who had studied the official documents of Rome understood some things that Livy did not. Our knowledge of old Greek and Roman history, even our knowledge of the Greek and Latin tongues, is imperfect indeed if we do not take in as an essential part of our course of study not a few writers who are now unduly neglected. Put them in their place; I do not ask for them more than their place; I only ask that it should be remembered that they have a place.

When we turn to mediæval writers, the evil is quite on the other side. Not a few students of mediæval subjects are still in the same state with regard to their authorities in which the men of the seventeenth century were with regard to earlier writers. Of course the difficulty is increased by the fact that everybody thinks himself qualified, if the fit should take him, to write on a mediæval subject, while happily it is comparatively few who think themselves qualified to write on classical subjects. Look at a book, say on some part of English history, whose author is not a mere compiler, not a copier of copiers, but who still has not reached the level of the real critical scholar; you will find his notes of reference crowded with the names of a vast number

of writers which seem thrown together anyhow. To
Augustine Thierry it is plain that any book older
than the invention of printing was as good as any
other. A great many people seem to think that a
fact becomes more certain merely because a great
number of writers have recorded it in the same way.
They do not stop to think which of these writers
had any means of knowledge which were not open
to, or were not used by, the earliest on the list, and
which simply copied those who went before them. It
is not uncommon to see a reference to the English
Chronicles followed by some such list as this—
Florence of Worcester, Simeon of Durham, Roger of
Howden, Roger of Wendover, Matthew Paris, perhaps
Matthew of Westminster. It seems to be thought
that all these are witnesses, and that their witness
adds something to the certainty of the fact. Now
it is always worth marking which earlier writers a
later writer chooses to follow; it is even worth
marking when a later writer misunderstands or per-
verts or colours the earlier writer ; nay, it ever and
anon happens that the later writer has got hold
of some real scrap of fact which the earlier writer
had neglected. It follows that the later writers are
by no means to be cast aside ; it is often very
important to see how they looked at the events
of earlier times. The point to be understood is
that they are not authorities, that they are not
witnesses, that a statement made by a contemporary
gains nothing in inherent value because it is copied
over and over again by a hundred writers who are

not contemporaries. Whenever a man at any date has special means of knowledge, he becomes so far an authority; a local writer or a man who has specially studied some particular class of subjects may be in this sense an authority, that is the nearest approach to an authority that we can get, even for times long before his own. He rises in short to the level of Plutarch or Diodôros. And of course a writer who is of no value for times before his own may be of the highest value for his own time, for times when he begins to be an authority. Matthew Paris is a precious authority for some years of the reign of Henry the Third; for the days of the Norman Conquest he is simply misleading; he awakens our curiosity to know where he found his fables, and that is all. And it is very curious to see how he, a strong Liberal, takes Roger of Wendover, decidedly a Conservative, and while copying his facts changes his views of things into conformity with his own notions. His story reads like a volume of Sir Archibald Alison corrected into agreement with the politics of Mr. Chamberlain. It does not very much matter whether Archbishop Hubert really made his famous speech on elective monarchy, or whether Matthew Paris invented it for him. On the whole perhaps it is better if it is the work of Matthew himself, as thereby the sound tradition of the old time is carried on a generation or two further. That the Waverley Annalist chose the Peterborough Chronicle as his guide is greatly to the credit of the Waverley Annalist; but the fact adds nothing to the authority of the

Peterborough Chronicle. That a crowd of later writers copied Florence's account of the election and reign of Harold rather than any of the alternative Norman fables, is an important fact in tracing the history of opinion on the subject ; it adds nothing to the weight of Florence's own statement. We must pick and choose equally among classical and among mediæval writers, but we shall not pick and choose on exactly the same principles. The secondary writers for the two periods—remembering that a man who is secondary for one stage often becomes of first-rate authority for a later stage—are for the most part quite different in nature and value. The secondary mediæval writers are on the whole very inferior in value to the secondary classical writers. There are few among them who answer to those writers of whom I said in my last lecture that, though not original authorities in themselves, yet they are original authorities to us, as reproducing the matter of lost writers who were original. It is but seldom that the later writers had any materials before them which are not open to ourselves ; for the most part they simply copied earlier writers by whom we can test them. There is hardly any mediæval writers like Plutarch, a direct authority for nothing, but the only substitute that we can get for a crowd of lost writers of the highest authority. The danger then is that of underrating the value of secondary writers in the earlier time and of overrating it in the later. I do not the least fear that, if I make a statement out of Thucydides anybody will get up and correct me out of Diodôros. But it has happened to me—and I have told the story in print —to bury my Conqueror according to the record of Orderic, who was living at the time and who had doubtless talked to people who were present, and then to be called in question because I had neglected to correct Orderic by the version of Paulus Æmilius, a rhetorician of the end of the fifteenth century.

I could say much more as to both the likenesses and the unlikenesses of the two classes of writers of whom I have been speaking, the so-called classical and the so-called mediæval writers. I trust that in times to come I may be able to speak of many of them more in detail. My business to-day has been only to insist on the fact that there is no real break between them. He who reads up to a certain point and reads no further does himself injustice, but it is an injustice that he may easily repair. Far worse is the case of him who flies off to later times, showy times, controversial times, with no sound and steady knowledge of the times that went before them. To all who have yet their line of study to choose, whether for the meaner purposes of an examination or for the higher purpose of improving and expanding their own minds, I would give a word of warning. Even reading for an examination may be of some use, if it is well directed, according to some rational system. He who is reading his Thucydides is well employed ; he is laying the best of foundations. He who is reading his Gregory or his Lambert is

well employed, if he has read his Thucydides before
them.   But he is not well employed who rushes off
to the sixteenth, seventeenth, eighteenth centuries,
without even a general knowledge of the fifth
century before Christ and the fifth century after.
I would cry aloud, if any will hearken, Be not led
astray by any temptations however seducing, listen
to no teaching however winning, which would tempt
you to fly off at once to times which are of the
deepest interest and importance, which are worthy of
all the attention that you can give to them in after
life, but which are utterly unsuited to be the beginning of your studies.   It is a grievous thing that
the fashion in this place now is—things were better
eight and twenty years back—to plunge at once into
these thorny times, more flashy perhaps, more showy,
and to neglect the steady work which is needed for
the study of earlier times, the sound knowledge
which is the result of that study.   Is there any one
here who has yet to choose his period, his subject,
his book ?   If he will hearken to me, I would say,
Begin at the beginning.   If he has to make his
choice for an examination, I would say, Begin as
near the beginning as the rules of the examination
will let you.   Do you want really to know about
Charles the Fifth, or the Peace of Westfalia, or that
most mysterious being in all history, Maria Theresa
Queen of Hungary?   Do you wish to know the
exact force of the acts which astounded the world
with an Emperor of the French and an Emperor of
Austria, an Emperor of Austria too who still kept

some glimmering notion that he was also Emperor-
elect of the Romans, King of Germany and Jerusalem ? You will never learn these things as they
should be learned, unless you grasp the great central
truth of all European history, the abiding life of
Rome and her Empire. Listen to no voice that
would tell you otherwise ; listen to no voice that
would bid you strive to crown the edifice, when as
yet you have not dug the ground for its foundations.
I bid you come with me and walk awhile in the
fellowship of Odowakar the Roman Patrician and of
Chlodowig the Roman Consul. They will guide us
on to Charles, Patrician, King, and Emperor, to Otto
answering the cry of an oppressed queen, to Henry
answering the prayer of a divided Church, to the
Frederick who fled from Legnano and who took
his crown at Arles, to the Frederick who won
his crown at Jerusalem and who sleeps in the
basilica of Palermo. From them you may well go
on to the voluntary fall of their latest successor ;
that path will be lighted by the true light of
sound historic knowledge — be not tempted to
stray from that narrow way by any *ignis fatuus*
which will only plunge you into a quagmire of
shallowness and half-knowledge, a quagmire out of
which it will be harder to find your way to solid
ground than if you were quartered in those "peni-
tissimæ paludes" where the Frank still dwelled in
the days of Sidonius but from which he had come
forth to do great deeds before the days of Gregory.

Q

LECTURE VI.

SUBSIDIARY AUTHORITIES.

In my lecture a fortnight back I pointed out the general character of the class of authorities of which I have to speak to-day. That class pretty well amounts to all sources of historical knowledge other than narrative histories. I speak of these as *subsidiary*, not as *secondary* authorities, because, while they are necessarily subsidiary in our use of them, they are anything but secondary in point of authority. Class against class, they are at least of equal authority with narrative writings ; in many cases they rise to even higher authority. Some classes of them are distinctly free from some of the sources of uncertainty which beset historical narratives, though it must be allowed that some classes of them bring in other sources of uncertainty which are altogether their own. One class of them, like the sources of the geologist's knowledge, can themselves neither err nor lie, but in return they are more likely to be misunderstood than a written record. Those of another class themselves rank among written records, and form a class of written records which are specially unlikely to err,

but are specially likely to lie. This wide range
of sources of knowledge, all, as I just now said,
which do not come under the head of historical
narratives, fall into two classes, capable again of
further subdivisions, which we may call the monumental and the documentary. Some branches of
our monumental evidences come very near to the
domain of the natural sciences; in fact they are the
application of natural science to serve as historic
evidence. Some examples of our documentary evidences are actually historical narratives, only preserved in a shape different from the ordinary shape
of a book. It is hard to draw the line between the
autobiographical records which have been left us by
the first and by the second Cæsar. The last Dictator
has left us the story of a large part of his life written
by himself in a book, on parchment or papyrus or
whatever was the material employed for the first
autograph. The first Augustus has left us the story
of his life, seemingly in his own words, graven by
his orders on the stones of a temple. There is no
difference between the two records, save any that
may arise from the difference of the shape in which
they appear; in each a man in authority records the
deeds which he himself did. So at the other end,
in regions altogether beyond the range of written
evidence, we have been taught that much has been
proved by the shape of the skulls found in ancient
graves. Now the nature of men's bones is in itself
purely a matter of physiology; but incidentally the
bones become a record, and tell the history of times

whose records have not been set down in writing.
The Monument of Ankyra and the contents of a
barrow are about the two ends of our subject to-day.
There are not a few links and shades between them.

I have used the word *monumental* to take in all
sources of knowledge which do not come under the
head of written records. Yet one doubts a little as
to reckoning the skulls among monuments. That is
to say, they are not works of man's skill in the same
sense as either a flint flake or a Corinthian capital.
In these last the shape is determined by the will of
the artist; but no one can, by any exercise of the will,
determine the shape of his own skull, or even of the
skulls of his children. This might seem to be a real
distinction; we have in some sort ruled that history
has wholly to do with matters which are under the
control of the human will, that will which deter-
mines alike the events which are recorded and the
shape of the records which record them. The skulls
seem rather to belong to the class of evidence
which is purely incidental, where the facts of some
other branch of knowledge may chance to throw
light on some historical question. And so in strictness it is; the evidence of the skulls is strictly of the
same kind as the incidental evidence on historical
matters which we may ever and anon get from the
strata of the earth or from almost any other source.
But the skull, though no more within the range of
the human will than the strata, is, unlike the strata,
part of the man himself, and therefore part of his
history in a way in which the strata are not. The

skulls form a kind of evidence which does not merely
come into play now and then, but which is abiding,
and may be applied in all times and places. The
evidence, in short, from the formation of man himself
is, as far as we are concerned, essentially of the same
kind as the evidence which we draw from the ruder
kinds of man's works. It is a kind of evidence in
which I venture to think that it is specially easy to
misinterpret the record; but it is certainly one in
which the record itself can neither err nor lie. Flint
axes have been forged no less than Old-English
charters, but I never heard of any doctrines as to
the succession of races in Britain being supported by
a forgery of brachykephalic or dolichokephalic skulls.
We will therefore place the skulls, and any other
parts of man's frame which are capable of giving
evidence of the same kind, among the most ancient
and primitive, no less than among the most modern,
of our monumental sources of knowledge.

Fast upon the evidence of man himself will come
the evidence of his works, especially his ruder works,
those primitive weapons, tools, and the like, from
which the primæval antiquary draws his division
into the stone, the bronze, and the iron periods. We
deal now with the flint arrow-head, the leaf-shaped
sword of bronze, the countless forms of primitive
utensils and ornaments, above all with the great monuments, funereal, religious, or defensive, which are often
works of no small mechanical skill, but which do not
reach the character of works of art in the higher
sense. Here comes the kist-vaen, the cromlech, the

dolmen, the hut-circle, the bee-hive house, the vitrified fort, the walls and gateways of primæval cities. Here comes the barrow by the broad Hellespont to which the sailor in days to come was to look up and think of the warrior slain by the hand of Hektôr ; here too comes the barrow looking down on sandy Severn which shelters the giants-chamber of the dead of whom none could tell the race or name when Ceawlin marched beneath it to receive the submission of Glevum after the great slaughter of the kings. Here comes the cromlech on Kentish soil to whose age a wrong has been done by calling it the grave of one so modern as Horsa the Æscing, and the cromlech in the wilder land of Gower, high on its ridge above the narrow seas, on which a like failure to tell the untold ages has bestowed the name of British Arthur. We may pass on by the vaster graves piled by unrecorded hands where Saumur, with all its later memories, rises above the rushing Loire ; we may pass on by Long Meg and her daughters on the Cumbrian moor, by the wonders of Avebury and of the Breton Carnac, to the roof and crown of the works of præhistoric man, to Stonehenge itself, dance of the giants, not more mysterious now than it was when Cynric smote the Briton by the ditches of the elder Salisbury. From works of which, save by the inferences of our own lore, we know not the name or race of the makers, we may pass on to the walls which fence in cities which have a name and a memory, walls which often, after so many ages, still keep watch over the dwelling-places of man. Time would fail to tell of cities once great and fenced up to heaven, which crown the hills of the Etruscan, the Latin, and the Hernican, which crown too the more famous heights of the elder Athens and the elder Corinth, which crown withal not a few of the heights of our own island on which no such wreath of fame as theirs has ever lighted. From the names which ring in our ears and kindle our souls as we tread the land of the wars of new-born Rome—from the stirring roll of the Thirty Cities in the lays of our own glee-man—from "Norba's ancient wall," standing empty of men from the days of Sulla—

> "From the gigantic watch-towers
> No work of earthly men,
> Whence Cora's sentinels o'erlook
> The never-ending fen,"—

from the stones of Signia, striving, like the stones of Tiryns, to fit themselves to that order of the self-sustaining arch, which men were feeling after but which as yet they had not reached—from the would-be cupola of Mykênê and the would-be cupola of New Grange—from the stones which gird the height of Tusculum and the stones which gird the height of Worlebury—we make our way to "the great group of village communities by the Tiber;" we pay our homage to the most renowned of all monuments of unchronicled days, the scarping-wall that bears the name of the wolf's nursling Romulus, and the mighty dyke that bears the name of Servius child of the fire.

Our roll-call of primæval works has brought us to

the very verge of recorded history; some may think
that it has overleaped the boundary. I have done so
of set purpose. It is of importance to mark that
the strictly monumental works of unrecorded and of
recorded times are in themselves evidence of exactly
the same kind. In each we have a work of man, a
work from which, even if it stands absolutely alone, if
we can bring no other sources of knowledge to bear
upon it, we can, with a fair approach to certainty, with
as near an approach as we ever reach in such matters,
make some inferences as to the state and habits of
the men who made them. When we can compare
several works of the kind, our knowledge increases ;
we can give no positive dates, but we can arrange
different modes of construction in chronological
order. The antiquary works with his buildings in
exactly the same way in which the geologist works
with his strata. He can say with very great confidence that A is older than B ; he cannot even
guess, without information of some other kind, without written records or something that may supply
their place, how much older A is than B. And the
argument from construction that A is older than
B applies only to different parts of the same building,
or at the outside to buildings in the same district.
Different countries did not develope their arts with
the same degree of speed; a ruder wall in Latium
is pretty certainly older than a more finished wall in
Latium; it may very likely be later than a highly-
finished wall in Etruria. We feel certain that the
Lion-Gate at Mykênê is older than the gateway of

the great Treasury; the gateway at Tusculum, with a piece of rock for its jamb, may, or it may not, be later than the Lion-Gate. If New Grange stood at Mykênê, we should say that it was the oldest thing there; standing, as it does, in Ireland, it may be ages later than the Pelopid empire, ages later than the Athenian democracy. The Reader in Anthropology will tell you that some nations are still in the stone age ; I have heard say that there are tribes in India that build cromlechs to this day. The monuments then themselves, by themselves, tell us a great deal ; but it is not till we get written records, or something that may take their place, that we can fix dates, even comparative or approximate dates. No man can fix the date of the walls of Tiryns; but we may safely say that they are older than the Homeric Catalogue; we may safely say that at the time of the Homeric Catalogue they were already ancient, already things that men wondered at.

Now when we have got as far as this, it is a great step in advance above the mere power of saying that A is older than B ; but it is a long way from having a building fixed by a record on stone or on parchment to the archonship of this man or the consulship of that. When we have reached this last point, we can begin to construct a science of architectural chronology, one of the branches, as I pointed out before, of the wider science of history. We know the dates of certain buildings, and we infer that certain other buildings which show the same characteristics must be of the same date. It was by comparing the written record with the abiding monuments that Professor Willis built up the science of which he was so unrivalled a master. It was by the same process applied to another class of objects that Dr. Guest brought to light the earliest history of England. With the written witness in their hands or in their memories, the one made columns and windows tell their tale, the other made mounds and ditches tell their more ancient tale. I have before now heard people contrast historical evidence and what they are pleased to call archæological evidence, almost as if they were things rival or hostile to each other. They talk as if the stones could speak with some mysterious voice of their own, a voice which is sometimes deemed to speak all the clearer without the help of written history. Now, as I have just shown, the stones, even by themselves, do speak with a voice; they do tell us something; but by themselves they tell us but little. Their voice is very indistinct, their tale is very imperfect, till written records step in to complete and to interpret it. The whole system, the whole science, if we like so to call it, of architectural chronology and architectural nomenclature rests on no other ground than the union of monumental and documentary evidence. Neither can stand for a moment without the other. It is indeed true that we should not hold that a single statement about a single building which might seem to be contrary to the whole received system of architectural chronology was enough to upset that system. We should not accept a statement that work palpably of the fifteenth century belonged to the twelfth. But why? Not because monumental evidence is distinct from or superior to documentary evidence, but because it is more likely that the author of such a statement was mistaken in his fact, more likely that we have misunderstood his meaning, than that a whole system of inferences from a great number of documentary statements should have gone utterly wrong.

I would here say a word or two more of this subject of architectural history, architectural chronology, and the like. There is something like a divorce between studies of this kind and the more direct study of history which is much to be lamented. The historian proper seems sometimes to think the antiquarian branches of knowledge beneath him; the student of buildings seems sometimes to fancy that he can get on in his own branch without any knowledge of general history. Now I cannot conceive how either the study of the general sequence of architectural styles or the study of the history of particular buildings can be unworthy of the attention of any man. Besides their deep interest in themselves, such studies are really no small part of history. The way in which any people built, the form taken by their houses, their temples, their fortresses, their public buildings, is a part of their national life fully on a level with their language and their political institutions. And the buildings speak to us of the times to which they belong in a more living and, as it were, personal way than monuments or documents of almost any other kind. Architectural monuments may be

studied, as anything else may be studied, in a weak
and unscientific way; only such weak and unscientific
study, whether of architectural monuments or of anything else, is really no study at all. To study them
worthily calls for an exercise as diligent of faculties
as high as any that is called for by the study of any
other branches of history short of the very highest.
There have been few minds of greater power, though
there have been some of wider range, than the mind
of Professor Willis; and we should not forget that
to the work for which I know him best, and for which
most people know him best, he also added the special
work of his own professorial chair into which I at
least am quite unable to follow him. And, on the
other hand, no delusion can be greater than that of
attempting the study of architectural monuments
without a sound grasp of general history. The most
grotesque blunders, the wildest theories, have come of
this most hopeless undertaking. Mr. Petit, whose
name I hope is not wholly forgotten, was one of the
keenest of architectural observers; every word that
he lets drop is precious; yet even Mr. Petit, though
he at once sees the fact, is a little puzzled by the fact,
that the architecture of Elsass is, as it could not fail
to be, not French but German. Since his time wilder
things have been done. We have seen elaborate
books in which the buildings, the Romanesque buildings, of those parts of the kingdoms of Germany, Burgundy, and Italy, which in our own century received
for the first time the common name of Switzerland,
are grouped together under a common head of " Swiss

architecture," and the facts that the architecture of Germany is German, that of Burgundy Burgundian, and that of Italy Italian, are gravely discussed as remarkable phænomena. This architectural speculation may be bracketted with another statement bearing on the same part of the world, one which I have seen in a political book by a public official of some importance, the statement that Duke Leopold at Morgarten commanded an Imperial army. So in a division headed " Scotch architecture," I have seen reckoned the church of Saint Magnus at Kirkwall, the head church of a Scandinavian earldom. This of course wipes out the real lesson of the building, namely how little the Scandinavian architecture of the twelfth century differed from the architecture of the lands in which Scandinavian builders would naturally seek their models. And I have myself had not a few strivings and fightings to make some minds grasp the very simple fact that the early Romanesque buildings of England, the examples of so-called "Saxon" style, are simply the same thing as the contemporary buildings of Western Europe generally. It was hard to break through one of the cherished dogmas of that curious faith which holds that Englishmen are anything else rather than Englishmen. It was hard to fight against the dogma that " the Saxons" were some strange and mysterious and altogether vanished race, who lived all by themselves without dealings with the rest of the world, and who seem, yet more unaccountably, to have all lived at the same time.

We are making our way gradually from the rudest forms of monumental evidence up to those highest forms of documentary evidence which are hardly to be distinguished from historical narratives. And at the point that we have reached, namely the discussion of architectural monuments, we are tempted to come to the subject of inscriptions strictly so called by way of the architectural monuments. Not a few buildings supply their own documentary evidence in the shape of inscriptions recording the date, and perhaps some circumstances, of their building. We may dispute about the name and the purpose of the great Pantheon at Rome; there is no room for disputing about its date or its founder, while the letters graven on the frieze declare that it was built by Marcus Agrippa in his third consulship. We have as little doubt about the memorable church and sundial of Kirkdale, that little minster of Saint Gregory which Orm the son of Gamel bought when it was all tobroken and tofallen, and set it up again in the days of Eadward the King and Tostig the Earl. But when a building in this way tells its own story by way of an inscription on its walls, it is something added to the building, something which is in no way essential to it. Though the building and the inscription have a physical unity, they are in idea quite distinct; the building is equally monumental without the inscription; the inscription is as strictly documentary when written on the walls of the building as if it had been written on an Egyptian reed or on a Pergamenian skin. The inscribed build-

ings therefore are rather cases of the two classes of
evidence brought into near neighbourhood with one
another than cases of real transition between the
two. There is another class of objects which are
among the most valuable kinds of evidence that we
have, and which seem more strictly to form a transition from the monumental class of evidence to the
documentary. I refer to coins. A coin is in its
own nature a historical monument, in a way in which
we cannot say that buildings or any of the other
classes of objects of which we have been speaking
are historical monuments. A building or a weapon
is not, unless quite incidentally, as when a building
commemorates a particular event, meant to convey
historical knowledge. It is meant to discharge its
own object, whatever that object may be. So too
the coin is meant to discharge its own very practical
object, but it cannot discharge that practical object
without also conveying historical knowledge. It is
part of its very essence that it should announce
certain facts. As soon as a coin gets beyond the
state of a mere lump of metal of a certain weight, it
needs the image and superscription, or something
equivalent to the image or superscription. It is the
legend, the image, the conventional badge of any
kind, which declares that the coin is struck by the
authority of such and such a king or commonwealth,
which makes it a coin at all, which gives it the
special nature and value of a coin, as distinguished
from a mere piece of metal of a certain weight.
And the declaration made by the legend, image, or

badge, is the declaration of a historical fact. The coin then is a historical monument, not merely in the sense in which the other monuments are historical, as illustrating either special historical events or a general state of things; it is historical directly and in its own nature. And when, from conventional figures and badges, we pass to a legend in writing, to the name of the king or city, sometimes to something more than the bare name, the coin becomes not only historical but documentary. The words of a coin are evidence of essentially the same nature as the words of an inscription or of a manuscript. The only difference is that the coin is a document which cannot accomplish its own object, unless many copies are made, while documents of the other classes may often accomplish their objects by means of a single copy. Coins therefore in their own nature form the transition from our monumental evidence which teaches otherwise than by writing to our documentary evidence which teaches by writing only. So far as the coin is a piece of metal put into a certain shape for a certain use, it ranks with weapons and implements; so far as it assumes an artistic shape, it ranks with other works of art. So far it is, like our other monumental evidence, a mere incidental source of history. As soon as it is stamped with the legend in writing, or even with the badge which has conventionally the same meaning as the legend in writing, as soon as it directly proclaims the fact, " I am the coin of Alexander the King" or "I am the coin of the city of Corinth," then it becomes documentary.

Of the value of coins for historical purposes it is needless to speak. There are periods of history for which the coins are almost our whole means of knowledge. Such for instance is the Greek kingdom of Baktria. I may give an instance from my own work of the way in which numismatic evidence and evidence of other kinds may be made to help one another. There is no extant list of the cities of the Achaian League in its later days, though we know the way in which their number was largely increased, not only by the admission of new members to the League, but by division of the greater cantons into several smaller ones. This is the same process which called into being Kentucky in the early days of the American Union and Western Virginia in our own time. By the help of the numismatic knowledge of Mr. Leicester Warren, I was enabled to put together, not a perfect list of the cities, but a list much nearer to perfection than I could ever have put together from my books only. And that list was not without political value. When we see the long list of insignificant towns which had equal votes in the Federal Assembly with Corinth and Argos, we better understand the great difficulty of a federal system in earlier times. This was the unavoidable alternative of swamping either the greater members or the lesser, the first attempt to grapple with which was made by the wise Confederation of Lykia, though the problem

R

was never fully solved till the creation of the
two-chambered Congress of the United States. It
is a very significant fact that in the first presidency
of Washington his head appears on the coin, while
in the second it appears no longer. Five and twenty
years ago a handful of French money was a living
lesson in modern history, such as you could hardly
get in any other way. Things were brought home
to you in the liveliest of all ways when, besides
intelligible kings and commonwealths, you traced
out the stages marked by "Bonaparte, Prémier
Consul," "Napoléon Empereur" with "République"
on the other side, "Napoléon Empereur" with
"Empire" on the other side, and again the Commonwealth of 1851 changing into the "Louis Napoléon
Bonaparte" of 1852, and that into the "Napoléon
III Empereur" of 1853. "Napoléon III" it was,
according to the peculiar arithmetic of revolutions
and restorations, though the most grubbing collector
has never unearthed a coin of Napoléon the Second
any more than one of Lewis the Seventeenth. Or
again it is pleasant to see on a coin of the great island
of Western Greece the legend ΚΟΡΚΥΡΑΙΩΝ. We
cannot help thinking with a smile of the small
scholars who buzzed about Mr. Grote—κόρακες ὡς
Διὸς πρὸς ὄρνιχα θεῖον—because he, knowing what he
was about, used the true local name *K*orkyra, while
they, not knowing what they were about, thought that
he was simply copying the Latin, and told him that,
if he used *K* at all, he ought to use the high-polite
Attic *K*erkyra, the only form that they had come

across in *their* reading. One wished to know whether
they would have quarrelled with *London* and insisted on *Londres*. Or again, our knowledge of the
Greek tongue is increased when we find that, though
Polybios talks of the men of Elis as Ἠλεῖοι, they
figure on their own coins as ϜΑΛΕΙΟΙ, with the
still abiding digamma. It comes to us as a strange
mixture of old and new, when we find this primæval
shape of the name in combination with the latest
political formulæ of independent Hellas, when the
coins of the Achaian canton of Elis bear the legend
ϜΑΛΕΙΩΝ ΑΧΑΙΩΝ. All these things, old and new,
come to us in a far clearer way when we thus
see them for ourselves on the coin than when we
simply read them in a book. None of the subsidiary
sources of history are of higher value than this of
coins, if they are only used rightly. And there is no
source of knowledge which there is so little temptation
to use wrongly, though there is a good deal of temptation not to use it at all. Though numismatics
are essentially a part of history, though, except from
the strictly artistic side, they have no value except
as part of history, yet their study needs a special
kind of knowledge; it has a special lore of its own,
which does not come by the light of nature to the
most diligent student of books. I can tell a coin
of King Antiochos, because I can read the Greek
name; but I can get no further. The professed
numismatist has signs by which he can tell which
Antiochos it is out of many. The students of coins
then, having this special knowledge, for which we

have to go to them, as men went to the pontiffs
before Gnæus Flavius wrote up his kalendar, are
sometimes tempted to separate their special pursuit
from the general study of history, and to look on it
as something which has a being by itself. There
is all the difference in the world between a numismatist who sees what his coins prove, and one who
does not trouble himself whether they prove anything
or not. The one is a scholar of a very high order;
the other is a mere collector with his hobby. There
is nothing drearier than people who talk to you about
"third brass" and "the Lower Empire," that flexible
"Lower Empire" which seems sometimes to mean
Carausius and sometimes Constantine Palaiologos.

We were on the verge of speaking of inscriptions
when we were speaking of buildings. Coins bring us
to them yet more directly. A building is often a
convenient place for an inscription, but inscriptions
are no part of its necessary being; a coin is hardly a
coin in the historical sense, unless it bears an inscription. Inscriptions naturally divide themselves
into two classes. There is the class where the inscription has some special connexion with the object
on which it is carved, and the class where it has
none. The inscription on a coin, on a tomb, on an
object such as Ælfred's jewel, the dedicatory or com-
memorative inscription on a temple or other building,
belongs to the particular object or building on which
it is graven; but for the sake of that object or building, it would not have been graven at all. In the
other class the inscription has nothing to do with the

particular place where it is set up; it is put there simply for safe-keeping, like a manuscript in a library. In the first class the inscription is monumental; it is put there to tell us something about the building or object and its contents. That is its primary object; it may incidentally tell us something else. The legend on the front of the Pantheon tells us the founder and the date of the building; but it tells us something more. It tells us something about the founder. Why Marcus Agrippa? Why not in full Marcus Vipsanius Agrippa? Because, so we are told, Marcus, thrice consul, did not care to blaze abroad more than he could help the name of the very obscure *gens* to which he belonged. He could put its name aside in a more respectable way than Englishmen in the like frame of mind are apt to do. An Englishman dissatisfied with the name of his forefathers, say Smithson or Bugg—names, in both cases, ancient and honourable—puts something else instead of his name. He gets rid of Smithson or Bugg, and calls himself Percy or Norfolk Howard. A Roman was not driven to those lengths. His *tria nomina* supplied him with easy means of dropping one. Marcus Vipsanius could not help being Marcus Vipsanius in a legal document where the *cognomen* Agrippa could come in only after the *prænomina* of his father and grandfather; but he was Marcus Agrippa in common speech, and he could, if he chose, call himself, in an inscription of his own making, only by the *prænomen* which he shared with countless ancient worthies and the *cognomen* which he had himself made illustrious. An inscription of this kind reveals to us the weakness of an eminent man more clearly than almost any other way could have done. Or take the tombs of the Scipios, the tombs which some one of the long series of infallible robbers has stolen to set up in his own house, and to record his own "munificence" in the stealing. This last inscription, to be sure, also proves something; but that is not the inscription of which I speak. I mean the elder ones, the most famous of which begins "Cornelius Lucius Scipio Gnaivod patre prognatus." The legend was carved to mark the tomb of Lucius, and to commemorate his exploits. To us it proves something more; it proves something about the history of the Latin tongue; according to some scholars, it proves that it could not have been written immediately after the death of Lucius. And it tells us also very clearly something about Roman history and its sources. It has often been remarked that the story of the exploits of Lucius Scipio given on the tomb is utterly unlike the story in Livy. Here we have a record, contemporary or nearly so, which says one thing; a much later narrative says another thing. But then the earlier narrative labours under the suspicion which attaches to its whole class, that of lying like an epitaph.

The legend on the front of the Pantheon is strictly monumental; it concerns only Agrippa and his building. It records a fact about them which nobody can have any temptation to doubt. Any further value that it has is purely incidental. But the legend on the grave of Lucius Scipio is in its own nature documentary. It is a piece of Roman history or of something that professes to be Roman history; it is a narrative, a meagre narrative certainly, but not more meagre than annals commonly are ; its very meagreness is something in its favour. The charm of the monumental inscriptions, pagan and Christian, at Rome and elsewhere in Italy is beyond words. They bring us home to the things and to the men. If we learn nothing more from the inscriptions of the Empire than the amazing scarcity of grandfathers, the way in which we find ten freedmen or more to one son, that is something. It is something more when we light at Cora on two inscriptions of different dates, one of which records the *prætors* of the still separate Latin town, the other the *duumviri* of the Roman municipium. It is pleasant to read the epitaph of the clinical doctor and surgeon at Assissi, how much he paid for a local magistracy, how much he left behind him, how much he spent on repairing the temple and how much on mending the roads. Such local patriots and benefactors seem not uncommon ; we feel brought near, and with feelings of deep friendliness, to a worthy man at Ferentinum of the Hernicans, whose inscription shows that, like Sir William Harpur at Bedford, he founded everything that in his day could be founded, even to a benefaction of nuts to be scrambled for by the boys of the town, bond and free. But beyond all inscriptions of this class that I have ever read in their own places come the epitaphs in the Volumnian tomb at the foot of

the hill of Perugia. I remember no spot where
letters graven on the stone seem to bring us so near
to looking with our own eyes on the fates of men and
the fates of nations.   There, amidst all the forms, all
the symbols, that mark a burying-place of the mysterious Etruscan race, stands the tomb of the Lucumo,
the head of his house, his sons and grandsons sleeping
in their tombs around their chief in death as in life.
They are all of one house, but they have ceased to be
all of one people or all to speak one tongue. Some of
the descendants of the Etruscan Lucumo have ceased
to be Etruscans. I claim no knowledge of that speech
which has so long refused to be pressed into our
service, which has refused to tell us the tale of a folk
who, though their written records are there before our
eyes, still speak to us almost wholly by the more uncertain voice of the symbolic forms of their monumental
art.   Yet here and there even one who has no claim
to be an expert can spell out a name or two in an
alphabet which, among some forms that baffle him,
might so often pass for one of the older forms of the
graven speech of Greece.   On one of those tombs we
may spell out the name of the Etruscan father, bearing, in letters traced from right to left, a name in his
own tongue, *Avle Felimne.*   By him is his son ; but
on the son's tomb the letters are the familiar letters of
Latium ; they are written from left to right, according to the common use of Europe ; the name needs
no more of painful spelling out than the name of
Marcus Agrippa ; it is a name which might meet us
in any year of the *fasti* of commonwealth or empire.

The son of the Etruscan Avle Felimne has become
the Roman Aulus Volumnius. That change, made
without comment, tells us that between father and son
a change had taken place of which we yearn indeed
to have fuller records. It needs an effort to believe
that in the days of Marius and Sulla those ancient
and mysterious forms of art and polity and religion
still lived on, and that it was only in that comparatively modern age, as the result of the great stirring
when Rome, head of the world, had again to strive for
the headship of her own Italy, that the old forms, the
old names, passed, with as slight a change as might
be, into names and forms which on that spot seem
those of a new and upstart people. And from the
first century before our æra our thoughts run on to the
eleventh century after it, when again sons bore names
of another type than the names of their fathers, when
the Englishman was content to veil his race under a
Norman garb, when it was no warrior from the land
of Rouen or the land of Coutances, but the man of
Hertfordshire, Robert son of Godwine, who cut a path
for King Baldwin through the ranks of opposing
paynimrie, and who died for his faith, by the death
of Eadmund and Sebastian, in the market-place of
the Egyptian Babylon.

Inscriptions like these have a charm when read in
their own place which hardly follow them into the
printed pages of the *Corpus Inscriptionum*. There
was after all a glimmering of truth in the singular
remark that some of us may remember, that the
pleasure of spelling out an inscription on the spot

was something like the slight pleasure of spelling out an autograph. The saying may rank with many other sayings of men who are just clever enough to catch at the most obvious side of a complicated question. The sight of the autograph, of the letters actually traced by the hand of a certain man, does seem to bring us nearer to the man himself than we are brought when we simply read about him. I shall not lightly forget seeing in the archives of Calvados the foundation charter of Saint Stephen's at Caen with the crosses traced by the very fingers of William and Matilda. The hand that could so well wield the war-club wielded the pen after much the same fashion; the two bold strokes traced by the hand of the Conqueror form a striking contrast to the slight spider-legs which mark the witness and consent of the Lady to her husband's gift. The autograph does after all put us in a kind of relation to the writer of the autograph, and thereby adds to the clearness of our historic conception. There is a likeness between the pleasure of spelling out an inscription and the pleasure of spelling out an autograph; but then, I think, scholars at least will allow that it is a likeness which tends rather to the honour of the autograph than to the disparagement of the inscription. It is perhaps not wise in the special students of inscriptions to talk of "epigraphy" as if it were a separate science, or at any rate a separate branch of knowledge. The division of labour is an useful thing, and it is well that some scholars should give special heed to what is written on stone and brass, as it is well that others should give special heed to what is written on parchment or papyrus. Each needs for his own immediate purpose a knowledge of some special details, some minute niceties, which are of less importance to the other, as well as of less importance to the more general scholar who is satisfied to use the results of the labour of both. All three are fellow-workers in the same field, though it may be convenient that one should hold the plough while another guides the horses.

It is in truth hardly possible to make too much of inscriptions as one of the sources of history; but it must be always borne in mind that their value consists in being one of the sources of history. The slighting comparison of the inscription to the autograph is forgotten in face of those great and famous documents on stone than which there is no higher class of evidence. There have been times and places where to engrave a public act on stone was as much the ordinary course of things as it has been in other times and places to write it on paper; the material on which it is written makes no difference. The words, the formulæ, the facts recorded or left unrecorded, will be exactly the same in the manuscript on stone and in the manuscript on paper, in the inscription on paper and in the inscription on stone. There are indeed some kinds of writings in which one might conceive that the difference between the two classes of writing, not so much in their materials as in their circumstances, has made a difference in style, perhaps even in matter. We must first part off certain records on the harder materials, in which the material is purely a matter of accident. The speech of the Emperor Claudius on behalf of the Gaulish senators was not composed with a special view to be written on brazen tablets; it was composed to be spoken in the Senate; it found its way to the brazen tablets only because that was deemed to be the surest way of handing down to posterity the fact that the speech had been spoken. And the document thus called into being is of no small value, both in itself and as showing how near to fact Tacitus thought it his business to come in reporting such speeches. He has carefully reproduced the general drift of the Imperial antiquary's argument; he shows us fairly what the general mind of Claudius was; but the actual words, and even the particular illustrations, as given by Tacitus, are quite different from those in the genuine document. But there is another record, of a still more directly historic character, which was distinctly composed to be graven on stone, and which owes much of its special character to that fact in its composition. Earlier in this lecture I placed together the autobiographies of two Cæsars, the first two of the series, which have come down to us on two different materials. One feels that the form given to the record of the deeds of Augustus in the monument of Ankyra is not exactly the same as the form which a record of the same deeds would have taken, if it had been written in a book by the prince

himself or by some other man at his bidding.   But
this is not a direct consequence of the difference of
material ; it is rather the result of the circumstances
which dictated the choice of the material.   The
record of Ankyra, surely not designed for Ankyra
only, but meant to be set up in the same form in
other places, was a record addressed to all the people
of the Roman dominions, that all might know what
manner of man their ruler was.   A book, like the
Commentaries of that ruler's legal father, would have
been addressed to a small class only, and would
therefore have taken another shape.   But the record
of Ankyra, though a literary composition of a very
peculiar kind, is still a literary composition; it
differs therefore from records, on whatever material
written, which are not literary compositions at all,
but purely documentary.   And in such cases stone
has the advantage, as it pretty well shuts out all
attempts at turning the document into a literary
composition.   The wonderful strains of Latin
rhetoric which usher in the practical substance
of the charter of an English king in the tenth century would certainly have been cut short if the
document had been meant to be graven on stone
or brass.   But that came of writing in a strange
tongue, and of the supposed necessity for showing off the writer's skill in that tongue, a necessity which gendered to a kind of Latin very like
the kind of English which we sometimes get from
Orientals trying to write in an unfamiliar speech.
When King Eadward or King William, Earl Harold

or Lady Edith, greeted men friendly in the kindly
English tongue, their will was as tersely set forth as
if it had been designed for stone and not for parchment. The charter of the Conqueror on which rest
the liberties of the city of London is of small bulk
indeed alongside of some trifling modern deed paid
for at so much *per folio*. There is no difference whatever for historical purposes between such a document on parchment and a Greek document on stone.
Both are original authorities, original authorities of
the very highest order, far higher in truth than any
narrative writer can be; we put the narrative writer
first, and call the documents subsidiary, simply because that is the way in which we are driven to use
them. We cannot read the history consecutively
in the documents ; that is the whole difference.

Meanwhile there are other inscribed documents
which are themselves pieces of history, our sole
authorities for memorable historic facts. Sometimes
they give us in full what the narrative gives us only
in a few words ; sometimes they reveal to us
great events of which narrative history has revealed
nothing to us. Even an editor, even a translator,
of Thucydides—we cannot help ever coming back
to the fountain-head, to the κτῆμα ἐς ἀεί, the abiding *eðel* or *allod* of every historical scholar, where
he makes his first home and whence he goes
forth in the *comitatus* of his lord to conquer other
fields—even an editor, I say, or a translator of
Thucydides will surely allow us to eke out or to
patch up his narrative with the very words of

the treaty, the ὁμολογία, by which Chalkis, after
its revolt, was allowed to come back to its old place,
or something less than its old place, in the dependent
fellowship of Athens. I well remember when the
words of the then newly discovered stone which records this piece of older Greek history were sent to
me as something new by one who has made no small
part of later Greek history, Charilaos Trikoupês,
now Prime Minister of the Hellenic kingdom [1].
The text of Thucydides records the fact of the
treaty; the stone gives us its terms. And terms
well worth study they are. Though the relation
between Athens and Chalkis can hardly be called
a federal one, yet those terms throw no small light
on federal politics. It shows that Reserved Rights
may still be Reserved Rights, even though they be
dwindled to the shortest span. Chalkis, by sub-
mitting to Athens, did not cease to be a separate
commonwealth; Chalkis keeps all rights that it does
not surrender to Athens; it may do any act that
a separate commonwealth can do, except when the
treaty forbids it to do so. Chalkidian action is the
rule, Athenian action is the exception; only the
exceptions take in every kind of external action and
all kinds of internal action of any importance. The
higher justice, for instance, is moved to Athens;
all grave matters are to go to be judged by Athenian
courts according to Athenian law. Chalkis is no
longer to see an assize or even a court of Quarter
Sessions; but nothing hinders any two Chalkidian

[1] November, 1884; unluckily not so in March, 1886.

magistrates from sitting to judge common assaults and petty larcenies according to the laws of Chalkis. Is not such a record as this, itself a co-ordinate text, a worthy commentary on the text, even of our father and founder? But the great volumes of inscriptions can give us more. We see how ruling Athens treated with dependent Chalkis in the fifth century B.C.; let us go on and see how the free city of Rome treated with the free city of Astypalaia late in the second century B.C. The treaty is well known, being in the great gathering of Boeckh; and I know it only there; I have not had the privilege, a privilege which I should greatly enjoy, of reading it in the autograph. But for me and for all of us the fact lives only in the inscription; there is no record of the transaction in any narrative Greek or Latin writer now preserved to us; it is the stones only which are alive to tell us the tale. Here, a good while after the mystic year 146 B.C., the fellow of the other mystic year 476 A.D., we find Rome making a treaty with a Greek city, a Greek city very far from being of the first rank, on perfectly equal terms. Rome and Astypalaia are to be true and faithful allies; neither commonwealth is to give any society, help, or comfort to the enemies of the other; nobody would find out from the document that Rome was a very great power and Astypalaia a very small one. In such an alliance were of course involved all the consequences which follow on alliance between the weak and the strong; it would have been well for Astypalaia if there had

been no Rome in the world; but, as Rome was in
the world, the downward path of Astypalaia was
a little smoothed by sinking gently from independence to dependence and from dependence to sub-
jection, instead of being, like some other cities,
stormed, sacked, enslaved, out of hand. The cause of
so much Roman graciousness is plain; Astypalaia had
a good haven, and, when Rome had to struggle with
the pirates, it was a gain that the haven of Astypalaia
should be open to the ships of Rome and not to the
ships of the pirates. But what a living light of historical teaching do the stones of the Astypalaian treaty
throw on the memorable and neglected age which
made Rome mistress of the Mediterranean lands.

Documents like these, formal treaties drawn up in
formal language, are, on the face of them, among the
most trustworthy of the materials of history. If they
mislead us as to the naked facts of the case, it must
be from our own ignorance. Thus the treaty between
Astypalaia and Rome might be easily misunderstood
by one who knew nothing of the state of the world
at the time. Such an one might be led to think that
the formal equality between Rome and Astypalaia
was much more of a reality than it was. Rightly to
apply a document of this kind we must know the circumstances of the times, and we must know the exact
force of the formal language employed. Such formal
language has sometimes been misunderstood, even by
the contracting parties to an engagement, as when
the Aitolians so rashly committed themselves to the
Roman Faith, without first finding out what the

words " Roman Faith " meant in a Roman mouth.
Disputes about δοῦναι and ἀποδοῦναι, about simple
homage and liege homage, may spring up in any
age of the world. And when the parties to a treaty
make any very exalted professions as to their motives, when they express any very fervent affection
either towards each other or towards each other's
subjects, we feel somewhat as a wary magistrate feels
when counsel begin to take a very high moral tone ;
he knows that there is some hole in the argument,
and he looks about to see where the hole is. But, on
the whole, treaties are not meant to deceive as to
mere facts ; each side commonly knows the facts too
well for that. For its own purpose therefore a treaty
ranks among sources of the very highest authority
for historical knowledge. So it is, within its own
range, with a law. As I said once before, though
English history cannot be studied in the statute-
book, yet it must be studied with the statute-book.
The statute-book often needs an interpreter in the
circumstances of the time ; but granting that interpreter, it does itself interpret the circumstances back
again. But when we come to manifestos, proclama-
tions, diplomatic documents which have not yet
reached the stage of treaties, the case is wholly
different. Here we are in the very chosen region of
lies ; everybody is, by the nature of the case, trying
to overreach everybody else. Yet they are instructive lies ; they are lies told by people who know the
truth ; truth may even, by various processes, be got
out of the lies ; but it will not be got out of them by

the process of believing them. He is of child-like simplicity indeed who believes every royal proclamation or the preamble of every act of Parliament, as telling us, not only what certain august persons did, but the motives which led them to do it; so is he who believes that the verdict and sentence of every court was necessarily perfect righteousness, even in times where orders were sent beforehand for the trial and execution of such a man. A little time back there was a sect of such confiding innocents who believed Henry the Eighth's reports of the inner workings of his heart. They were prophesied against beforehand by Gibbon, by Sismondi, and by Hallam; but we may go back earlier still; we may go once more to our great leader, and learn from him the charitable form of rebuke, μακαρίζοντες ὑμῶν τὸ ἀπειρόκακον οὐ ζηλοῦμεν τὸ ἄφρον. Yet in the most modern history of all, the history of the last two days[1], we have seen in high places a like memorable instance of the harmlessness of the dove unluckily not combined with any trace of the wisdom of the serpent. Within these last few days, the cry has once more come into our ears, the familiar cry of the oppressed and the betrayed, " Come over into Macedonia and help us." And the Foreign Minister of England deems it an answer to that cry to say that he has just met the Turkish Ambassador, that the Turkish Ambassado assures him that there is no ground for any cry at all, that his Imperial Master is full of the most benevolent designs, and is daily carrying them out in the

[1] November 1884.

most benevolent acts, in those favoured regions of the earth which are happy enough to be placed under his rule. The official words of an Ambassador, even when yet unwritten, are in some sense a document. In such a document the Foreign Secretary believes with the same child-like faith as the believers in King Harry. A slight knowledge of man's nature, a slight knowledge of men's deeds, that knowledge of good and evil which is gained by the study of historic records, and not least by weighing the utterances of high diplomatic personages, might have hindered displays of innocence so beautiful and so baleful as that which believes the official words of Henry the Eighth in a past age and that which believes the official words of the Grand Turk in our own.

Against such unhappy delusions either as to past or present, the sound study of history, the careful weighing of evidence, the thorough sifting of documents, is the best guard. In the present lecture we have looked hastily at a vast stock of sources of knowledge of various kinds. We have dealt with skulls, with weapons, with walls, with architecture of the more artistic kind, with inscriptions, with documents written or spoken. All are among our materials. I trust that I have shown that, if the necessities of our mode of study constrained us to give the precedence to narrative historians, it has at least not been out of any undervaluing of other sources of knowledge. It is something to have one's words printed in a book; it is something more to have them graven with an iron pen and lead in the rock for ever.

LECTURE VII.

MODERN WRITERS.

WE come now, drawing near as we are to the end of our course, to a class of writings which, from one point of view, it might have not been out of place to reckon among those subsidiary means of knowledge of which I spoke in my last lecture. We now come to the modern writers of history. I do not now mean the writers of modern history. A man living in the nineteenth century, and writing the history of the nineteenth century, ought in theory to be an original authority just as much as if he had lived in the ninth century and written the history of the ninth. In practice he will never fill quite the same place. I suspect that he never will really fill it; at any rate he will never seem to his own contemporaries to fill it. It needs a little effort to take in the fact, but we ought not to forget that Thucydides himself was not to his contemporaries all that he is to us. That is no blame to his contemporaries; it could not be otherwise. It is not merely that no age can look on men of its own age as it looks on men of a past age. The difference goes deeper. A writer of contemporary history in times like ours comes much nearer to the position of a writer of past history than a writer of contemporary history did in earlier times.

In the same measure he departs from the position of
a contemporary historian of the elder class, from the
position of an original authority. The extent to
which he writes from his own personal knowledge is
likely to be much smaller; it will certainly be much
smaller, if we compare him with those writers of
earlier times who were themselves spectators and
actors. Under personal knowledge we may fairly
reckon, not only those things which a man sees and
hears himself, but also those things which those who
have seen and heard them have made known specially
to him and not to the rest of the world. Now in the
wider world of modern times, a world in which the
means of communication have grown so infinitely,
even a spectator and actor of the first rank, if he
sits down to write the history of his own times,
will have to write, far more than a writer of earlier
times had, from sources of knowledge which are
open to all the world. Such an one can, if he
chooses, tell us, from his personal knowledge as just
now defined, many things which none of us here
know anything about; but he will surely put
together a large part of his story from materials
which are as much open to us as they are to him.
And when an ordinary man, who has no such secret
stores of knowledge, sits down to write contemporary
history, he does it in very much the same way as if
he were writing past history. His personal knowledge, even in the sense defined above, will go but a
little way; he has to collect and to examine, to weigh
and to judge, a vast mass of written and printed

materials, just as if he were writing the history of a thousand years back. The chief difference is that his materials will be infinitely greater in amount, incomparably harder to deal with, than if he were writing the history of a thousand years back. There will not really be so many chances of mistaking this and of leaving out that, for such chances will necessarily be thicker in the earlier time; but there will be many more people able to correct anything that is really mistaken or left out, and still more people who will think themselves called upon to correct a great deal that may be perfectly right. He who undertakes to record a war of our own times has to set to work, not quite in the same way as if he were about to record the wars of Sparta and Athens, but in very much the same way as if he were about to record a war of two or three centuries back. The position of Mr. Kinglake comes much nearer to the position of Lord Macaulay than it does to that of Xenophôn. In the actually contemporary time which is dealt with by Mr. Kinglake, and in the time a little while back which is dealt with by Lord Macaulay, there is the same endlessness of materials, the same lack of one great centre-piece round which to hang everything. The old Greeks were not in the same way overwhelmed by materials; Thucydides had nothing to help his own memory and the memories of his personal informants beyond here and there an inscription read in the very freshest autograph. We cannot in these days have contemporary histories like that of Thucydides, or even like that of Procopius.

Yet I have sometimes, in reading the contemporary
narratives of the Greek War of Independence, especially in reading the Greek History of Spyridôn
Trikoupês, felt as if I had gone back to Procopius
at least, if not to Polybios.   Perhaps the nature
of the story, the country in which it was laid,
in the case of Trikoupês the language in which
it was written, helped to throw a certain illusion
over the whole thing.   Gordon, Trikoupês, Finlay,
were all, not only contemporaries, but actors in
the events which they describe.   Finlay moreover
comes a step nearer to Procopius in another way.
In the scathing judgements on particular men
which he has mixed up with the general record of
the time, in the ever-lifted rod which comes down
with such force on most Greeks, most Englishmen,
and all Bavarians, we might almost seem to be
reading the Gothic War and the Anecdotes entwined
together in a single narrative.

   But of the writers of modern history, in the sense
of writers of contemporary history, I have to speak
to-day only so far as they may unavoidably depart
from that character of original authorities which, it is
to be supposed, will belong to them in ages to come.
I have to speak of them only so far as they may
approach to the character of the class of writers with
whom I am this day concerned.   These are those
writers of modern times who are confessedly not
original authorities, but who write the history of
past ages from such materials, narrative or otherwise,
as there may be for the particular times of which

they write. They are a class in which I have somewhat of a personal interest ; it may be well then if,
instead of only telling you how they look in my eyes, I
tell you how they looked in the eyes of a very discerning
man, a man who did indeed love learning for its own
sake, who has but lately passed away from among
ourselves. I have before me the *Christian Remem-
brancer* for January, 1845. I had not looked at the
number for many years, but it contains three articles
which I well remembered when I came to glance at
them. The articles deal severally with Gregory of
Tours, Archbishop Laud, and the Vice-Chancellorship
of Dr. Wynter. All three, I imagine, come within
the lawful range of a Professor of Modern History; but
just now I have nothing to say on the two specially
modern subjects. But the article on Gregory of
Tours I had remembered well during all these years,
and I read it again with both pleasure and profit
now that I have entered into a specially intimate
relation with the historian of the Franks. I did not
know who was the author, but I now find that it is
an early work of the late Rector of Lincoln College. In
1845 Mr. Pattison was still hardly more than a young
man; but he had already made his way to a very firm
grasp of the position of Gregory and his age, and of
the contrast between Gregory and Bæda. But it is
not to what he says of Gregory and Bæda that
I wish to draw your attention now, but to what
he says about the position and the destiny of modern
writers of past history. Here are the opening words
of his article ;

"Whether or no there be any perfect ideal of historical composition, the one best form of writing history for all ages and countries, if we look to experience, we find that in fact each age has ever had a fashion of its own, differing from that which preceded and followed it. We do not speak of writers contemporary with the events they write of. Such, even though the most jejune of annalists, must always have an interest independent of their form. But we speak of regular history, complete accounts of nations or countries, compiled in later times from books and records. Such history is a distinct species of composition, a work of art, having its own principles of taste to be guided and judged by.

"Such history, almost more than any other branch of literature, varies with the age that produces it. Contemporary history never dies; Thucydides and Clarendon are immortal; but, on the other hand, no reputation is so fleeting as that of the 'standard' historian of his day. A review of the historical literature of any nation will discover an endless series of decay and reproduction. The fate of the historian is like those of the dynasties he writes of; they spring up and flourish, and bear rule and seem established for ever; but time goes on, their strength passes away, and at last some young and vigorous usurper comes and pushes them from their throne. It is not because new facts are continually accumulating, because criticism is growing more rigid, or even because style varies; but because ideas change, the whole mode and manner of looking at things alters with every age; and so every generation requires facts to be recast in its own mould, demands that the history of its forefathers be rewritten from its own point of view. When Hume superseded Echard, his admiring contemporaries little thought that Hume himself would so rapidly become obsolete. Hooke was considered to have exhausted the history of the Roman Republic, and his Roman History to be the final book on the subject; but great as is the distance between him and Arnold, it is inevitable, in the course of things, that the next century will have to compose its own 'History of Rome.' And these mutations of popular favour involve the smaller satellites as well as the great planets of the historical heaven; Mrs. Trimmer and Goldsmith pale before the rising light of Keightly and Mrs. Markham, as the subs of office quit their desks when premiers deliver up their portfolios."

Mr. Pattison has here pronounced the doom of a great many. It may even be that among them he has pronounced the doom of those who write about Isaac Casaubon as well as the doom of those who write about William Rufus. We are all creatures of a day. I felt that truth keenly when I first attended a debate in the Greek Assembly, where the only word I could catch was σήμερον, and when some time after I attended a debate in the Italian Senate, where the only word I could catch was *oggi*. Still in our little day we can do something. We can at least make ready the way for those who are to supplant us, and we may even do somewhat towards the more pious work of prolonging for some small space the posthumous lives of those who went before us. One duty of the father is surely to keep up the dignity of the grandfather in the eyes of the grandchildren. If any one will listen to me, there is no precept on which I must insist more strongly than that he should listen to those to whom I once listened. Thirlwall, Arnold, Kemble, Palgrave, Guest, Willis— these are names which shall not die, as long as a voice from this chair can do anything to keep them alive. And as the generations of historians pass away like the generations of leaves, they do themselves become part of history. We should not forget that the history of opinion about facts is really no small part of the history of those facts. Doubtless there is no position in the world so triumphant, while it lasts, as the position of the author of the last German book. He is the oracle ; all must bow down to him.　He is like the dweller among the trees of Aricia,

> " Those trees in whose dim shadow
> The ghastly priest doth reign,
> The priest that slew the slayer,
> And shall himself be slain."

The author of the last German book, like the *Rex Nemorensis*, has set aside all that were before him, and reigns till some one comes to set aside him also. But I doubt not that Aricia kept careful *fasti* of her slaughtered kings, and the author of the last German book is commonly careful to embalm the memories, not only of those whom he has himself slain, but of those whom they had slain in their day.　It is like the old Maori creed, in which the brightness of the star into which the eye of the canonized chieftain passed, was made up of the brightness of all the eyes which he himself had eaten and of all the eyes which those whose eyes he had eaten had themselves eaten in their day.　So we all have a chance ; like flies in amber, we may hope to live in the records of our conquerors and of our conquerors' conquerors.　For my own part, I stand before you as the mere mummy of a professor, dead and buried already.　Some time back I read my own sentence, pronounced by one of the infallible judges of such matters, that my work was done, that I could now only repeat a thrice-told tale.　Be it so ; yet even the thrice-told tale may have its use.　Falsehood is hard to root out ; it has more heads than even Hêraklês alone can crush. Every fresh assertion of the thing that is not is reason enough for a fresh assertion, even for the thousandth time, of the thing that is.

In fact the extract from Mr. Pattison's article which I read to you, full of truth as it is, hardly does justice to this singular power of falsehood, to the amazing life of a bad book. There is the memorable fact that, when the School of Law and Modern History was set up in Oxford, Hume's History of England was recommended, not by the University, not by the Examiners, but in a wonderful paper that went about, without authority, without signature, but which all undergraduates, many graduates, some heads of colleges, mistook for a statute of the University. That was the paper which, as I mentioned in an earlier lecture, recommended William of Malmesbury, seemingly as the one original authority that the writer of the paper had heard of. I know not whether anybody in Oxford reads Hume now; but I know that, not many years back, a real scholar was, in the vain hope that something might come of putting new wine into old bottles, set to correct the Student's Hume. How well I remember when I first heard that Hume had been chosen as the easiest book with which to begin the easy study. I at once asked whether in the other school they had burned Thucydides and taken to Mitford. In that comparison I did injustice to Mitford. For Mitford, with all his blunders, all his unfairness, all his advocacy of the worse cause against the better, had the great merit of being the first to see that the old Greeks were not mere names

in a book or statues in a gallery, not beings of
some other nature, above us or below us or in some
way apart from us, but real men like ourselves,
capable of calling forth the same feelings as the men
of our own day. If a man could not bring himself
to love Dêmosthenês, it was a great thing to be able
to hate him.   <u>Hume</u>, to be sure, could slander Dunstan
yet more foully than Mitford slandered Dêmosthenês;
but that was not because he had any such living
conception—living, however mistaken—as Mitford
certainly had of Dêmosthenês; Hume slandered Dunstan out of simple blind hatred of a system which, in
his ignorance, he fancied that Dunstan represented.
I should not recommend anybody to go to Mitford
for the facts of Greek history; but in the more
curious study of opinion about the facts of Greek
history, Mitford holds a marked place, and one not
altogether discreditable.

Now, what is the real place of modern writers of
long-past history during that little day which is all
that Mr. Pattison's rule allows to them, at any rate
to the good ones among them? Their only true
position is that of commentators, illustrators, har-
monizers, of the original texts. Myself a somewhat
voluminous writer of narrative histories, I claim no
other place. I wish no one to read me instead of
my authorities; I wish simply to send readers to
my authorities, and to help them in their study of
them. <u>In theory</u> the <u>original authority</u> should be
<u>read first</u> and the <u>modern commentator afterwards</u>.
In practice it is by no means easy always to do this.

The meagreness of our authorities for some periods and the overwhelming mass of them for other periods both join to hinder such a rule from being followed. It is only here and there that it is possible. Where it can be done, it is well to do it. A man would do well to read the Peloponnesian War or the Gothic War in his Thucydides or his Procopius first of all, and to turn to his Grote or his Gibbon afterwards. That, if he wishes to bring his story to any kind of natural finish, he must eke out the narratives of the great masters by the narratives of Xenophôn and Agathias is no difficulty. Xenophôn and Agathias, though writers immeasurably below the level of Thucydides and Procopius, are original authorities just as much as they are. Between Herodotus, Thucydides, and Xenophôn, it is possible to read a large and very important piece of Greek history consecutively in original writers. And I should say to every one, Read the text first and the comment afterwards. I do not say, Wait till you have finished the whole text before you look at the comment; but I do say, Get your first notion of each main portion of the story from the text before you look at the comment. Yet even in these cases, it is hardly possible, it is hardly desirable, that any student should get his very first notions of Greek history from the original writers. We should hardly condemn our sons and daughters to remain utterly ignorant of Athens and Sparta, and of anything that happened in them, till they have reached the stage in which they can master such a Greek text as that of Thucydides and illustrate it by such an English comment as that of Grote. And, as I have already said, there are large periods of history for which we have no such consecutive original guides, periods where the original authorities are so meagre and so piecemeal, that the student, the learner as distinguished from the finished historical critic, cannot be reasonably expected to get his first impressions of the time from such authorities as we have. In such cases we cannot help turning things about; some modern narrative unavoidably becomes the text, and the original sources are unavoidably treated as the comment. And considering that, as we ruled long ago, no man can read all history in original authorities, it follows that, whatever periods he chooses, the periods between and around those which form his own special subjects, must be mainly read in modern writers. In truth the rule of reading the original writers first, a rule to be followed wherever we can, can be carried out only within very narrow limits. We must, oftener than not, get our first impressions of any period of history from modern writers and not from original sources.

The modern then, properly a commentator, will often find himself turned, by the necessity of the case, into the opposite of a commentator. He is driven in many cases to step into the place of his authorities and himself to do what they ought to do. But one of his functions, one part of his duty to his lord, he need never lay aside. If he cannot always act as a commentator, he can always act as a guide.

He can always show the way to his authorities, and exhort every one to follow that way for himself. If he does not do this, he fails in his duty. He fails in his duty if he ever lets it be forgotten that he is simply the prophet of somebody else, the guide to somebody else. And it is by no means needless to proclaim that fact. I spoke some weeks back of the great difficulty that there is in making many people understand the nature of an original authority, in making them understand that there are any original authorities for large parts of history. The modern writer must protest against every attempt to treat himself as an authority. He must thrust back all idolatrous worshippers. He must never allow himself to be looked on as a mysterious source of knowledge, having private revelations which are all his own and which are not equally open to everybody else. He must make his hearers and readers understand that what they are he once was, and that what he is they may by due pains become. The means by which he has gained his knowledge are as free to the rest of the world as they are to himself; he invites all who will to join him in working at them, more fully if so be, more accurately, than he has worked at them himself. He will let every reader see, if the reader chooses to take the trouble to look, the process by which he reached his conclusions, and he will thereby give the reader the power of coming to other conclusions, if he thinks good. For himself he will claim no advantage over any other man, beyond those advantages which are the natural result of experience.

T

He may perhaps venture to think that experience may have given him a certain tact, perhaps a certain instinct, at any rate a certain power of dealing with his authorities, which may entitle his conclusions to some measure of respect. He may go so far as to think that, after long years of teaching himself, there is a certain prescription in favour of his conclusions, such as hardly belongs to the conclusions of those who begin to teach others at a time when he was humbly learning, and who rush off at a speed which he cannot follow to the very latest pages of the story. But he claims for himself nothing more than this ; nay, he claims nothing more than this for the elders at whose feet he himself has sat. While yielding them all due respect, he never surrendered his right of judgement; and while venturing to claim some respect as due to himself, he asks no man to surrender his right of judgment to him.

γηράσκει δ' ἀεὶ πολλὰ διδασκόμενος.

He will have learned enough to grasp the great truth of all, how much he has still to learn, and he will never scorn to learn even from those whom he is set to teach.

Such is my view, perhaps a lowly one, of the position of the modern writer of history. He refuses to be made an idol of himself, and he refuses to make an idol of anything else, even of the latest German book. But I cannot help telling a story which seems to show the somewhat different view which some people seem to take of his position. You will not be surprised to hear that I have in my time received

many strange letters, asking me many strange questions. One of the very strangest came from a painter,
whose name I have forgotten, but who, I conceive,
was minded to paint a picture of the fight on Senlac.
I know not whether he ever did paint it; if he did,
I hope he made it more like the facts than the painter
of a picture which I have seen, in which Harold is
shown falling from a horse,—more like them than a
whole series of pictures in which Edith Swanneshals,
who, according to a sum that I once did, must have
been full forty years old in 1066, is painted as quite a
young girl,—more like them than one picture specially,
in which she is represented as finding the King's body
under a great rock, seemingly close by the sea-shore.
I can only conceive that this last picture was painted
by an ingenious writer in the Edinburgh Review, who
fancied that the exploit of Taillefer, and so, I suppose, the whole ebb and flow of the great battle,
happened at the very moment of William's landing
—it could hardly be his landing on the shore of
Pevensey. But to come back to my painter, who
I fancy had read my third volume, which the Edinburgh Reviewer could hardly have done. He wanted
to know what kind of looking man the Conqueror
was, and what kind of weather it was on the day of
Saint Calixtus. On the former head I referred him
to the Bayeux Tapestry and to William's coins,
perhaps also to the personal description of him given
by William of Malmesbury, though that belongs to a
later time of his life. But it was the question about
the weather which specially struck me. In some

battles the weather did great things, say at Trebia,
at Trasimenus—who does not remember Arnold's
picture of it?—and at Crécy.   But as to the weather
on the day of Senlac, our own Chroniclers could
hardly be expected to dwell upon it, and even William of Poitiers and Guy of Amiens hold their peace.
Had the day been either remarkably bright or remarkably stormy, the chances are that they would
have found something to say about it ; so we may
perhaps guess that the elements were in that neutral
state which I have heard described as no weather at
all.   But my painter clearly thought that I knew all
about the matter, only that, for some unexplained
reason, I kept my knowledge to myself.   So Boswell
clearly thought that Johnson knew all about the
other world, only he did not choose to tell him.   Now
I am not one of those who can carpet the earth with
daisies which are not recorded in any book, nor can I
light up the sky with stars when haply the heaven was
clouded over.   But I should certainly have been well
pleased either to light up my picture of the great battle
with the rays of a blazing sun, or to shroud it in clouds
and darkness, if only those who were there to see
had handed down any witness either way.   Surely
the state of mind attributed to me by the painter
was as odd an one as any man can lightly fancy.   I
was thought to have got hold of a piece of knowledge
of no small value for the effect of the very central
point of my whole story.   But it was further thought
that—why I will not presume to guess—I had wilfully
kept back that piece of knowledge from the mass of my

readers, but that I might perhaps be ready to reveal it in a private letter to an unknown correspondent.

I would therefore have all who hear me fully grasp the fact that we who have written large volumes of history are no oracles, but simply fellow-workers with themselves, companions who at most have got a little ahead of them on a road on which it is perfectly open to them to follow. It may be their luck to catch us up, and, according to Mr. Pattison's rule, to supplant us, alive or dead, in any position that we may have won. Yet I would venture to hint that, in the minds of impetuous searchers after novelty, in the minds of those who somehow seem not to find time to think before they speak, to read before they criticize, as in times past we were taught to do, and as we tried to do,—in such minds as these this process of supplanting and "superseding" seems to go on rather faster than Mr. Pattison would have approved. Mr. Pattison's words read as if he allowed a century as a possible life for a modern historian's reputation. The term of power of a French ministry, the life of a new system of Oxford examinations, might seem to be nearer the mark. I am sure that my dear friend John Richard Green never wished his admirers in the newspapers to say that he was the first man who did anything for early English history, at any rate that he was the first man who threw any life into early English history, its events or its characters; before him, we were told, all was "fossil." I felt somewhat humbled, as believing that I had myself thrown some little life into some

of the characters and events of early English history;
and I felt somewhat amazed, as being yet more certain that Sir Francis Palgrave had done a good deal
in that way before me. I could only guess that the
smart writers had never read a word of Sir Francis
Palgrave ; I think they would have found him anything but " fossil " if they had tried him. I could
prove too by very distinct evidence that there are
men who think themselves qualified to talk about
early English history, perhaps even to teach early
English history, who have never looked at a page of
Kemble or Lappenberg. Yet Lappenberg, Kemble,
Palgrave, Guest, those are the men who built the
house, the men without whose help we should be a
long way indeed from any clear notion of the history
and the ways of our forefathers. I have the Bishop
of Chester with me here ; he used always to speak
of John Mitchell Kemble as his " model scholar."
And the Bishop of Chester himself, a portrait-painter
at once so truthful and so brilliant, is not altogether
a " fossil " either. But then fancy a writer who has
to enlighten all mankind in the columns of the newspapers stopping to enlighten himself by a reading of
the great prefaces. But believe me, you who have
still your line of study to choose, you will be well
employed, you will be gaining real knowledge, you
will be giving your minds a true and sound discipline,
if, as soon as you have well mastered the facts of
early English history, you take Kemble's Saxons in
England and Palgrave's History of the English Commonwealth, not as oracles, not as idols, but as writings

from which you will learn not a little, if you use
them as they should be used, comparing and weighing them with one another, and above all, verifying
their references to original authorities at every step.
So to do will be something like making a lodgement
in the fortress of sound learning.   And then, as a
lighter exercise, you may go on and read Palgrave's
History of Normandy and England, which you will
not be able to test by verifying the references to
original authorities, forwhy there are no references
to verify.   But read the book all the same; only
use on it those powers of judgement which by
this time you will surely have gained.   Mark, as
I have often done, some perplexing and provoking
passage, where you are inclined to curse the writer
for not giving you a reference.   Keep it in your
mind; search for it in places likely and unlikely;
you will find it sooner or later, for Sir Francis Palgrave, at that stage of his life, never wrote a word
for which he could not have given a reason; the
search will be useful to you in many ways, and, when
you have found the reference, judge how far it proves
the writer's point.

But you will some of you say that I am bidding
you to read too much, that I am bidding you to
read everything.   I am not bidding you to read
everything.   I would warn every one, save the most
advanced students, to forbear from reading Augustine
Thierry's History of the Norman Conquest; and,
if you can so steel yourselves, forbear from reading
Ivanhoe.   When you reach the stage of studying,

not early English history, but the history of opinion
about early English history, then read Thierry and
even Ivanhoe, but not till then. The literary
fascination of two such masters of tale-telling is
too great; the early reading of such books simply
gives a great deal to unlearn. But let me do
justice even to Thierry. To say nothing of his base-
less theory, few writers oftener go utterly wrong in
points of detail. Yet Thierry was not a careless
writer; least of all was he negligent of authorities.
I do not believe that he ever wrote anything for
which he did not believe that he had the witness of
something which he looked on as an authority. Only
he was utterly uncritical; to him one book older than
the invention of printing was as good as another; he
would gravely put forth statements from the latest
and most worthless writers—that is, of course, if they
helped to patch up his theories—as if they were of
equal value with contemporary narratives and documents. He would kill a man by one name in one
page and bring him to life by another name in a later
page, each time with a perfectly good reference;
he simply had not learned the art of probing and
weighing his references, and finding out either what
they meant or what they were worth. Now Palgrave, though I think he sometimes gives the reins
too freely to his imagination, though he does not
always distinguish the different value of different
authorities, though he sometimes makes his authorities prove too much, still, at least in his mature writings, never blunders like Thierry. We may accept

his conclusions or not ; we have seldom anything to
say against his statement. Kemble has no narrative
work to compare with that of Palgrave ; but the
Saxons in England may fairly be compared with the
History of the English Commonwealth. They are
two great works, works of two great scholars, who
assuredly are not yet superseded. They will give
you two sides of the same general story. Read them,
weigh them ; most likely you will come to think with
me that the union of the views which they severally
maintain comes nearer to the truth than either view
by itself. But Kemble is, if not purely English, at
least purely Teutonic ; Palgrave is œcumenical. It
is from him, directly or indirectly, that all we who
have learned it at all, have learned the great central
truth of history. He knew, as all do not know yet,
how it is to Rome that all paths lead, how it is from
Rome that all paths start again. Do not, I would
pray you, believe that Sir Francis Palgrave is as yet
supplanted or superseded. *Pro reverentia imperii,*
he is still the father and teacher of us all.

Before Palgrave wrote Hallam. There is something, to my mind at least, thoroughly touching in
the way in which the elder man, in his Supplemental
Volume to the Middle Ages, acknowledges his obli-
gations to the younger. Hallam shows that mark of
true greatness, that he could allow himself to have
been wrong. In the strictly mediæval part of
Hallam's writings he belongs to a distinct school
from Palgrave ; he represents another way of looking
at things. Hallam, as he himself once says, was

brought up in the teaching of the eighteenth century. He shows that teaching in its very best shape, accompanied by singular discretion, and by no small reading within his range. But Palgrave is the beginner of the fuller enlightenment of which I hope we are all partakers. Hallam was not strong on the side of imagination, and imagination, if kept under proper restraint by more sober companions, is one of the most essential elements of historical research. He never thoroughly took in either the Imperial or the ecclesiastical element in history; if I say that he did not thoroughly take in the Teutonic element either, it might seem that I leave him no standing-ground at all. And whither shall he seem to vanish, if I add that he never shows that same kind of thorough knowledge of original authorities, that mastery of them, that delight in them, which stands out in every line of Kemble and Palgrave? Hallam had nothing of the spirit of the antiquary; he had not, I should say, very much of the spirit of the historian proper. Yet Hallam was a memorable writer, whose name ought to be deeply honoured, and a large part of whose writings are as valuable now as when they were first written. I distinguished in an earlier lecture two classes of lawyers, one class who are among the worst foes of historical learning, and another class who are among its best friends. We may safely put Hallam as the patriarch of the second class. He did not attain to the world-wide grasp of some of our modern masters of the study of institutions; but he showed, perhaps first after Selden, what an English lawyer, a lawyer who did not take away the key of knowledge, might do for English history. Bringing to his work all the advantage of the lawyer's professional training and professional knowledge, without any trace of the lawyer's professional narrowness and prejudice, bringing too a judgement, not of so wide a range as that of some others, but admirably clear, sound, and impartial, within its range, Hallam did indeed a great work. In that part of English history in which such qualities as these are preeminently needed, say from the reign of Edward the First onwards, I know no writer who so fully discharges a certain very valuable function. If I wish at a pinch, when there is no time to turn over many books, to find a clear and trustworthy account of a matter, I can commonly find what I want in Hallam. And I know no one who more commonly utters some sentence of quiet wisdom, which we carry off and dwell upon. We better understand the solid strength of Hallam when we turn to the feeble talk of his continuator.

Of some of the greatest modern writers of past history I spoke incidentally in an earlier lecture. As I have fallen into the critical vein to-day, I will speak of one or two more. I know few books more delightful and more instructive to read than Milman's History of Latin Christianity. And none better discharges the work of a guide, both to the original authorities, and, what we cannot neglect, to modern German writers. Milman is emphatically a strong writer, a writer with a wide grasp of many subjects, many lands, many ages. The strange thing is that among those subjects, lands, and ages we cannot place any age of English history. It is strange how his mind seems wholly to dwell on the continent, how his strength fails him whenever he touches his own island. In England he seems never either to grasp the general position of a time or to master its details. But in mere detail Milman is nowhere strong. His matter and his style are singularly alike. Few compositions are more effective, as few are more vigorous, than the massive and emphatic sentences in which he brings before us the great features of some character or some event. Dissect those sentences according to the rules of grammar, and in a great number of cases they cannot be parsed. So, irrespective of mere style, Milman's way of putting the general aspect of anything is invariably vigorous, thoughtful, instructive. Yet every page is crowded with mistakes in detail, petty errors as to names, titles, dates, family relations, small points of every kind. They are mere errors on the surface, errors which a moment's thought would have set right, errors which one might go through the book with a pen and correct. They are quite unlike some other kinds of errors, which go through the whole work from top to bottom, where no amount of correction in detail could turn a record of falsehood into a record of truth. Yet it is strange indeed that such errors should be found in such a book. It is hardly possible that the book went forth to the world without the writer ever reading over what he had written, either in print or in manuscript. It hardly can be so; yet Milman's mistakes are just of the kind which might be found in the first rough draught of the most accurate writer. Only such a writer would commonly set them right before they met any eye but his own. For please to remember that the accurate writer is not he who makes no mistakes, for there is none such; it is he who finds out his own mistakes for himself on his own manuscript, and does not leave them for other people to find out in print.

Among Milman's many merits we cannot reckon a thorough grasp of the position of the Roman Empire in the history of the world. And this is the more strange, as he is thoroughly at home in so many particular aspects of the endless questions between Popes and Emperors. But from the œcumenical point of view, Milman is a decided falling back from Palgrave. It fell to the lot of another writer, the faultiest of all of whom I have spoken, but one who has none the less wrought as great a work as any, to do, in a kind of incidental way, for Eastern Europe much the same as Palgrave did for Western Europe. George Finlay, more perhaps than any other modern writer, belongs to the same class as those earlier historians who began a story of remote ages and carried it on into times and scenes in which they were themselves spectators and actors. Living in Greece, reposing after the great struggle in which he had taken a part, not hitherto a strictly historical student, a student rather of law and political œconomy, a practical man too,

a soldier and a tiller of the ground, Finlay looked at
the state of things which he saw at his own door;
he felt a call to trace its causes, and he found that
the tracing of those causes led him back at least to
the days of the Macedonian Alexander. The result
was that great series of volumes on Greece under
Foreign Domination, which form the sad counterpart
and contrast to Grote's great series of volumes on
Greece in the days of her independence. And the
contrast in subject was not the only contrast. While
Grote put forth volume after volume amid the
general applause of scholars, Finlay toiled on at his
thankless task, amid every form of neglect and
discouragement, till he made a few here and there
understand that there was a Roman Empire of the
East. Full of faults his book is, in form, in matter,
in temper; but it is a great work all the same.
Some little way he must have made even where it is
hardest to make way. I have seen Leo the Isaurian
made the subject of a flourish in a leading article.

I have compared Finlay and Grote. I believe
I had the latter great writer in my eye when I
spoke a little time about the hasty way in which
the jaunty critics of our time fancy that a great
scholar is "superseded," because forsooth they have
not mastered his writings. I have already mentioned in print, but I cannot help mentioning it
again—it is so beautifully illustrative—the calm
saying of the smart writer who told the world that
Thirlwall had been "superseded" by Grote. Bishop
Thirlwall himself, in his modesty, once said some-

thing of the kind; but he was the only man who had a right to say so. The judgement is specially instructive, because it shows how little the judge knew of the two great scholars on whom he presumed to sit in judgement. Somebody has perhaps gone on to say that Grote is "superseded" by Curtius. Such a saying would be as silly as to say that Thirlwall is superseded by Grote. For of these three great writers each is so manifestly the best of the three in particular parts and in particular aspects, that none of the three can supersede any other; we must have all of them. But it rises almost to the dignity of a joke to say that either Grote or Curtius has superseded Thirlwall. The part cannot supersede the whole. The man who wrote the whole tale of independent Greece cannot be superseded by men who wrote only parts of it. The critic of course had not the faintest notion what Bishop Thirlwall had written about, or what there was for him to write about. The strength of Thirlwall as clearly lies in the history of Alexander and his successors as the strength of Grote lies in the political history of Athenian and Syracusan democracy, as the strength of Curtius lies in the geography, in the artistic side of things, in the general picture of that age which was the glory of Athens, but which, as the disciples of Finlay know, was an age of decline for Hellas in the wider sense. Curtius, perfect master of his own lore, but a babe when he ventures to meddle with the lore of Grote, does not even touch that part of Greek history in which

Thirlwall was strongest. <u>Grote</u>, historian of democracy, was unfair alike to the earliest and to the
latest parts of Thirlwall's story, to old Achaians at
one end, to Macedonians and new Achaians at the
other end. The successors of Alexander he barely
touched; Alexander himself he would have done
well to leave alone. Yet he is said to have "superseded" Thirlwall, because a careless writer had not
taken the trouble to read Thirlwall, or even to find
out what he wrote. He might indeed have said
that the early parts both of Thirlwall and Grote
were superseded by the growth of Comparative
Mythology; but that might have been too obvious
a truth to reach the regions of infallible criticism.
Indeed I am told that the early parts of Curtius,
which seemed so novel not many years back, are
already superseded by sciences beside which Comparative Mythology seems ancient.

Let then no student of history scorn the guidance
of the great Bishop of Saint David's, any more than
he will scorn the guidance of the living Bishop of
Chester. I know not whether Thirlwall is good
for the schools; I know that he is good for sound
learning, when read alongside of Arrian, Diodôros,
Plutarch, and Polybios. But in speaking of him
I have indeed run into the jaws of the lion; I have
dared to speak freely of one of the great masters
of German learning. I spoke some time back of
the fashionable idolatry of the last German book.
One has sometimes heard of the question "Have
you read the last German book?" being put under

circumstances which might suggest as a reply the more searching question, "Have you read the first English book?" Now it is a fact, a fact that we may perhaps set down among "things not generally known," but still a fact, that the last German book is sometimes not equal to the German book that went before it, sometimes—may I dare to say it?—not equal to some English book that went before either. Yet we cannot afford to cast aside either the last German book or the German book last before that. Each, while going about to show some other writer to be wrong, is sure to bring out some point or other which one is glad to see brought out; the only grievance is that one has to read from one end to the other to find out what the points are. We must read the German books; if Stubbs is the Waitz of England, Waitz is the Stubbs of Germany. I only demand the right to keep our independence, and to believe that on many matters of historical learning an Englishman—an Englishman on either side of Ocean —is better fitted to judge than a German. A Swiss or a Norwegian may judge of the workings of free constitutions in old Greece, in Italy, in any other land, because he, like the Englishman, has daily experience of their working in his own land. But these things are mysteries to German professors, because they are mysteries to German statesmen also. The German scholar simply reads in a book of things which we are always looking at and acting in. He therefore utterly fails to understand many things at Athens or Rome or anywhere else which come to us like our ABC. Look at Curtius, so great in his own line, so helpless in face of the great political truths which were Grote's daily bread. Sometimes he writes as if he had never read Grote, sometimes as if he had read him but had failed to grasp the simplest points in his meaning. Because Grote used his critical independence in the matter of the generals at Arginousai, Curtius fancied that he was defending the conduct of the Assembly, whereas he condemned it in the strongest terms. As Ranke can make so little of English institutions when he directly grapples with them, so Curtius and a crowd of other German scholars show in every page the lack of that practical understanding of free institutions which can be gained only by living among them.

And now that we have dared so far as this, let us fly at the highest game of all. I have spoken my mind about Mommsen, matter and manner, in other shapes. I have lately had need to read a great deal of him over again, with greater attention than I had ever before given to him. And let me pay all becoming homage to the greatest scholar of our times, well nigh the greatest scholar of all times. In all learning that comes under the head of scholarship in the widest sense, we may surely all be glad to sit at his feet. Surely no man of our times has ever taken in so wide a range of subjects, all brought with the happiest effect to bear upon and to support one another. Language, law, mythology, customs, antiquities, coins, inscriptions, every source of knowledge of every kind—he is master of them all. Nor does he shut up his researches within any narrow bounds; he is as much at home with Cassiodorus and Jordanis as he is with an Iapygian inscription or with the fragments of Appius the Blind. And to all this he adds some of the highest qualities of the historian proper. Few can surpass him in wide and sure grasp of historic sequence; and, when he chooses, he can put forth deep and far-reaching thoughts with the full power of the noble tongue of his birth. I know no piece of historical painting that outdoes the wonderful passage near the beginning of the second volume of the Roman History, which sets forth how, through the weakening of the Macedonian kingdoms, the barbarian powers of the East again came to the front, how "the world had again two lords," when Rome had to gird herself for the strife with Parthia. What then is lacking in one endowed with such mighty gifts, and who for many purposes makes such a splendid use of them? What is lacking is political and moral insight, the moral insight which is born with a man, the political insight which is gained only by living in communities of freemen. One mourns to see in such a scholar's historic judgements only the morals of Macaulay's Avaux; one mourns to see in him the politics of an œcumenical Jingo, falling down and worshipping brute force wherever he can find it. The chosen object of Mommsen's scorn is the honest man, the patriot

of a small state, who finding his native land plotted
against by a foe whose irresistible power does not
make him ashamed of the lowest tricks and false-
hoods, strives, even against hope, to preserve the freedom and the dignity of his people, to hinder their
fall if he can, at any rate to delay it or to make
it less bitter.   That the weak can have any rights
against the strong never enters the mind of one
who has had in his own person some experience
of the rule of blood and iron.   The wrath of Mommsen against a righteous man of old is equalled only
by his wrath against any man of our own times who
ventures to admire those who refused to bow to
the Baal or Moloch of brute force.   And the whole
thing is as shallow as it is immoral; it all goes
on the principle that a man of the second century
B. C. was bound to see as clearly that things were
coming as a man in the nineteenth century A.D. can
see that they did come.   But, in some strange and
happy way, the true Teutonic tongue refuses to be
the means for putting forth thoughts of this kind.
When a righteous man has to be reviled, it can,
it seems, be done only in a half-French jargon which
makes us more than ever disposed to echo the words
of the old Swabian, "Lond us tütsch blyben : die
wälsch Zung ist untrü."   Against boisterous dog-
matism clothed in epigrams it is easy to make
epigrams back again.   When we are told that those
who do not see that Gaius Gracchus aimed at kingship must have no eyes at all to see with, it needs
no effort to say in turn that those who see any-

thing of the kind must be looking through the coloured spectacles of their own arbitrary fancies. When Mommsen gets puzzled over the union between Appius Claudius and Gnæus Flavius, between the high aristocrat and the innovating freedman. I have often wished that I could have had him with me at the Northampton election of 1841, and could have shown him the Tories and the Chartists —may I say Appius Claudius and Gnæus Flavius?— marching friendly in one procession to the strife against the friends of free trade and moderate reform —may I say, against Quintus Fabius and Publius Decius? From Mommsen let me go back to Niebuhr, who perhaps is now "superseded." Well, I do not ask any one to accept all his divinations; but I do ask all to remember what they owe to an illustrious scholar who knew all the learning of his generation, and who added to his learning a good share of that real political insight in which his illustrious successor is so grievously lacking. Niebuhr had not lived in a free country; but he had seen many men and many lands; he lived in a stirring time, and if not exactly an actor in its events, he was able to see them nearer than most men. And now in many things the axe is being put to the root of Mommsen's argument by a countryman of his own who is also almost a countryman of ours. I will not claim for Ihne the power or the genius of Mommsen; I do not share his excessive tendency to doubt, or his somewhat needless eagerness to prove Mommsen in the wrong. But he is a scholar of no mean mark, a wary and prudent scholar, and he has gained an insight into many political matters which to Mommsen are the blackness of darkness. But how did he gain that insight? By long dwelling in a land of free institutions and carefully marking the institutions of the land in which he dwelled. Ihne's long sojourn at Liverpool has taught him a thing or two which Mommsen has never been able to understand. Had the sojourn been at Manchester or Birmingham instead of at Liverpool, it might have taught him a thing or two more.

I had meant to end what I had to say about modern writers with a word or two about one class of them, namely the makers of translations, what in my day were called cribs. The subject is an interesting and instructive one; but we have no time for it to-day. After dealing such heavy blows at the great fishes, we may let the small fry go. We must keep to those among modern writers who at least profess to put forth their own thoughts in their own tongue. And these surely have their use in historical study, if only their use is rightly understood, their use, not as themselves authorities, but as guides to the real authorities, as commentators on them. If a man wishes to begin the study of any particular period of history, the advice that I should give him would, in most cases, be something like this. Get hold of the best English writer on the subject that you can find. If he really deserves that name, his references will send you

both to the original writers and to those German
commentators whom, I repeat, we cannot do without. The names that at first seem strange to you
will gradually become familiar; the books themselves will gradually become cherished companions.
One book will lead to another; you will gradually
find how vast and how fascinating a field is opened
to you by almost any period of history that you
may choose. Only once again, whatever period you
choose, do not isolate it; bind it, if only by a
narrow thread of general knowledge, to other periods.
For this last work you will often have to use modern
writers, not only as guides, but as substitutes. And
it may sometimes happen that a guide of a generation or two back may not be wholly useless. Bear
with me in that hard saying. Speaking myself as
a superseded fossil, I cannot altogether keep down
my fellow-feelings for the superseded fossils that
were before me. If we are good for nothing else,
we are at least good for the history of opinion. I
venture to hold that many of those who went before
me were good for something more. When I call
on you, as I did at the beginning, to "praise famous
men and our fathers that begat us," natural piety
bids me claim a place among them for the teachers
of my own youth.

LECTURE VIII.

GEOGRAPHY AND TRAVEL.

I now come to the last stage of the course which I have chalked out for the present term. I wish last of all to speak of certain means towards the acquisition of sound historical knowledge which yield to none in importance, as they certainly yield to none in the inherent charm of their study. I have headed this lecture *Geography and Travel*. Now geography, in its bearings on history, has two meanings, or rather two aspects, which, though they often run into one another, are clearly distinct in idea. Geography, in one of its aspects, is simply a branch of history; in the other it is a precious help to history. In one aspect, it is a form of knowledge which may be mastered in the study by books and maps; in the other, it is a matter of travel, a matter of seeing things with our own eyes. The former aspect is that of which I have myself treated in a special work, a thick volume of Historical Geography, with a thin companion volume of maps. This side of geographical know-ledge amounts to the knowledge of the political divisions of the earth at different times. It comes very largely to be a matter of nomenclature; what

was the meaning of such and such a geographical
name at such and such a time? Did it mean the
same extent of the surface of the earth which it
means now? Did it reach further than it does
now or not so far? Or did it, as sometimes happens,
mean some other part of the earth from what it
means now, some part which may not have an inch
of ground in common with the land to which the
name is now commonly given? That knowledge of
this kind forms part of the very A B C of historical
study hardly needs to be proved. The thing seems
almost childish to insist on; it is obvious, as the
phrase goes, to the meanest capacity. So it is in
theory; in practice the case is somewhat different.
There is no part of our study in which there is more
to learn and to unlearn, and in which both learning and unlearning are harder tasks, than in the
right employment of geographical terms, according
to the usage of successive times. There is no subject about which we have so often to say the same
thing over and over again, and about which we
must so little shrink from saying it over again,
even, if need be, till seventy times seven. For
there is no subject on which error crops up again
so constantly, because so unconsciously; there is
no subject on which accuracy of expression, and
that accuracy of thought which cannot be without
accuracy of expression, calls for more constant and
more painful efforts. For it is needful to unlearn
at every step; every time we open our mouths,
we have to watch our words and our thoughts; for

the temptation constantly besets us to use some word or other in the manner which comes most naturally to our lips, but a manner which would at once lead others astray. Bear with me, if I counsel you here, as I have counselled some beyond Ocean, not to be discouraged if your striving after truth is rewarded with the name of *pedant*. The pedant, as the word is commonly used, is the man who does his best to make his words agree with his thoughts and to make his thoughts agree with facts. Without pedantry, that is, without accuracy, we can make no way in any matter, least of all can we make any way in this matter of Historical Geography. For its very first lesson is that we must not be startled at the use of a word in some sense other than that to which we are most accustomed, that we must not be startled at being told to use one word when it comes far more naturally to us to use another. At such teaching the natural man revolts; he asks what mere names matter; if he knows his facts, is not one name as good as another to express them? Now there is in truth no such thing as a mere question of names; every question of names is a question of facts; for names are facts. In one sense indeed it is perfectly true that one name is as good as another; that is to say, at the very beginning of language, if we can conceive a beginning of language, it did not the least matter by what sound an idea came to be expressed. But when the sound and the idea have become connected by long usage, when the sound at once suggests the

idea, when the two have become practically insepar-
able, an inaccurate use of a name implies an inaccurate impression as to facts. When a certain name
as applied to a country conveys the idea of a certain
state of things in that country, to apply that name to
it at a time when that state of things did not exist,
at once conveys a false impression; it suggests that
the state of things which the name implies existed
at a time when it did not exist. The inaccurate
use of the name does not necessarily imply abiding
ignorance on the part of the man who misuses it; but
it does imply at least momentary forgetfulness on his
part, and it may lead to abiding misconception on
the part of those who hear him. The simplest instance of all is the best; to say, as we often hear,
that Cæsar landed in England does not necessarily
imply abiding ignorance of the great facts of the
history of our island on the part of him who says
it. But it does imply at least momentary forgetfulness of them. He who says that Cæsar landed
in England cannot have present to his eye at that
moment all that is implied in the word *England.*
He cannot be conscious at that moment that, though
the land in which Cæsar landed was the same land
as that in which Cnut and William landed, yet the
people who defended the land against Cæsar were
not the same people as those who defended the land
against Cnut and William. He may himself be
perfectly able to correct his own slip in his next
moment of accurate thought; but he may meanwhile have given an abiding false impression to

some hearer who may not be able in the same way to correct it. He may himself need only to unlearn a careless habit; he may lay on others the duty of unlearning an utterly confused view as to the history of their country. Here the remedy is the easiest in the world; there is nothing needed but to use another word, not quite so usual, but quite as intelligible. We have only to say *Britain* instead of *England*. That is to say, we have only to use the abiding geographical name that applies to every part of the island at every time, instead of the shifting political name which has at different times applied to different parts of the island, but which did not apply to any part of it at the time when Cæsar landed. Here then nothing is needed but a little thought; but even that little thought implies some slight effort, and that slight effort might be rewarded with the name of pedant at the hands of some one for whom even that slight effort is too much.

But in many cases of the kind far more effort is needed than this. It is really a hard task to use some geographical names, those of France, Burgundy, Austria, pre-eminently among them, so as at once accurately to set forth the state of things at the time of which we are speaking, and at the same time to have a chance of conveying the meaning that we wish, or any meaning at all, to the mind of an ordinary hearer. The only thing is to educate the ordinary hearer, to make him unlearn what is false and learn what is true, till the accurate use of words conveys to him a meaning, and that the right meaning. For we cannot alter the names to please him. In altering the names we should be sinning against the facts; we should be giving him not bread but a stone; we should be telling him the thing that is not, because he is not yet ready fully to take in the thing that is. In other words, if history, past or present, is to be understood, nothing must be more carefully studied than Historical Geography. Now we might almost define Historical Geography to be the knowledge of the names which different parts of the earth's surface bore at different times. If under knowledge of the names we may reckon knowledge of the ways in which the names came to be borne, the definition will do thoroughly well. Than the neglect of Historical Geography, than the lax and inaccurate use of the names of countries and nations, there has been no more fertile source of historical error. Nor is this all; the lax and careless use of names constantly leads to the most mischievous misunderstandings of the most important questions of the present; the misuse of a name has even helped to prolong the bondage of nations. No one can doubt that the use, careless or designed, of the word *Turkey* to express the lands under bondage to the Turk has done much to blind men's eyes and to deaden their natural feelings in the great strife for the deliverance of South-eastern Europe from its oppressors. As long as that name is used, so long will men unconsciously think that the Turks are to Turkey as the English are to England or the French to France. Learn to speak, as history and fact require us to speak, not of a Turkey which has no being, but of enslaved Greece, enslaved Bulgaria, enslaved Servia, and we have taken one step, a step by no means to be scorned, towards the reunion of the enslaved lands to free Greece, free Bulgaria, free Servia. Those who are more nearly concerned know the force of a name. On Greek lips Epeiros and the other enslaved Greek lands are never called Τουρκία; they are ἡ δούλη Ἑλλάς.

Perhaps no geographical names are more likely to lead astray than such familiar names as *France* and *Austria*. *Francia* in Latin is a very old name, much older than *Anglia*; but it is a speaking fact that it has never settled down as the received name of the land so thoroughly as *Anglia* has. I fancy that no classical purist would be so precise as to refuse to speak of *Anglia*, while any one writing in Latin would prefer *Gallia* to *Francia*, unless he had to bring in the King's style, or in some pointed way to distinguish *Francia* from some other land. This vague feeling is an instructive expression of the real difference between the history of Gaul and the history of Britain. A large part of Gaul never became *Francia*, except in a sense in which *Francia* takes in a great deal besides Gaul. No part of Gaul ever became *Francia* in the same sense in which a great part of Britain became *Anglia*. For there is no part of Gaul in which a Frankish people, keeping the Frankish tongue, really became the folk of the land. We may translate *Anglia* by *England* from the first moment that the word *Anglia* is used; it would be very dangerous to translate *Francia* by *France*, at any time before the end of the ninth century. We should make strange havoc of our meaning if we used the word *France* to translate either the *Francia* of Claudian, the *Francia* of Einhard, or the Φραγγία of Constantine Porphyrogennêtos. But when France in the modern sense, the duchy and kingdom of Paris, sets out on her career of aggrandisement, it is the right thing to extend the use of the name with every extension of the power. As to the name of *Austria*, besides other uses of the name which have nothing to do with the *Eastern Mark* of Germany against the Magyar, the name, as applied to that still existing archduchy, has an use exactly opposite to the use of the name *France*. As it is needful to extend the use of the name *France* with every extension of the French power, it is equally needful not to extend the name *Austria* with every extension of the present Austrian power. For every land that came under the dominion of the French king was formally incorporated with the French kingdom, and every such land sooner or later became French really as well as formally. But every land that came under the dominion of the Austrian archduke was not formally incorporated with the Austrian archduchy, nor have the mass of such lands ever become Austrian in any practical sense. Lyons, not French before Philip the Fair, has been French ever since. We must shape our language so as to express both facts. But Venice and Ragusa have never been Austrian, though Venice once formed, and Ragusa still forms, part of the dominions of the sovereign of Austria. We must shape our language so as to express those

facts also. Of two advancing powers, each of which
has annexed a crowd of other lands, one has really
made its annexed lands part of itself; the other has
failed to do so. Look at the map; there is now no
special local France; *France* is the aggregate of all
the departments from the North to the Low Pyrenees;
the word has no other meaning, either formal or
popular. But *Austria* is still a word of doubtful
meaning. There is still an archduchy of Austria with
ascertained boundaries, which forms but a small part
of the dominions of the archduke to whom it still
gives a title. There is also a so-called Empire of
Austria, greater, we may suppose, than the archduchy, but which at any rate does not take in all the
dominions of the so-called Emperor. For assuredly it
does not take in the kingdom of Hungary and its
partes annexæ. When, speaking of the present day,
we apply the name France to all the European territories of the sovereign or the commonwealth of
France, we are expressing a political and historical
truth. It is as essential to accuracy so to apply the
name now as it is to apply it otherwise in speaking
of times three or four hundred years back. But if, as
people often carelessly do, we apply the name Austria
to all the possessions of the sovereign of Austria, we
are expressing a political and historical falsehood. It
is as essential to accuracy in speaking of present times
as it is in speaking of times three or four hundred
years back, so to shape our language as to express
the very important political fact that, while all lands
over which French rule has been spread have become

both formally and practically French, all lands over
which Austrian rule has been spread have not either
formally or practically become Austrian.

Thus far we have been dealing with cases of
bondage to the modern map. Nowadays there is no
excuse for bondage to the modern map. It was
otherwise when I was young. We used then to
have the "Ancient" and the "Modern Atlas," and
nothing between them. The "Ancient" atlas was
to do for all "classical" times; the divisions of the
world in the days of Xerxes, of Alexander, and of
Trajan—but I am not quite sure whether Trajan is
"classical"—were thought to have been exactly the
same. The "modern" Atlas was to show the state
of things as it was at that moment, a state of things
which has happily changed a good deal since that
moment. There was indeed a map of "France in
provinces" as well as of "France in departments," and
I know one atlas which went so far as to show both
the divisions of Europe as they stood at the beginning
of the French Revolution and the divisions of Europe
as they stood in 1815. But with me at least the comparison of these maps led only to the most helpless
puzzledom. Any one who has ever tried to make
historical maps knows the problem of problems, the
problem from which, as far as our own day is concerned, we were relieved by the events of 1866.
How shall I draw a map which shall clearly show
the extent of the Roman Empire or of the German
Confederation, and at the same time clearly show
the extent of the dominions of the sovereigns of

Austria and Prussia, both within the Empire or
Confederation and without it ? It is excessively hard
to mark both without confusion. Now among the
maps of my youth, those which professed to show
the older state of things marked the extent of the
Roman Empire, perhaps rather of the Kingdom of
Germany, plainly enough. But will it be believed
that in those maps there was no Austria marked at
all, while there was a very visible kingdom of
Hungary, and that no Prussia was marked save a
little one bordering on the *Frisches Haff* and *Kurisches
Haff*? There was not a hint that the Kings of
Hungary and Prussia held any territories within the
bounds of Germany. Why or how should it be hinted ?
That the Kings of Hungary and Prussia, as well as
the Kings of Great Britain, Denmark, and Sweden,
were also princes of the Empire, holding German
lands, was a fact of politics, not a fact of geography.
The accident that the King of Prussia was also
Elector of Brandenburg no more made Brandenburg
part of Prussia than the accident that the King of
Great Britain was also Elector of Hannover made
Hannover part of Great Britain. In a map of Europe
which showed Germany as a whole, and did not profess
to go into its internal divisions, there was no need to
show a separate Austria any more than to show a
separate Reuss-Schleiz. Only, when I tried a little
eighteenth century history, my map puzzled me a
good deal. I could make nothing of a King of Prussia
whose kingdom lay quite away from Germany, but
who seemed to have so much to do in the middle

of Germany and to be so very much at home there.
I am bound to say that with my map I had no
difficulty as to Maria Theresa being Queen of Hungary; my difficulty was to understand about the
Queen of Hungary being so many things besides.
But remember that the maps that led me thus
astray were, as regarded Germany, formally quite
accurate; it was otherwise when they represented
Italy as all one thing.   For Germany was a political
whole, though the connexion of its parts might be
very loose ; Italy was a mere geographical expression,
laxly used to express several kingdoms, duchies,
and commonwealths which did not form any political
whole.   Nor, when I turned to the map of 1815,
did I get any more help towards understanding the
newer state of things.   The great Germany of the
former map had vanished.   A great part of it seemed
to have been joined to an enlarged Prussia, which
now lay in two great pieces, one of which touched
France.   The impression conveyed was that Prussia
had, besides any doings in Poland, conquered a large
piece of Germany.   On the other hand, Hungary
was gone; it seemed to have changed its name to
Austria, and to have added great pieces of Poland,
Germany, and Italy, to say nothing of its running
in a wonderful way down the east coast of the
Hadriatic.   Nobody then knew much of these last
lands, and it might be hard to find a map of the
exact year 1813, which should show that dream
of oppressed right which for that moment was a
fact, a free Slavonic Cattaro, haven and capital of

X 2

Tzernagora. As for Germany, the new map sometimes confined the name to those parts of Germany
which had not been moved within the Prussian or
Hungarian border; sometimes the name Germany
ran across the lands which were also marked Prussia
and Austria, in a way that was not a little puzzling.
As for times before 1789 we were left to shift as we
could. I once indeed saw a map marked " Europe
in a period intermediate between Ancient and
Modern." As far as I remember, it did not represent any period exactly, but it perhaps came nearer
to the days of Charles the Great than to any other.
In those days we were left to find out what we
could about the territories of Burgundian dukes and
Angevin kings. As for the lands between the
Hadriatic and the Euxine, let me tell you of a little
book which I was happily set to read in the year
1836. This was " The History of the Overthrow of
the Roman Empire, and the Foundation of the prin-
cipal European States," by William Cooke Taylor,
LL.D. of Dublin. The overthrow of the Roman
Empire there spoken of was that which was finished,
not in 476 but in 1453. By this time Dr. Taylor
has most likely gone the way of historians great and
small, as described by Mr. Pattison. But it may be
that some of you are not the worse for the fact that,
eight-and-forty years ago, some years before Mr.
Finlay had written anything, I learned from him
that there was a Roman Empire of the East.

In these times no one need go through these
difficulties of an elder day. The facts of his-

torical geography are now open to all ; they may be
learned by the same processes of study as other
facts ; and, if the study has some difficulties special
to itself, the same may be said of any other branch
of study. I wish only to insist on its pursuit as
one of the most essential parts of our general work.
It ought to be taught from the beginning, so that there
need be no painful unlearning of the modern map.
Yet sometimes there is a painful unlearning needed
the other way. We have lately heard a good deal
of a land called Soudan—*the* Soudan ; why it has
the article I know no more than why the newspapers
always talk of *the* Tyrol, or why, when a land that
I knew very well as Crim or Crim Tartary suddenly
became famous thirty years ago, the newspapers
always spoke of it as "*the* Crimea[1]." When I heard
of Soudan as being somewhere near the Red Sea,
I was as puzzled as if I had heard of Germany being
somewhere on the Euxine. In the maps of my youth
" Soudan or Nigritia " lay a long way to the west,
nearer certainly to the Atlantic than to the Red Sea.
Soudan to be sure does not, as Crim does, lie within
my immediate range of work, and I have found no
one to tell me how the name shifted in this sort.
But I envied those who had no difficulties about the
matter, those who had nothing to unlearn. To say
the least, it saved trouble never to have heard of
Soudan before 1884, as it certainly saved many
people a great deal of trouble never to have heard
of the Tauric Chersonêsos before 1854.

[1] In Gibbon it is " Crimea " without the article.

I have spoken of bondage to the modern map; but that is not the lowest form of bondage. There are some parts of the world, some parts of our own island, in which mastery of the modern map is all that is needed to get rid of error. The history of Strathclyde, Cumberland, all that part of Britain, by whatever name we call it, is at all times puzzling enough, and it might have better fallen in with any notion of natural boundaries, if Lancashire—that modern shire of which Domesday knows nothing—had not reached beyond the sandy estuary of Morecambe Bay. But, as a matter of fact, it does so reach; yet it is hard to convince men's minds of the fact; it is hard to convince them that a large part of the coast of Winandermere is in the same county as Manchester. It is more puzzling to guess why a large part of West Somerset is commonly conceived to be Devonshire; against that danger the English Chronicler long ago put forth an express warning. He marks Porlock, the scene of Harold's landing, as lying on the borders of Devonshire and Somerset. Yet I have before now read in a book that the Barle is the best trout-stream in Devonshire, though assuredly every inch of the course of the Barle lies in Somerset. But these are lesser difficulties compared with the crowning difficulty of persuading mankind that Mont Blanc is not in Switzerland. It is hard to see the origin of this superstition, except on the doctrine which I believe some seriously hold, that, wherever Alps are, there is Switzerland. But the land of the Old

League of High Germany, and of those allies and subjects, German, Burgundian, and Italian, who have in later times been admitted to share in their Confederation, is the chosen stronghold of error in this whole matter. The real history of the land, its folk and its name, is singular enough. That parts of the three Imperial kingdoms should detach themselves from the general mass of each, to form for all political purposes a real artificial nation, but without any one of the three dropping its natural tongue—that the body thus gradually formed should remain for ages without any formal collective name—that the name of one member, and by no means the greatest member, should become the popular name of the whole body, but that it should not be taken into formal use till the present century—all this is strange enough in itself. But the story, if strange, is simple ; it is easy to be understood, if only people will remember that the old German lands and towns, first three, then eight, then thirteen, are the kernel of the League, and that its Romance members are allies and subjects who have been raised to Confederate rank. The name of the one land of Schwyz had, even in Philip of Comines' time, come to be applied in popular use to the whole League ; but it never found a place in the formal style of the Confederation till 1803. Yet no errors are harder to get rid of than the notions that there has been from the beginning of things a Swiss people, occupying seemingly the present extent of the Swiss Confederation—that the German people of the Three Lands had something to do with the Helvetii of Cæsar—that the struggle against the dukes of Austria was in all its stages a struggle against the Empire. Alas for those warriors of Morgarten whom King Lewis so warmly thanked for the blow dealt against the Austrian rebel. I spoke in an earlier lecture of Mr. James Fergusson's wonderful discourse on "Swiss architecture," and some may remember Dean Stanley's idea that the legendary Lucius, by becoming Bishop of Curia Rætorum, Chur of the Grey League, in the second century A.D., thereby became a "Swiss bishop." In that borderland of the Imperial kingdoms, that schoolroom of Europe which some strangely call its playground, I believe geography is formally forbidden. At least I have heard of an Oxford man on a Swiss journey accompanied by other Oxford men, who at some stage put the very natural question what canton he was in. His companions jeered at the question. What had Switzerland to do with cantons ? In Switzerland he should not have been thinking about cantons ; he should have been thinking only about *cols* and *horns,* and the best way of breaking his neck among them.

I started from the map, from the study of geography on the map, and from that I have wandered to the more living study of geography on the very soil of the lands and cities whose history we are studying. This is that second aspect of geography as applied to history of which I spoke at the beginning. For my own part, it has never seemed to me to be strange, I have never travelled with com-

panions to whom it seemed to be strange, to make it
my first business to know where I was, in what
canton or other division, and to make out all that
one could make out as to the physical look of that
canton or other division, and the light which that
physical look throws on its history. I am not
sure that going to the top of an Alp is the best
way to find out. I once tried a Pyrenee—Orosius
will justify the singular number; I went up in
the same state of mind as the last Philip when
he climbed Hæmus—Livy seems to look on Hæmus
as a single peak—in the hope of seeing the Euxine
and the Hadriatic at once, and thereby of doing
great things in the way of planning campaigns.
So I went up my Pyrenee, not with any purpose
of planning campaigns, but in the hope of seeing
Aquitaine, and perhaps Septimania, spread like a
map at my feet, of seeing Garonne wandering
hither and thither, perhaps—as Mr. Green saw
Runnymede from Château-Gaillard—of looking at
Toulouse and Bordeaux at a single glance. King
Philip came down disappointed from his Hæmus,
and I came down disappointed from my Pyrenee.
I had seen nothing and learned nothing; I came
down with no more knowledge of the geography of
Southern Gaul than I took up. But that was
because I had gone too high. From a moderate
height, from the top of Cotswold or Mendip, from
the castle-hill of Carlisle, the castle-hill of Stirling,
and the castle-hill of Domfront, from the more famous
heights of Athens and of Corinth, there you may

indeed learn history. I would almost say that, without such climbings as these, you cannot fully learn history. Beyond doubt the finished historian must be a traveller; he must see with his own eyes the true look of a wide land; he must see too with his eyes the very spots where great events happened; he must mark the lie of a city, and take in, as far as a non-technical eye can, all that is special about a battle-field. Yet I have been asked within the last few years at Exeter, at Norwich, and at Lincoln, whether I had ever seen those cities before. I wondered a little that I was not asked the last time I was at Battle whether I had ever been there before; and I do remember a reviewer who gave me credit for unusual energy in having ever taken the trouble to go thither. And I have read a very learned German discourse on the topography of Ravenna, accompanied by many maps and fully discussing many points, written by a professor who had never set his eyes on the mosaics of Saint Apollinaris or on the cupola under which Theodoric once lay. But anyhow in holding that, thoroughly to understand a land or a place, you must see it with your own eyes, I have good companions. Had not Lord Macaulay seen Derry? did not Asser ages before him walk along the height of Ashdown the better to tell of Ælfred's day of victory? And I may add that only this last summer the last new made fellow of All Souls rode away from my house on his three wheels to get up the battle of Lansdown on the spot. You cannot, so

I at least have found it, fully take in the history
of the world, its lands and its cities, except by
working at each historic spot on the spot itself.

Among those spots there are some whose interest
is œcumenical. In them the whole world, at least
the whole world of Aryan Europe, lies before
you as in a figure. The history of creeds and
tongues and races rises more clearly before our
sight, as we tread the Marble Way of Palermo,
as we think how tall ships once rode at anchor
on either side of us, as we pass from the haven
where the men of Canaan first made their home,
by the palace of the Emirs to the palace of the
Kings, to the church which holds the dust of the
Wonder of the World, to the arch which records
the victories of the last Augustus who planted the
cross of Christendom and the eagle of Rome on the
shores which had seen the conquests of Agathoklês,
of Regulus, and of Roger. From the tomb of Frederick and the trophies of Charles we may go back
to the noblest centre that any city of man can
show; under the shelter of the four guardian virgins,
we look up to the mountains on three sides of us,
to the mid sea of Europe on the fourth; we look
up to the height on which the Thunderbolt of Carthage, Hamilkar Barak himself, kept his camp where
men now go to do homage to Saint Rosalia; we
look up to the western height, to the Royal Mount
which William the Good crowned with his wondrous
minster; we cast our eyes over the plain where
Metellus won his spoil of Punic elephants, to the

hill down whose slopes marched Garibaldi and his
Thousand. The pages of the whole world's history
are opened to us within the walls of the city thrice
won for Europe, once won for Christendom, by the
Epeirot, the Roman, and the Norman ; the rival nations of the earth seem gathered in their meeting-
place within the Happy City of the Threefold
Tongue. There we see the great cycles of man's
history alive before us ; we see the Byzantine Greek,
the African Saracen, carrying on the memory and
the work of the colonists of old Hellas and old
Phœnicia, till they could rest for a while from the
eternal strife of Aryan and Semitic man, till each
could flourish unharmed after his own fashion beneath
the equal sceptre of kings of Teutonic blood and
Roman speech.

Or again, would we see a spot where the whole
artistic history of the world—and, first and foremost, the art of the great days of transition—is
stamped for ever on the stones of a single building ?
We shall find it in a land to which, when our Professor of " Classical" Archæology comes, I would send
him as his first errand, that he may there learn a
yearning to cast away the ungracious adjective which
may go far to mar his usefulness. Let him seek the
eastern shore of Hadria, let him stand in the everlasting court of Jovius, and there let him ask himself whether he has not come by an easy path from
Segesta to Pæstum, from Pæstum to Athens, from
Athens to Rome, from Rome to Spalato. And let
him ask himself again whether he can withstand the

call which bids him go yet further on his journey
—the call which bids him again, not to the Rome
of Trajan but to the Rome of Constantine, and
which calls him on from Rome by Ravenna, Lucca,
Pisa, by Schaffhausen and Toulouse and Durham and
Oakham, till he is held firm in the gentle grasp of
the saint of Witham and Lincoln, till he finds himself
hurried along the path which will leave him only
under the vault of our own Divinity School, or
beside that tall pillar by the staircase at Christ
Church on which the latest times of all have laid
so strange a burthen. On that spot, between those
ranges of arches, the most epoch-making of the
works of the builder's art, our thoughts go back
from the house that became a city to the city that
became a house; they go back from the home of
Diocletian by the shore to the home of Romulus
by the river's bank; they pass back to the days
when the Illyrian coast became Rome's pathway
to Eastern influence and Eastern dominion, till she
herself moved from the seven hills by the Tiber
to the seven hills by the Bosporos. We see the
fleets of the Eastern Rome sail from the haven of
Long Salona to win back the elder Rome to the
obedience of her own Augustus. We pass on to
the days of invasion when Salona became heaps
and the house of Jovius became a city of refuge;
we pass on by Servian kings and Venetian doges,
till, sad ending in such a line of memories, last
link of base metal in a golden chain, we turn away
with shame and sorrow from the tablet which pro-

claims the rule of the stranger, the oppressor, the impostor—the tablet which tells how a man who had held the foremost place on earth, Teutonic king and Roman Cæsar, he who had been the last to don the purple of Augustus and to wear the diadem of Jovius, could sink to be described in the very land and home of so great a predecessor as *Austriæ Imperator et Dalmatiæ Rex.*

Or do we seek for earlier memories? Pass down the shore of Hadria, thread the channels between its islands and peninsulas, pass by a thousand spots each of which has its tale which I may find other days for telling; pass on into the seas of Greece herself, land by the new Corinth, make your way by the seven columns of the old, columns already ancient in the days of Timoleôn, not wholly new perhaps in the days of Periandros—climb the "cloud-capped akropolis," with all its memories, all its relics, from the primæval wall to the Turkish mosque; there indeed we may learn history as before we never learned it; look eastward over the gulf where lie Aigina and Salamis; it is feeble reading in a book how the elder naval power grudged the rising greatness of the younger. To the men who climbed the hill of Corinth the growth of the rival city was not a tale of books, of letters, of telegrams; from the hill of Corinth they could on a bright day see the very hill of Athens; they knew the presence, the nearness, of their rival, not only by the hearing of the ear, but by the sight of their own eyes. Do we then wonder that when the day of vengeance

came, Corinth was fiercer against a foe whose enmity
was thus ever present, than Sparta who had felt
the might of Athens on the waves, who knew well
the prick of her sting and scourge at Pylos, but
who did not on the banks of Eurôtas see daily
with her bodily sight that danger was making ready
for her by the banks of Kêphisos? Or climb the
hill of Athens itself; there I must indeed put rein
on ten thousand memories, on ten thousand points
of deathless history, every one of which becomes
ten thousand times more living as we see them
written for ever on the everlasting page of the
soil, the hills, the sea which men reckoned as having
itself become a part of the Attic soil. But there we
may learn one lesson above all, a lesson which we
may learn in a manner on the map or on the printed
page, but which can never come home to us on the
map or the printed page as it comes home to us
when we look out from the rock of Athênê upon
the loftier hills which gird it round. We there
learn how great and wonderful, how contrary to
all Greek instincts, was that revolution of early
days which made Attica a single whole, which
made Athens the political home of a greater number
of free and equal citizens than any other Greek
commonwealth, the political home of a number of
free and equal citizens as great as could discharge
the duties of free and equal citizenship in their
own persons. We look out, and we see, hemmed
in with hills, the land which, according to Greek
ideas, would be the natural territory for the one

city of Athens. We see not the land of Marathôn and the land of Eleusis; they are cut off from us; we feel that a day must have been when they were as distinct from Athens as Plataia and Orchomenos were from Thebes; and we the more wonder at the wisdom of the primitive lawgiver who ruled that Marathôn and Eleusis should not be to Athens as Plataia and Orchomenos were to Thebes, the wisdom which gave the world, not a loosely-bound confederation of Attica, but the one commonwealth of Athens.

Let us again flit back to the mid peninsula of Europe; climb the hill of Brescia, that outlying spur of the vast Alpine wall which seems specially placed there as the historian's gazing-place. Look out on the plain of Lombardy; see the tall slender towers rising on every side, towers each of them marking the whereabouts of a city which once was a commonwealth as free as any commonwealth of the elder land of freedom. Why was their fame only for a moment? Why was not Milan as Athens? Why was the rule of Visconti more abiding and more wide-spread than the rule of Peisistratos? The reasons are many, but one above all is borne in upon us by the outlook from the Brescian height. The cities of Greece stand each on its hill, in its valley, on its peninsula or island, with the separate territory of each marked by the hand of nature. The cities of Lombardy seem dotted here and there by the hand of chance; the territory of each might seem to end as naturally at one point as at another.

Doubtless there were reasons for the site of each city, for the extent of its territory, but they are not such obvious and abiding reasons as those which placed Athens on a lowlier hill and Corinth on a loftier, and which bade Aigina float on the waves of the gulf that lay between them. And then, to crown our study of the world's history, go to the *arx* of Tusculum; from that primæval height look down on the younger city that supplanted the ancient head of Latium. There indeed we grasp the truth, the central truth of all history, the truth that the whole fate of the world of which we are a part was ruled by the physical fact that certain of the hills of Latium were nearer together, lower in height, and nearer to the river's brink, than their fellows. Tusculum on her one lofty hill could never become the head of the world; Rome, on her seven lowly hills, could and did. The men on the height of Tusculum might have confederates; they might have enemies; they had not neighbours with whom the only choice was union closer than confederation or warfare more deadly and more unceasing than ordinary enmity. The Latin of the Palatine, the Sabine of the Capitol, learned to change the meeting-place of fight into the meeting-place of council; they became one city, one power; the work of union went on; hill after hill, land after land, was called into equal fellowship; Latium, Italy, the whole Mediterranean world, were merged in one state, we might say, in one city, a city whose walls sprang lightly over mountains and seas, and kept one

bastion at Nisibis and another at Lugubalium. What
Tusculum could not be, what Athens could not be,
Rome was; it was so because the very shape of
the earth's surface ruled that so it should be.

It is hard to stop ; but the time would fail to tell
of all the lands, of all the cities, in Greece and Italy,
in Burgundy and Aquitaine and France and Germany,
in the island that is our own, in the Norman land that
feels all but our own, each of which has its tale to tell,
a tale which can be heard in its fulness only on the spot
which is its home.   Names and memories press on me ;
but I must bid them stand aside.   But there is one
land, a land of which I have spoken earlier in this
lecture, where yearly in the spring-tide, in the last
days of April or the first days of May, a sight may be
seen such as can be looked on nowhere else on earth.
I must be the only man here who from the Athenian
akropolis has looked on the Athenian Dêmos in his
own person, and heard the voice of a nation calling for
its headship to be entrusted to the worthiest of its sons.
That I saw and heard on the day when Hellas ruled
that Constantine Kanarês should grasp the helm of
Hellas.   Dêmos was indeed there with his old voice
and his old power, but he was not in his old seat ; he
was not marshalled in his old order, and the voice
that he uttered had to wait for an answer from the
lips of a foreign king.   But go, on the fitting spring-
tide morning, to the meeting-place of Glarus or
Unterwalden, to the market place of Trogen on its hill,
to the plain of Altdorf between its mountains.   There
you may see something nearer to us than the Dêmos

of Athens; you may see the Germans of Tacitus face to face. On the shore of the lake of the Four Cantons, with the view shut in by the mighty mass of Saint Gotthard, we learn geography and history past and present at one stroke. As we see the free-men of Uri gathered to exercise in their own persons the powers that greater commonwealths and king-doms have to place in the hands of a chosen few, we learn many things, and, not least, we learn the place of the powers of nature in the political world. The lowly heights by the Tiber ruled that universal dominion should fall to the lot of Rome; the heaven-reaching heights by the Reuss ruled that abiding freedom should fall to the lot of Uri. To the geologist, to the Alpine climber, the final cause of Alps will doubtless seem different. One who has twice seen the Landesgemeinde of Uri may be pardoned if he deems that the final cause of the everlasting mountains is that they may stand as the guardian walls of an everlasting commonwealth.

And now I have done for a season. I have gone through my platform for this first term, fairly thoroughly I hope, as far at least as my own will and my own efforts have been concerned. And I have heartily to thank the faithful ones, the three hundred who lapped and did not draw back, who have had the strength to abide with me, week by week, through a somewhat lengthy course. And in the summer term of next year, I trust, if we live and prosper, that some at least of you will be found active enough, even in that busy and sportive season, to follow me through another course, somewhat more solid, it may be, than this, on the main periods of European history. Meanwhile in Hilary term—the name calls up pleasant memories of Poitiers on its peninsula—I trust to go on with more solid work still, with my reading of Gregory of Tours. Such is the will, and I think it a wise one, of the select few who have followed me steadily through three books of his History of the Franks. They ask for more; they think it well to go on further with his great story rather than as yet to make any fresh adventures into other fields. To those select few I must pay all honour and all thanks; but I could wish that the number of the gathering had been larger. It is not for my own sake that I wish it, for our little meetings have been very pleasant, and I hope not unprofitable, to the professor himself certainly not so. I have had in my class men to whom it is an honour to lecture, men before whom one feels it somewhat dangerous to lecture, men who are already masters of history or of language, men therefore who know so much that they are fully aware that they have still something to learn. And I have had also younger men in whom is the right spirit and the true zeal, men who have come within the fold themselves and who are eager to bring others with them. But I should like to enlarge both classes. To the masters of history I should be glad to add some of its official teachers. Times pass so fast, modern progress is so supernatural, that it may be that forty years' work in my generation may come to less fruit than half-a-dozen years' work in the present; only on the other hand, there are some of the present generation, and those not the meanest of its children, who certainly think otherwise. And to my younger hearers—I think I have some—I would offer a repeated, even a ten thousandth, voice of warning. Once more then, be not led astray; follow not after shadows; do not attempt the building without the foundation. If any man, whoever he may be, tempts you to build after that fashion, if he bids you rush off to the study of the later times before you have mastered the earlier ones, you have your answer. A choice is not denied you; you are not compelled to fly off at once to some fourth period, some fifth period, some seventy-seventh period, which may perhaps contain the exact boundaries of the borough of Mile-End Old Town. Believe me that your study of the Palaipolis of Mile-End will not unfitly begin with the ἄστυ of Athens and its surrounding δῆμοι. It may go on through Gaulish *civitates,* Old-English *marks,* Burgundian *communes,* South-Swabian *gemeinden.* The *cité* and *ville* of Limoges, the borough and *foreign* of Walsall, the Englishry, Welshry, and *foreignry* of Kidwelly, may haply help towards mastering the last problem in municipal and parliamentary life. I have seen some bits of very modern history, at home and abroad, in the very working; I have always found that I understood them the better, by tracing them, like Finlay, back to the ν

then you wish really to know anything of the
later times themselves, begin at the beginning.
And, as a sure way of beginning as near the beginning as circumstances will let you, come and
hearken to the Bishop of Tours, the Senator of
Auvergne. Hearken to no voice that would bid
you do otherwise. If the voice comes in any shape
that you may not like to contradict in your own
name, contradict it in mine. I venture to think
that my experience may possibly be the longer and
deeper of the two. And I do not stand alone. I
am strengthened by the advice and encouragement of
men who have a right to speak, men who, having
really climbed the heights of learning, have no interest in shallowness, no lingering love for easy
studies, men whose work has lain in later periods
than mine, who assuredly do not undervalue the
work of their own lives, but who feel that that
work is something distinct from ordinary academic
study, who feel with me that, for laying the foundations, for disciplining the mind, their own later
periods are not so well suited as the earlier times.
Men like these bid me to go on as I have begun, to
do all that one man can do to stop the torrent, and
to strive to win back even a few to a path that may
more surely lead to the end that is sought. Believe
me then; believe no man who says otherwise. Begin
at the beginning; lay the foundation; ear the ground;
the rest will follow. Take the proffered help of one
who believes that he can guide you, because he has
walked the path himself; one whose official duty it

is to guide you along it, if only you will walk with him.   A professor is not a teacher for Examinations; he has nothing directly to do with Examinations; but his teaching will at least not hinder you for Examinations.   You can, if you will, choose the first period rather than the hundredth.   Choose it, and accept my help in mastering it.   I cannot promise you classes and fellowships; but I do not think that my teaching will stand in the way of them.   And at any rate, I can promise you something better; I can promise to show you a path which, if you do not wilfully stray from it, may lead you to the house of sound learning.   And I can show you means which on the way may help you to something better than learning itself, to the discipline of your own minds.

INDEX.

[P. T. O.

BY THE SAME AUTHOR.

Historical and Architectural Sketches; chiefly Italian. Illustrated by the Author. Crown 8vo. 10s. 6d.

Subject and Neighbour Lands of Venice. Being a Companion Volume to "Historical and Architectural Sketches." With Illustrations. Crown 8vo. 10s. 6d.

English Towns and Districts. A Series of Addresses and Essays. With Illustrations and a Map. 8vo. 14s.

Comparative Politics. Lectures at the Royal Institution. To which is added "The Unity of History." 8vo. 14s.

The Office of the Historical Professor. An Inaugural Lecture read in the Museum at Oxford, October 15, 1884. Crown 8vo. 2s.

History of the Cathedral Church of Wells. As Illustrating the History of the Cathedral Churches of the Old Foundation. Crown 8vo. 3s. 6d.

Old English History. With Five Coloured Maps. New Edition, revised. Extra fcap. 8vo. 6s.

The History and Conquests of the Saracens. Six Lectures. Third Edition, with New Preface. Crown 8vo. 3s. 6d.

The Growth of the English Constitution from the Earliest Times. Fourth Edition. Crown 8vo. 5s.

General Sketch of European History. New Edition. Enlarged, with Maps, &c. 18mo. 3s. 6d. (Vol. I. of *Historical Course for Schools.*)

Europe. 18mo. 1s. [*Literature Primers.*

Disestablishment and Disendowment. What are they? Popular Edition. Crown 8vo. 1s.

MACMILLAN AND CO.: LONDON.